Ethical Economy

Studies in Economic Ethics and Philosophy

Volume 61

Ethical Economy describes the theory of the ethical preconditions of the economy and of business as well as the theory of the ethical foundations of economic systems. It analyzes the impact of rules, virtues, and goods or values on economic action and management. *Ethical Economy* understands ethics as a means to increase trust and to reduce transaction costs. It forms a foundational theory for business ethics and business culture. The Series *Ethical Economy. Studies in Economic Ethics and Philosophy* is devoted to the investigation of interdisciplinary issues concerning economics, management, ethics, and philosophy. These issues fall in the categories of economic ethics, business ethics, management theory, economic culture, and economic philosophy, the latter including the epistemology and ontology of economics. Economic culture comprises cultural and hermeneutic studies of the economy. One goal of the series is to extend the discussion of the philosophical, ethical, and cultural foundations of economics and economic systems. The series is intended to serve as an international forum for scholarly publications, such as monographs, conference proceedings, and collections of essays. Primary emphasis is placed on originality, clarity, and interdisciplinary synthesis of elements from economics, management theory, ethics, and philosophy.

The book series has been accepted into SCOPUS (March 2019) and will be visible on the Scopus website within a few months.

More information about this series at https://link.springer.com/bookseries/2881

Jermo van Nes • Patrick Nullens
Steven C. van den Heuvel
Editors

Relational Anthropology for Contemporary Economics

A Multidisciplinary Approach

SUPPORTED BY
GOLDSCHMEDING FOUNDATION
MENS • WERK • ECONOMIE

Springer

Editors
Jermo van Nes
Evangelische Theologische Faculteit
Leuven, Belgium

Patrick Nullens
Evangelische Theologische Faculteit
Leuven, Belgium

University for Humanistic Studies
Utrecht, The Netherlands

Steven C. van den Heuvel
Evangelische Theologische Faculteit
Leuven, Belgium

The research for this book was funded by the Goldschmeding Foundation, who supported both the projects "Hope as an Incentive" and "Homo Amans: A Relational Anthropology for Work and Economics".

ISSN 2211-2707 ISSN 2211-2723 (electronic)
Ethical Economy
ISBN 978-3-030-84692-3 ISBN 978-3-030-84690-9 (eBook)
https://doi.org/10.1007/978-3-030-84690-9

This Springer imprint is published by the registered company Springer Nature Switzerland AG
The registered company address is: Gewerbestrasse 11, 6330 Cham, Switzerland

Foreword

Homo economicus is a character. He is said to act in accordance with his own interests and aim for personal wealth and well-being. *Homo amans* is said to act on different instincts and motivations, such as love, hope, care, and sympathy. One only has to look at some of the problems facing our present global society to see that change is needed. This book provides a remarkably interesting and intelligent exploration into the world of *Homo amans*. Is *Homo amans* a potential alternative to *Homo economicus*, the authors of this volume ask? In light of today's economic, social, and environmental challenges the question is important to raise but, as the book shows, difficult to answer. Isn't it the case, Wildman asks in this book, that "any large culture plays host to a great variety of mutually inconsistent anthropological visions"? One can even take this question one step further and ask whether *Homo economicus* and *Homo amans* aren't interdependent and need each other on the path towards a more humane and dignified life for all? Why don't we start this exploration with something that is laudable in the context of a humane society: respect for human rights – and, specifically, access to healthcare as a human right.

Article 25 of the Universal Declaration of Human Rights reads as follows:

> Everyone has the right to a standard of living adequate for the health and well-being of himself and of his family, including food, clothing, housing and medical care and necessary social services, and the right to security in the event of unemployment, sickness, disability, widowhood, old age or other lack of livelihood in circumstances beyond his control.[1]

The right indicates that all humans should be able to live without having to worry about the basic requirements for a free, humane, and dignified life related to physical, mental, and social health. Having a right to primary goods and services related to our health and well-being is only the first condition for ensuring that humans are able to access and enjoy the benefits of these goods and services. The second condition is that these goods and services are actually available and accessible. As signatories to the declaration, governments have a responsibility to provide their citizens and other inhabitants of their countries with what is necessary to live a life

[1] https://www.un.org/en/universal-declaration-human-rights/

in dignity – sufficient medical care, food, shelter, and other goods. With the limited resources that they often have, they rely partially on the commitment and support of business and civil society to respect and promote the implementation of human rights. This sharing of responsibility is already implicated in the preamble of the Universal Declaration of Human Rights that calls on "every individual and every organ of society" to promote and respect human rights. International law scholar Louis Henkin noted in 1999 that "every individual and every organ of society excludes no one, no company, no market, no cyberspace. The Universal Declaration applies to them all."[2] In many official documents relating to the principles and practice of business, including but not limited to the OECD Guidelines for Multinational Enterprises or the UN Guiding Principles on Business and Human Rights, the focus is mainly on *respecting* Human Rights. It will not be difficult to argue that it is in the interest of the company to do so.

Increasingly, however, a plea is made for a more active role for business in *promoting* human rights and a dignified life for all. A recent example is the UN General Assembly Resolution A/RES/70/1, adopting "Transforming our world: the 2030 Agenda for Sustainable Development," which outlines the Sustainable Development Goals.[3] In its introduction, the declaration calls for an inclusive approach to implementing the agenda:

> It is "we the peoples" who are embarking today on the road to 2030. Our journey will involve Governments as well as parliaments, the United Nations system and other international institutions, local authorities, indigenous peoples, civil society, business and the private sector, the scientific and academic community – and all people. Millions have already engaged with, and will own, this Agenda. It is an Agenda of the people, by the people and for the people – and this, we believe, will ensure its success.

Already in the preceding Addis Ababa Action Agenda that was adopted in July 2015, governments and business had agreed to support the UN development agenda by making commitments to sustainable development, inter alia through the provision of (blended) finance. One of those business organizations was Philips, the company that was previously known for its lighting and household appliances – ranging from TV sets to electric shavers and toothbrushes – and recently transformed into a medical appliances company. As its core mission, it wants to "make the world healthier and more sustainable through innovation."[4] To make that mission more tangible the company's expressed goal is "to improve the lives of three billion people a year by 2030." In addition, it wants to be "the best place to work for people who share our passion. Together we will deliver superior value for our customers and shareholders."[5]

---

[2] https://www.business-humanrights.org/en/business-human-rights-a-brief-introduction

[3] https://www.un.org/en/development/desa/population/migration/generalassembly/docs/globalcompact/A_RES_70_1_E.pdf

[4] https://www.philips.com/a-w/about/company/our-strategy/how-we-create-value.html

[5] Ibid.

The transformation of Philips did not turn the company into a charitable organization, thereby disposing of the conception of a human being as *Homo economicus* and replacing it by one of *Homo amans*. On the contrary, Philips is still a company that aims to create value for its shareholders by doing the things it is good at. As the mission and vision of companies like Philips demonstrate, mainstream businesses very gradually become more susceptible to the needs of society and the contribution they can make to "human flourishing." They continue to perceive human beings as rational and as focused on their personal wealth and well-being, while at the same time acknowledging that making profit is not the sole purpose of a business in a dynamic society. For some, it is not the purpose of the business at all to make as much money as possible for shareholders.[6] These enlightened companies see business as vehicle for producing goods and services for (consumers in) society, for which, obviously, a business has to be profitable. Without profits, there is no well-being for society. But the opposite also matters: without demonstrably creating value for society, the company believes it will have no future.

This book calls for a transformation of our thinking in, inter alia, economics, business, civil society, and politics in order to revalue the notion of a human being. We are invited to perceive human persons for what they are: individuals engaging in multiple relationships that add meaning to their life. The value of these relationships, and additional values, is not only perceived in terms of self-interested wealth creation but also in terms of mutual respect, care, love, and hope. The book wants to revitalize the idea of morality in business in the way that, for instance, Adam Smith was able to combine and align his economic and moral thinking. Yes, it does make sense to promote the division of labor to allow for specialization, without forgetting that, as human beings, our purpose in life is not to create as much personal wealth as possible.

Since the 1950s, our global economy has gradually become saturated with the belief that economic wealth creation is the alpha and omega of value creation in society – despite the pleas of critics challenging such a narrow view of what – and who – should count in the dominant economic and political domains of life. More recently, and partly as a result of the major social, environmental, economic, and financial crises that our society has faced and faces still, the economy is changing to one that is inspired by a sense of human dignity and flourishing. More and more, new concepts emerge, displaying and endorsing ways of management that promote values other than self-interest. The "commitment of the will to the true good of another" – McCloskey's definition of love – is increasingly found to inspire key players in the economy. Excellent examples are set by social entrepreneurs and businesses aimed at promoting the common good. Even though these movements bring together important business leaders, their impact on the economy is still

[6] Recently Danone, the French multinational dairy company, announced it was becoming an "entreprise à mission" thereby aligning its social and environmental objectives with its purpose. Nonfinancial objectives have become as important as financial objectives: https://www.danone.com/about-danone/sustainable-value-creation/danone-entreprise-a-mission.html

marginal due to the size of their operations. It is when a B Corp like dairy multinational Danone, or a major medical appliances company like Philips, steers towards a more humane economy that we can hope to make some progress. The word "hope" is quite appropriate in this respect. Over time, changing the prevailing economic paradigm has always been seen to be a rocky road towards – what the incumbent leaders of previous times believed to be – a better future.

In this respect, we need the aforementioned companies to do more than make sure that human rights are protected and that people are granted the right to health and well-being. Respecting rights is important but not sufficient for promoting human flourishing. It is precisely because Philips promotes access to healthcare in Africa through its Community Life Centers, and Danone works together with the Grameen Foundation to produce Shokti Doi, a nutritious yogurt providing the most needed vitamins and nutrients to young children, that we see progress materializing. These advances can clearly be seen as expressions of *Homo amans*, since the companies are not making any money on these activities. They are merely undertaken because of the social value that they create – although the companies hope to benefit strategically from these investments in a distant future.

It is in the intelligent combination of the strengths of economic development and the recognition of its weaknesses and limitations, that steps are made towards a more humane economy. This is a slippery path, however, asking us to continuously secure the progress that has been made, while simultaneously exploring ways of advancing further. In climbing the path towards this more humane future, it is not so much that *Homo amans* should take *Homo economicus* by the hand. Nor can *Homo amans* replace, or be an alternative to, *Homo economicus* in our present economic system. What is needed is an engaged conversation between the two on the purpose and values in life that matter for our global society and on the path that will lead us there. The attempts at this conversation that we gradually see being made – and the first signs of a changing paradigm in today's business practice – still have something about them of the deaf *supporting* the blind, and vice versa. They are interdependent and therefore need each other. As Gerrit Glas argues in his contribution "new theories, concepts, and paradigms are a precondition for change, but they do not bring about change by themselves. What is needed is a change in the practices themselves, a change that is both personal and comprehensive." It is precisely here that *Homo amans* can inspire economic practice, while at the same time diligently looking for support and guidance within current economic practices that will induce change and lead to an economy that promotes love, care, sympathy, and hope. The current economic, social, and environmental crises might actually be helpful in spurring change: these crises increasingly help to deepen the understanding of leaders of government, business, and civil society that there are limits to having wealth accumulation as the only purpose of their practices.

This book offers delicious food for thought for a profound and inspirational conversation among academics and between academics and practitioners. It nourishes all those currently walking within the economic landscape, heading for greener and more humane pastures. One can only hope for a sequel, a future volume that would report on the fruits of the conversation along the way and the progress that has been made on the road towards a more humane and flourishing economy. It is only when inspirational leaders point the way, and practical leaders simultaneously take action to actually create, implement, and secure change, that progress is made.

I began this contribution by referring to the right to adequate healthcare. This can help us understand how self-interested and other-interested behavior can go hand in hand and may even benefit from each other. Ever since it was proclaimed by the General Assembly of the United Nations in December 1948, the Universal Declaration of Human Rights has been an extraordinary and important signpost for human development and respect for every single human living on this planet. Over time, however, we have learned that a mere declaration is not enough to secure access to the most basic needs that humans need to live a life in dignity. Action is needed to promote the interests of others within the context of the current political, economic, environmental, and social boundaries. That context, the authors in this book have convincingly argued, is to a large extent still dominated by *Homo economicus*. Replacing *Homo economicus* by *Homo amans* is very likely not the best way of achieving a more humane economy and of promoting human flourishing. A dialectic relationship, leading to a constructive discourse between the self-interested *Homo economicus* and the other-oriented *Homo amans*, is more likely to clear the path towards the change that is needed in our current society. We have a long and interesting walk and talk ahead of us.

Maastricht University
Maastricht, The Netherlands

Harry Hummels

Contents

About the Editors and Contributors

Editors

Jermo van Nes is Assistant Professor of New Testament at the Evangelische Theologische Faculteit (ETF), Leuven, Belgium. At ETF, he was Senior Researcher in the Institute of Leadership and Social Ethics. He is also a Research Associate in the Department of New Testament Studies at the University of Pretoria, South Africa. His research has been published in academic journals such as *New Testament Studies, Zeitschrift für die neutestamentliche Wissenschaft, Novum Testamentum,* and the *Journal for the Study of the New Testament.*

Patrick Nullens is Full Professor of Systematic Theology with a focus on Christian Ethics, and former Rector of the Evangelische Theologische Faculteit (ETF), Leuven, Belgium. He is the founder of ETF's Institute of Leadership and Social Ethics. He is also Extraordinary Professor of Leadership Ethics and Humane Society at the University of Humanistic Studies, Utrecht, the Netherlands. As a widely published author in the field of theology, ethics, leadership, and humanistic management, his research focus is on the need for new leadership and governance to carry out the urgent transitions in sustainability and social justice.

Steven C. van den Heuvel is Associate Professor of Systematic Theology with a focus on Christian Ethics at the Evangelische Theologische Faculteit (ETF), Leuven, Belgium, and Director of ETF's Institute of Leadership and Social Ethics. He published inter alia on the theology of Dietrich Bonhoeffer and ecological ethics. Furthermore, he edited a number of scholarly volumes, published by Springer, Palgrave, Peeters, and Routledge. At ETF, he is involved with various research projects on (theological) anthropology, including "The Hope Project" and "*Homo Florens,*" both funded by the Goldschmeding Foundation.

Contributors

James Beauregard Rivier University, Nashua, NH, USA

Emilio Di Somma Evangelische Theologische Faculteit, Leuven, Belgium

Gerrit Glas Vrije Universiteit, Amsterdam, The Netherlands

Harry Hummels Maastricht University, Maastricht, The Netherlands

Rebekka A. Klein Ruhr-Universität Bochum, Bochum, Germany

Dennis L. Krebs Simon Fraser University, Burnaby, BC, Canada

Deirdre Nansen McCloskey University of Illinois Chicago, Chicago, IL, USA

Patrick Nullens Evangelische Theologische Faculteit, Leuven, Belgium
University of Humanistic Studies, Utrecht, The Netherlands

Hendrik Opdebeeck Universiteit Antwerpen, Antwerp, Belgium

Steven C. van den Heuvel Evangelische Theologische Faculteit, Leuven, Belgium

Jermo van Nes Evangelische Theologische Faculteit, Leuven, Belgium

Joke van Saane University of Humanistic Studies, Utrecht, The Netherlands

James A. Van Slyke Fresno Pacific University, Fresno, CA, USA

Wesley J. Wildman Boston University, Boston, MA, USA

Chapter 1
Introduction

Jermo van Nes, Patrick Nullens, and Steven C. van den Heuvel

Abstract Discussing the rise and fall of the anthropological concept of *Homo economicus*, which is still a dominant model in the field of economics, this introductory chapter provides a framework for understanding the contributions in this volume. In response to a white paper in which a complementary model entitled *Homo amans* is proposed, they altogether reflect on the status of the *Homo economicus* model in contemporary economics from a multidisciplinary perspective.

Anno 2020, business is among the most popular fields of study for students in higher education, at least in Europe and the United States.[1] Already in 2013, however, Wharton professor and best-selling author Adam Grant was alerting us that the study of economics was in danger of discouraging prosocial behavior, referring to a number of studies showing that the study of economics was quashing cooperation and generosity.[2] It appears, for instance, that US professors of economics donate less money to charity than their peers in other fields (Frank et al. 1993), and that economics students, in comparison with students from other majors, are more

[1] See https://www.onderwijsincijfers.nl/kengetallen/internationaal/leerlingen-en-studenten/aantallen-ingeschrevenen-in-het-hoger-onderwijs-naar-studierichting-in-europa (accessed 2 July 2021), and https://nces.ed.gov/fastfacts/display.asp?id=37 (accessed 2 July 2021).

[2] Adam Grant, "Does Studying Economics Breed Greed?", Psychology Today, 22 October 2013, https://www.psychologytoday.com/us/blog/give-and-take/201310/does-studying-economics-breed-greed (accessed 2 July 2021).

J. van Nes (✉) · S. C. van den Heuvel
Evangelische Theologische Faculteit, Leuven, Belgium
e-mail: Jermo.vannes@etf.edu; steven.vandenheuvel@etf.edu

P. Nullens
Evangelische Theologische Faculteit, Leuven, Belgium

University for Humanistic Studies, Utrecht, The Netherlands
e-mail: Patrick.nullens@etf.edu

J. van Nes et al. (eds.), *Relational Anthropology for Contemporary Economics*, Ethical Economy 61, https://doi.org/10.1007/978-3-030-84690-9_1

willing to deceive for personal gain (Frank and Schulze 2000), more easily rate greed as morally good (Wang et al. 2011), and have less concern for fairness (Marwell and Ames 1981; Carter and Irons 1991). Experiments further demonstrate that altruistic values among economics majors drop over the years (Gandal et al. 2005); that economics students become more selfish during their studies and gradually expect worse of others (Frank et al. 1993); and that just thinking of economics can make people less caring (Molinsky et al. 2012).

One of the reasons for the destructive effects of studying economics in the twenty-first century, as Grant points out, is that certain (neoclassical) economic models still rely on the assumption that every person is essentially a "*Homo economicus*", i.e. a rational being who attempts to maximize his or her utility for both monetary and non-monetary gains. The history of this theoretical construct – a "universal bogey," as Lionel Robbins (1932, p. 90) called it – is complex. While the term *Homo economicus* came into use as late as 1883 (Hengstmengel 2020, p. 177), the idea of economic man can be traced all the way back to Xenophon of Athens (c. 430–355 BCE) as his treatise *Economicus* includes a Socratic dialogue in which Socrates – wisdom personified – helps the economist Kritoboulos to see "that he cannot do good for himself if he is not doing good for the *polis*: his own well-being and that of the *polis* are not separate enterprises" (Wilson and Dickson 2012, p. 16). Accordingly, Wilson and Dickson (2012, p. 22) see the idea of *Homo economicus* foreshadowed in Xenophon's *Economicus* as both are personifications of instrumental activity directed towards ends or values outside themselves.

Joost Hengstmengel (2020, pp. 45–64), however, argues that the idea of *Homo economicus* could never exist in classical Antiquity as true happiness and 'the good life' were connected to immaterial things. At that time, economics was a moral 'science'. It was normative, being allowed to tell how people should act yet realistic about people's capacities. All human economic activity was evaluated in terms of the cardinal virtues of prudence and justice. With the rise of Christianity, the virtue of charity was added. Accordingly, in Antiquity and early Christianity an economics of sufficiency and love were promoted respectively in which self-interest was condemned when it harmed others and did not contribute to the good life of the community as a whole. This "prelapsarian" state of economics, as Hengstmengel (2020, pp. 14–16) calls it, slowly but radically changed during the early modern period (c. 1500–1650) due to three major transitions: (1) communities changed into societies, (2) man changed from a community being into an economic being, and (3) living the good life in terms of a virtuous life changed into the ideal of living a life maximizing one's utility and pleasure. These transitions were encouraged by the emergence of the Renaissance spirit, which exposed man's allegedly 'true nature' to be addictive to power, pleasure, and profit, as well as the rise of political economy as a modern science, which suppressed the normative status of economics as the ties with moral philosophy and religion were slowly cut.

As a result of these important shifts in early Modernity, the sense of community was supplanted by economic individualism as the social and religious stigma attached to self-interest gradually disappeared from political discourse. Inspired by the political writings of Thomas Hobbes (1588–1679), whose social contract theory encouraged that submission to an absolute sovereign was in people's best interest as the sovereign secured protection and property, all sorts of (British) intellectuals ranging from clergymen to politicians in the 'long' eighteenth century (c. 1650–1800) started to promote the social value of self-interest. Some tentatively argued that self-interest is only one of man's inherent drives and is controlled by a natural balance of motives. Others proposed that self-interest constructively organized the movement of human bodies in society. Yet others contended that self-interest brings about a natural division of labor and results in higher collective productivity (Myers 1983). The gradual legitimation of self-interest in this age of Enlightenment is what Hengstmengel (2020, p. 14) calls "the Fall" of economics as self-interest was turned from vice into virtue.

The most important intellectual writer on the (moral) question of how individual self-interest can be a constructive force for the collective welfare in the eighteenth century was the Scottish philosopher Adam Smith (1723–1790), who is generally considered to be the father of modern economics and founder of the classical school of economics. In his most famous studies *The Theory of Moral Sentiments* (1759) and *An Inquiry into the Nature and Causes of the Wealth of Nations* (1776), Smith – standing in a long tradition of virtue ethicists – sought an economic solution to what is in essence a moral question: Can individual self-interest be a constructive force for the collective welfare? Answering in the affirmative, Smith attempted "to reconcile economic and moral behaviour in the emerging system of market capitalism and to quell the anxiety this market gave rise to" (Comyn 2018, p. 29). Acknowledging the complexity of human nature yet arguing that people are predominantly driven by self-love and self-interest, Smith discerned mainly egocentric forces in economics (Hengstmengel 2020, p. 166).

While the term *Homo economicus* was not coined yet by the turn of the nineteenth century, many scholars (e.g. Ridder 1941–1942) see the spirit of free market capitalism as reflected in the writings of Smith as the delivery room of the concept. John Stuart Mill (1806–1873) was among the second generation of classical economists who continued to explain economic behavior by means of self-interest, but consciously abstracted it from other human motives. As Mill (1844, pp. 137–138) notes on the ever-growing science of political economy:

> It does not treat of the whole of man's nature as modified by the social state, nor of the whole conduct of man in society. It is concerned with him solely as a being who desires wealth, and who is capable of judging of the comparative efficacy of means for obtaining that end. It predicts only such of the phenomena of the social state as take place in consequence of the pursuit of wealth. It makes entire abstraction of every other human passion or motive; except those which may be regarded as perpetually antagonizing principles to the desire of wealth, namely, aversion to labour, and desire of the present enjoyment of costly indulgences.

This famous quote implies two important methodological assumptions: (1) economic behavior can be explained solely in terms of people's pursuit of wealth, and (2) economic decisions in terms of ends and means are judged rationally by people. Mill himself was very clear about the hypothetical and imagery character of his anthropology, but insisted on its necessity if political economy wanted to develop into a science of equal status as the natural sciences: "Not that any political economist was ever so absurd as to suppose that mankind are really thus constituted, but because this is the mode in which science must necessarily proceed" (Mill 1844, p. 139).

In response to Mill, Charles Devas (1883, p. 27) was the first to use the term *Homo economicus* in noting that "Mill has only examined the *homo oeconomicus*, or dollar-hunting animal." He abstracted "'economic man', who is under no ethical influences and who pursues pecuniary gain warily and energetically, but mechanically and selfishly" (Marshall 1890, p. vi) and "whose activities are determined solely by the desire of wealth" (Keynes 1891, p. 16). Mill's conceptual 'invention' of *Homo economicus* was by no means adopted by every economist, but it further stimulated economics to develop into a theoretical, deductive, and abstract discipline in which moral philosophy was no longer needed to study the relationship between self-interest and happiness. Accordingly, the traditional virtue ethical concerns were slowly but steadily replaced by the emerging ideal of utilitarianism – to maximize happiness and well-being for all affected individuals. This resulted in a 'positive' form of economics, which was consciously amoral (Hengstmengel 2020, pp. 173–187).

Assuming that agents make consumption choices so as to maximize their happiness or utility, economists like Stanley Jevons, Léon Walras and Carl Menger formalized Mill's ideas into a set of axioms in the late nineteenth century. This "guaranteed the internal coherence of economic assumptions and allowed the use of mathematics to deduce testable implications from those assumptions" (Rodriguez-Sickert 2009, p. 224). The field of study that emerged from this mathematical enquiry is known as rational choice theory, which is particularly associated with the Chicago school of economics. The basic premise of this theory is that the decisions made by individual actors collectively produce aggregate social behaviour. Proponents of rational choice theory also assume that individuals have preferences available and choice alternatives. Advocates of rational choice theory do not (cl)aim to describe the choice process, but rather help predict the outcome and pattern of choice. They consequently assume that the individual is self-interested and comes to a decision that maximizes personal advantage by balancing costs and benefits (Friedman 1953, p. 15). As such, the idea of *Homo economicus* is still very much alive in contemporary economics, at least in this branch of the discipline (e.g. Becker 1976; Jensen and Meckling 1994).

On 6–7 June 2019, the Institute of Leadership and Social Ethics, a research institute of the Evangelische Theologische Faculteit in Leuven, Belgium, organized a symposium in the Peace Palace in The Hague, the Netherlands, to address the importance of reflecting on the status of the *Homo economicus* model in contemporary economics from a multidisciplinary perspective. In order to kindle a constructive dialogue, a discussion paper drawing on anthropological research in the life sciences, social sciences, and humanities was prepared that outlined the contours of what could potentially serve as a refined version of *Homo economicus*, preliminarily entitled "*Homo amans*" – the human person as a loving being. A number of keynote speakers and respondents working in various academic disciplines were invited to interact with this paper. Most of the contributions in this volume were presented during the symposium; others were written later, by invitation. As a result, some of the essays do not directly engage with the discussion paper but reflect on relevant themes evoked by it; others dialogue directly with some of the ideas presented in the discussion paper; and there are some that interact with someone else's paper.

In the second chapter, Patrick Nullens and Jermo van Nes open the discussion by addressing the problem that overall human flourishing is hindered by the ongoing dominance of the *Homo economicus* paradigm in contemporary economics. They believe the *Homo economicus* paradigm overemphasizes people's rational capabilities at the cost of their relational qualities. By way of suggestion, Nullens and Van Nes develop the contours of the holistic concept of *Homo amans* as phenomenologically constituted by the virtues of faith, hope, and love, since multidisciplinary study has shown that human persons are searching, expecting, and relational beings. They also suggest that people are able to search for meaning, project their longings into the future, and relate meaningfully to others by means of their ability to trust.

The contributions by Dennis Krebs and James Beauregard in Chaps. 3 and 4 respectively support the overall idea of *Homo amans*. Rejecting the common claim that evolutionary theory implies that all animals are selfish by nature, Krebs argues that social animals can propagate their selfish genes in psychologically unselfish ways. As such, the central function of morality is to uphold adaptive systems of cooperation. Throughout human history, as Krebs explains, primitive psychological sources of moral behavior such as perspective-taking and moral reasoning have helped the human species to evolve. From a personalist perspective, James Beauregard offers a robust anthropological vision which presents the human person as a dynamic unity – active, and capable of learning, and living the virtues of faith, hope, and love. He also believes that neuroscience can inform the *Homo amans* model, but warns about its conceptual limitations.

In Chaps. 5, 6 and 7, contributors (in)directly engage with the argument of the discussion paper. Deirdre McCloskey argues for the connection between free will in Abrahamic theologies and free action in liberal ideologies. In God's eyes, she insists, a free-willed person should be free from human interference in religion as well as behavior and business. This implicitly critiques the *Homo amans* model as living up to the virtues of faith, hope, and love may interfere in people's freedom. Rebekka Klein questions whether the nature of love is truly phenomenologically discussed in its ambivalence. Drawing on Kierkegaard's phenomenology of love, she argues that love cannot be clearly distinguished from selfish acts without reference to an external party. Gerrit Glas sides with the concerns raised by Klein, adding that thinking that science helps in validating and legitimizing a biblically informed concept of love is committing a naturalistic fallacy. In addition, he seriously questions whether academic disciplines by themselves will be able (and should be expected to be able) to transform deeply ingrained, institutionally anchored economic practices. What is needed more, Glas insists, is a change in economic practices themselves, a change that is both personal and comprehensive.

More specifically, the contributions in Chaps. 8, 9 and 10 address the notion of virtue and reflect on the potential of the *Homo amans* model. James Van Slyke focuses on the virtue of love as altruistic concern, arguing on the basis of psychological studies that this type of love uniquely informs the virtue of humility, as it puts people ahead of or before the self. In the context of business, humility is formed through the development of relational values and is best expressed in how superiors show concern for others. Those who value the intrinsic worth of other persons are less likely to express the various vices of pride and will more readily demonstrate humility towards others, as was demonstrated in moral exemplars, such as Holocaust rescuers. Emilio Di Somma focuses on the notion of trust. Using Taylor's concept of "social imaginary", he argues that in order to implement the *Homo amans* model a desire for trust among people and institutions is to be instilled in people first. This takes courage as it requires the affirmation of the objective goodness of virtues such as faith, hope, and love. According to Hendrik Opdebeeck, a paradigm shift from *Homo economicus* to *Homo amans* is not a utopia as long as the models are not considered as rivals. With the right attitudes, as advocated in the *Homo amans* model, a rational economy can turn into a responsible economy, or, in his words, a "u-globia".

Wesley Wildman and Joke van Saane, in Chaps. 11 and 12 respectively, discuss the transformative power of the *Homo amans* concept in economics. Wildman argues that relationality and self-awareness are necessary corrections for the individualism and cognitive error found in contemporary western human self-understanding. He also believes that love as *agape* and *karuna*, and wisdom as knowledge and humility could be two spiritual translations of these corrections. Reflecting on how the envisaged transformation in ideas about human nature could be implemented, Wildman concludes that the anthropological insights of philosophers would be best served by a partnership with education and policy experts. Van Saane agrees with Wildman's analysis concerning the structural failures in human functioning caused by individualism and cognitive errors, but counters that we better acknowledge our individualism and failing cognitions. This creates opportunities for personal leadership, as only individuals are real game changers.

In the final chapter, Patrick Nullens, Jermo van Nes, and Steven van den Heuvel reflect on all the contributions and revisit the discussion paper. As a result, they reply to some of the questions brought up in the overall discussion, including the possible restriction an anthropological model may have on human freedom, the relationship between *Homo economicus* and *Homo amans*, the nature of love, the danger of committing a naturalistic fallacy, and the need for a theory of change. They end the conversation by refining the *Homo amans* model and pointing to new directions of study.

Acknowledgments The publication of this volume in this series as a result of the symposium in The Hague offers the opportunity to express our sincere gratitude to a number of people. First of all, many thanks are due to all contributors for shaping our thoughts on relational anthropology by means of their worthy contributions. Second, we thank all our honored guests at the symposium for their active participation. Many of the questions and stimulating discussions have helped us in the process of refining our thoughts. Third, as we look back on a wonderful symposium, we say a big "thank you" to its general director, Erik de Baedts, and his staff, for hosting us in the beautiful context of the Peace Palace. Fourth, we thank our colleague Cees Tulp, as well as Kay Caldwell, for their editorial assistance in preparing the manuscript. Fifth, we thank the anonymous peer reviewers of the manuscript for their suggestions on how to improve the manuscript. Sixth, we wish to express our gratitude to the series editors for accepting this book in their prestigious series. And last but not least, we gratefully acknowledge the Goldschmeding Foundation for their ongoing support for this project. Special thanks are due in this regard to Michiel de Wilde, Wim Janse, Martijn Roos, Aart Jan de Geus, and Suzanne Ekel.

References

Becker, G.S. 1976. *The Economic Approach to Human Behavior*. Chicago/London: The University of Chicago Press.

Carter, J.R., and M.D. Irons. 1991. Are Economists Different, and If So, Why? *Journal of Economic Perspectives* 5 (2): 171–177.

Comyn, S. 2018. *Political Economy and the Novel: A Literary History of "Homo Economicus"*. Cham: Palgrave Macmillan.

Devas, C.S. 1883. *Groundwork of Economics*. London: Longmans, Green & Co.

Frank, B., and G.G. Schulze. 2000. Does Economics Make Citizens Corrupt? *Journal of Economic Behavior & Organization* 43 (1): 101–113.

Frank, R.H., T. Gilovich, and D.T. Regan. 1993. Does Studying Economics Inhibit Cooperation? *Journal of Economic Perspectives* 7 (2): 159–171.

Friedman, M. 1953. *Essays in Positive Economics*. Chicago/London: The University of Chicago Press.

Gandal, N., S. Roccas, L. Sagiv, and A. Wrzesniewski. 2005. Personal Value Priorities of Economists. *Human Relations* 58 (10): 1227–1252.

Hengstmengel, J. 2020. *De Homo Economicus: Een familiegeschiedenis*. Amsterdam: Boom.

Jensen, M.C., and W.H. Meckling. 1994. The Nature of Man. *Journal of Applied Corporate Finance* 7 (2): 4–19.

Keynes, J.N. 1891. *The Scope and Method of Political Economy*. London: Macmillan.

Marshall, A. 1890. *Principles of Economics*. London: Macmillan.

Marwell, G., and R.E. Ames. 1981. Economists Free Ride, Does Anyone Else? Experiments on the Provision of Public Goods, IV. *Journal of Public Economics* 15 (3): 295–310.

Mill, J.S. 1844. *Essays on Some Unsettled Questions of Political Economy*. London: Parker.

Molinsky, A.L., A.M. Grant, and J.D. Margolis. 2012. The Bedside Manner of *Homo Economicus*: How and Why Priming an Economic Schema Reduces Compassion. *Organizational Behavior and Human Decision Processes* 119 (1): 27–37.

Myers, M.L. 1983. *The Soul of Modern Economic Man: Ideas of Self-Interest – Thomas Hobbes to Adam Smith*. Chicago: The University of Chicago Press.

Ridder, J. 1941–1942. De oorsprong van het begrip van den homo economicus. *Philosophia Reformata* 6: 128–144; *Philosophia Reformata* 7: 58–63, 123–127.

Robbins, L. 1932. *An Essay on the Nature and Significance of Economic Science*. London: Macmillan.

Rodriguez-Sickert, C. 2009. Homo economicus. In *Handbook of Economics and Ethics*, ed. J. Peil and I. van Staveren, 223–229. Cheltenham/Northampton: Elgar.

Wang, L., D. Malhotra, and J.K. Murnighan. 2011. Economics Education and Greed. *Academy of Management Learning & Education* 10 (4): 643–660.

Wilson, D., and W. Dickson. 2012. *A History of Homo Economicus: The Nature of the Moral in Economic Theory*. London/New York: Routledge.

Chapter 2
Towards a Relational Anthropology Fostering an Economics of Human Flourishing

Patrick Nullens and Jermo van Nes

Abstract Basic capabilities and human interests that are directed towards the ideal of human flourishing now seem at odds with the concept of *Homo economicus* as once defined by John Stuart Mill – a rational being pursuing wealth only for his own self-interest. This popular paradigm still dominates economic theory and practice, but a growing group of academics consider its underlying model of human behavior to be inaccurate. As a result, scholars across various disciplines have expressed the need for a more refined anthropology in relation to contemporary economics. In response, the holistic concept of *Homo amans* as phenomenologically constituted by the virtues of faith, hope, and love is introduced, since multidisciplinary yet complementary study suggests that human persons are questing, expecting, and relational beings. Whether or not *Homo amans* could serve in the future as a complementary model to *Homo economicus* remains to be seen, because several aspects of human relationality that are relevant to contemporary economics are in need of future study.

2.1 Introduction

Amidst the many environmental and societal problems facing our world today, there is growing awareness and recognition in both academia and society that economics should aim to foster human well-being. But how do we substantiate the good life? Is it more than freedom of choice? Is it a matter of fulfilling our needs? Is it about commitment to an idea or ideal? The capability approach offers a potential way to move ahead. Inspired by the political/economic works of Amartya Sen (1992,

P. Nullens (✉)
Evangelische Theologische Faculteit, Leuven, Belgium

University for Humanistic Studies, Utrecht, The Netherlands
e-mail: Patrick.nullens@etf.edu

J. van Nes
Evangelische Theologische Faculteit, Leuven, Belgium
e-mail: Jermo.vannes@etf.edu

J. van Nes et al. (eds.), *Relational Anthropology for Contemporary Economics*, Ethical Economy 61, https://doi.org/10.1007/978-3-030-84690-9_2

1999), Martha Nussbaum (2011, pp. 33–34) proposed a list of ten core capabilities that will enable people to flourish. These are being able to (1) live, (2) enjoy good health, (3) move freely, (4) use the senses to imagine, think, and reason, (5) relate emotionally to things and people, (6) reason practically by engaging in critical reflection, (7) affiliate to others on the basis of self-respect and non-humiliation, (8) live in relation to the natural world, (9) play, and (10) have control over one's environment in terms of politics and property. In a similar vein, Christian Smith (2015, pp. 181–82) identified six universal goods that define basic human motivations and interests: (1) bodily survival, security, and pleasure, (2) knowledge of reality, (3) identity coherence and affirmation, (4) exercising purposive agency, (5) moral affirmation, and (6) social belonging and love. Without these, Smith (2015, p. 240) argues, no human being can develop: "[f]or persons to be rejected, excluded, and isolated, outcast, invisible, untouchable, and irrelevant, leaves them retarded, wounded, or deformed in their personhood." This implies that one can flourish as a person only by seeking the good for oneself and others, in other words, by seeking the common good.

Yet, in both academia and society the dominant approach to human behavior continues to be that of economic man or *Homo economicus* – "a model of human agency in which the individual actor maximizes his own well-being given the constraints he faces" (Rodriguez-Sickert 2009, p. 223). The term came into existence as late as 1883 (Devas 1883, p. 27), and though the concept can be traced all the way back to Xenophon of Athens (c. 430–355), it was the writings of the British theorists Adam Smith (1723–1790) and John Stuart Mill (1806–1873) that made the idea of *Homo economicus* popular and influential.[1] While Smith (1759, 1776) developed a nuanced version of economic man whereby well-being is not exclusively related to material goods (McCloskey 2016, pp. 172–96), it was Mill (1844, p. 137) who defined *Homo economicus* as "a being who desires wealth, and who is capable of judging of the comparative efficacy of means for obtaining that end." Mill's focus on accumulation, leisure, luxury, and procreation, was to make his version of economic man the more popular and dominant one over time.

While the concept of economic man as introduced and developed by eighteenth- and nineteenth-century British intelligentsia makes sense against the background of Enlightenment thinking in general, and the American Revolutionary War (1775–1783) as well as the French Revolution (1789–1799) in particular, it makes less sense today. The utilitarian model of behavior underlying this concept not only embodies a commitment to methodological individualism (i.e. the individual more than the social system is the basic unit of analysis), but also accepts that human nature is essentially rational, a-moral and unsocial (Bovenberg 2018, p. 25). However, from the twentieth century onwards, the mechanical worldview advocated by Mill (and his followers), in which people are isolated yet rational beings acting in an environment populated by like-minded individuals, has been criticized in many different disciplines (Kirchgässner 2008, pp. 185–218; Ng and Tseng 2008,

---

[1] For an historical overview of the concept of *Homo economicus*, see Hengstmengel (2020).

pp. 269–71; Rodriguez-Sickert 2009, pp. 225–26; Klein 2011, pp. 101–109). Sociologists, for example, have insisted that the *Homo economicus* model is too narrow since it does not allow for human behavior to be explained by social norms (Dahrendorf 1958), social interdependence (Frank 1985), social relations (Granovetter 1985), moral codes (Sen 1982), and/or institutions (Bowles 1998). Behavioral economists (e.g. Forsythe et al. 1994; Gintis et al. 2005) have found that people sometimes act irrationally and/or reciprocally, something that goes beyond mere rational self-interest. More recently, neuroscientists have claimed that altruism is a genetically based human capacity (Krebs 2012). The same is true for emotions, which seems to affect human behavior (Haidt 2003). Because emotions "are generated spontaneously in the limbic system outside the conscious control of the individual" (Kullberg and Singer 2012, p. 249), they sometimes contradict the rationality of human nature.

With the concept of *Homo economicus* being criticized on so many fronts,[2] Kate Raworth (2017, pp. 88–100) represents a growing group of scholars who have asked that Mill's caricature of human nature be replaced by a more refined anthropological model allowing for our sociality (instead of self-interest), fluid values (instead of fixed preferences), interdependency (instead of isolation), approximating (instead of calculating), and embeddedness in life (instead of dominion over life).[3] As Raworth (2017, p. 82) urges,

> …it is time to meet ourselves all over again by taking his [Mill's] cartoon depiction out of the economic gallery and painting, in its place, a new portrait of humanity. It will turn out to be the most important portrait commissioned in the twenty-first century, mattering not just to economists but to us all. Its preparatory sketches are under way and, just as in Leonardo's workshop, many artists are collaborating in piecing them together, from psychologists, behavioral scientists and neurologists to sociologists, political scientists and, yes, economists.

Yet responding to Raworth's call is anything but easy. Arguably the major challenge is finding a common language that enables scholars working in various disciplines, each with their own worldview and (religious) background, to think deeply about how human flourishing can be increased. This chapter is nothing more than a modest attempt to encourage a multidisciplinary dialogue on anthropology in contemporary economics by (1) rethinking human personhood, (2) introducing the concept of *Homo amans* as a complementary model to *Homo economicus*, and (3) exploring some dimensions of human relationality that deserve future study.

---

[2] For popular critiques on the *Homo economicus* model, see especially Cohen (2012), Papadogiannis (2014), and Fleming (2017). Already by 2000, a survey of 64 participants had revealed that even ordinary people question the model on the basis of common sense, as they generally believe that "the human being is free, changeable, influenced by the subjective world of experience, a product of the environment, and best understood from a holistic perspective" (Hochwälder 2000, p. 611).

[3] Other critics who have asked for the *Homo economicus* model to be replaced include Drucker (1939), Arendt (1958), Dahrendorf (1958), Elworthy (1993), O'Boyle (1994), Doucouliagos (1994), Bowles and Gintis (1998), Dinello (1998), Thaler (2000), Pearson (2000), and Girgerenzer and Brighton (2009), to name but a few.

2.2 What Is a Person? Rethinking Human Nature

The centuries-old quest for the meaning of being human has given rise to many different and sometimes rival theories about human nature (Stevenson et al. 2018). Focusing on the Western intellectual tradition, Joseph Torchia (2008, p. xiii) distinguishes four distinct periods in the history of philosophical anthropology: (1) the classical period, ranging from the pre-Socratics to Aristotle, during which the first metaphysical accounts of humanity were developed; (2) the Middle Ages, when key Christian thinkers such as Augustine and Thomas argued for the fundamental psychosomatic unity and relationality of human beings; (3) Modernity, which saw the emergence of Descartes' mind-body dualism and the subsequent critique of the notion of mind in British empiricism as represented by David Hume; and (4) Postmodernity, during which a new brand of dualism emerged in terms of biological humanity versus moral personhood.

It appears that, during the long history of philosophical anthropology, the question of what it means to be human has been approached from different angles – the religious, the scientific, and the philosophical. Torchia (2008, p. 1) observes that from the very beginning two competing answers have been given, and these continue to be expressed in various forms: (1) *teleological* perspectives that endorse "a metaphysical distinction between an immaterial mind and a material body," recognizing "an order and a purposiveness in human existence by virtue of an appeal to something which transcends our physical being" (Torchia 2008, p. 1), and (2) *mechanistic* perspectives that ultimately reduce "our mental life and decision-making capacity to no more than highly complex neurophysiological processes", suggesting that "there is no difference between mind and brain, or between thinking and brain-wave activity" (Torchia 2008, p. 1).

Drawing upon the works of the Scottish philosopher Alasdair MacIntyre (1981, 1988), Torchia (2008, p. 10) himself endorses the view that "only a teleological understanding of human nature and the virtuous life rooted in the Aristotelian/Thomistic tradition of inquiry" allows for making moral judgments. This being the case, he stresses the importance of recovering a human *telos* to form the basis for our view of happiness. Accordingly, human lives are to be interpreted as coherent narratives directed toward the realization of their final ends. Torchia (2008, p. 11) questions whether "a purely reductionist account of human nature and personhood explain[s] everything we are capable of doing in cognitive, volitional, and affective terms." Personhood is not a matter of arbitrary interpretation, nor is it definable on the basis of biological or behavioral characteristics alone. Instead, Torchia (2008, p. 11) argues:

> In my reckoning, "human being" is correlative with "being human," the mode of existence appropriate to persons as dynamic centers in their own right who participate in human nature even as they transcend it in their uniqueness. This touches on the mystery inherent in our way of being, a mystery that can only be revealed and appreciated by entering in the experience of the other through the intimacy of interpersonal relationships. In the face of such a penetrating mystery, a metaphysical explanation alone suffices, since this type of

account attunes us to the luminosity of an inner life that always eludes attempts at complete empirical analysis.

Similarly, Christian Smith (2010) dismisses mechanistic anthropologies that reduce all reality to natural laws inherent in matter and energy and in doing so neglect the reality of moral values, meaning, and the spiritual dimension of life. Preferring a teleological understanding of human nature, Smith (2010, p. 15) argues "that human beings as they exist in the world embody a particular constitution – they have a human nature rooted in nature more broadly." They are characterized by properties, abilities, and qualities that are unique to human personhood. Assuming the essentially social condition of humanity, Smith believes that human personhood emerges through the social interaction, communication, and communion between people. The concept of emergence is a daily phenomenon, referring to "the process of constituting a new entity with its own particular characteristics through the interactive combination of other, different entities that are necessary to create the new entity but that do not contain the characteristics present in the new entity" (Smith 2010, pp. 25–26). One could think, for instance, of hydrogen (H) and oxygen (O) merging into water (H_2O).

In support of his thesis for the emergence of personhood, Smith relies on three key theoretical resources: (1) critical realism, (2) personalism, and (3) anti-scientistic phenomenology. First, critical realism as introduced by the English philosopher Roy Bhaskar (1997), searches for a middle way between empirical positivism on the one hand and postmodern constructivism on the other. It makes a distinction between the real, the actual, and the empirical: the real is the objective being, material or non-material, which exists apart from our human awareness of it; the actual is what happens in time and space, whether we experience it or not; and the empirical is what we experience directly and indirectly. Critical realism critiques the conflation of these three aspects. It is critically aware of our limited understanding and at the same time aware of a reality, apart from our limited understanding. Smith (2010, pp. 92–93) summarizes the core ideas of Bhaskarian critical realism as follows:

> Critical realism's central organizing thought is that much of reality exists independently of human consciousness of it; that reality itself is complex, open, and stratified in multiple dimensions or levels … ; that humans can acquire a truthful, though fallible knowledge and understanding of reality through various forms of disciplined conceptualization, inquiry, and theoretical reflection; that (social) science is rightly concerned with, first, identifying what is real and, second, understanding and explaining real causal capacities, mechanisms, and processes that operate in reality to produce various events and outcomes of interest … ; and, finally, that knowledge and understanding of the truths about reality position knowers to critically engage the world in normative, prescriptive, and even moral terms in ways that may overcome the traditional fact-value divide and intentionally try to shape the world for the better.

Being strongly anti-reductionistic, critical realism respects the many dimensions and causal interactions of what is real and actual. Smith (2010, p. 54) presents a list of no less than 30 human capacities that structure themselves hierarchically in five categories: (1) "existence capacities" (e.g. subconscious being), (2) "primary experience capacities" (e.g. mental representation), (3) "secondary experience capacities" (e.g. emotional experience), (4) "creating capacities" (e.g. language use), and (5) "highest order capacities" (e.g. interpersonal communion and love). To understand the interrelation of these capacities and to avoid all forms of reductionism, the reality of emergence is crucial. The 30 human capacities "are the stuff out of which human personhood exists emergently" (Smith 2010, p. 59).

Second, the core belief underlying the philosophy of personalism as it originated in the United States and continental Europe in the late nineteenth and early twentieth century respectively, is that human beings are real entities with an ontological being that exists in nature. We are truly persons. This ostensibly simple claim has serious implications as it entails that we are more than "rational, self-interested, exchange-making calculators of costs and benefits" (= *Homo economicus*); more than "the constituents of functional social orders"; more than "discursively constructed positions of shifting identities pieced together in the flux of variable meanings and power relations"; more than "corporeal sites through which regimes of power express themselves through bodily discipline"; more than "strategic, dramatic presenters of performances driven by culturally specified scripts"; more than "biological carriers of "selfish" genetic material that has been naturally selected upon for its superior reproductive fitness and that seeks to perpetuate itself through behavioral determinism"; and more than "egos struggling to manage the id in the face of the superego" (Smith 2010, pp. 102–103). Smith (2010, p. 104) approvingly quotes Karol Wojtyla (1993, p. 211), better known as Pope John Paul II, who notes that personalism believes "in the primordial uniqueness of the human being, and thus in the basic irreducibility of the human being to the natural world."

Third, anti-scientistic phenomenology as developed by the Canadian philosopher Charles Taylor (1989) challenges common assumptions of naturalistic scientism in terms of materialism, objectivity, and reductionism that discount "people's phenomenological experience as a guide to valid and reliable knowledge about reality, including human life" (Smith 2010, p. 105). Smith counters that no single scientific view should dominate, but that priority should be given to our lived experiences of being human. He argues that we are beings who want to make sense of our lives, because we are by nature morally and spiritually committed. We are always searching for "the best account" of our lives, referred to as "the BA [best account] principle" (Taylor 1989, p. 58). We need to search continuously for the best account that makes sense of our phenomenological experiences and immaterial realities, including value, meaning, morality, and personhood. Such accounts are best "arrived at by challenge, discussion, argumentation, reflection, criticism, vetting, that is, by testing against the clarity of experience, including through systematic observation and the discipline of reason" (Smith 2010, p. 112).

Smith also engages critically with the popular theory of social constructivism introduced by the sociologists Peter Berger and Thomas Luckmann (1966), who argued that all reality, including someone's personality, is socially constructed. This implies that what normally is taken for granted as "natural" and "factual" is nothing but a cultural artifact. As such, all theories regarding human nature, whether religious or scientific, are creations of people engaged in patterned roles and behaviors that become habituated or institutionalized. While Smith (2010, p. 121) recognizes that social constructivism is "an important instrument in the sociological toolkit," it overstretches relativistic claims when it becomes dominated by poststructuralism and postmodernism. By way of an alternative, Smith proposes a weak or realist version of social constructivism: "All human knowledge is conceptually mediated and can be and usually is influenced by particular and contingent sociocultural factors such as material interests, group structures, linguistic categories, technological development, and the like – such that what people believe to be real is significantly shaped not only by objective reality but also by their sociocultural contexts" (Smith 2010, p. 122). Yet these human capacities are not without limits. Human beings are finite creatures. It is in the tensions between human capacities and their limits that patterns of lived practice emerge, and eventually these become social structures. This entails that human goods or values are not conditional, and each society or individual is free to choose them.

All of these deliberations make Smith (2010, p. 61) define a human person as "a conscious, reflexive, embodied, bodied, self-transcending center of subjective experience, durable identity, moral commitment, and social communication who – as the efficient cause of his or her own responsible actions and interactions – exercises complex capacities for agency and intersubjectivity in order to develop and sustain his or her own incommunicable self in loving relationships with other personal selves and with the nonpersonal world" (Smith 2010, p. 61). He stresses that the fusion of these elements is not just a mix of component parts but constitutes a distinct personal being. This thick notion of human personhood grounds *eudaimonic* ethics, i.e. the understanding of the human good as the realization of our nature. Smith gives a foundation to a morality that profoundly acknowledges personal agency, sustaining a social context of loving and nurturing relationships that enable human persons to flourish. This involves an ethics that moves beyond a set of rules or procedures to a realistic type of teleological personalism: "Moral life that is tuned to reality thus begins with a correct understanding – whether intuitive or reflexive – of the real human condition, actual human potentialities, and the right telos of personhood" (Smith 2010, p. 414). It requires virtue ethics "to become our real and best selves" (Smith 2010, p. 418). And for this purpose, no new moral system is needed; it simply requires the rediscovery of the wisdom of old moral systems that are already often in line with our own intuitions. Universal traits such as love, justice, generosity, etc., should be enacted and developed continuously. They enable us to flourish, and their absence from our lives threatens our very personhood.

2.3 Faith, Hope, and Love: Introducing *Homo Amans*

The studies of Torchia (2008) and Smith (2010), as outlined above, acknowledge the complexity of human nature and resist the reductionist tendencies in contemporary scholarship when defining human personhood. They both stress the importance of virtue. In the Judeo-Christian tradition, human personhood is marked, ideally, by the virtues of faith, hope, and love. They are mentioned in one breath by the apostle

Paul in 1 Corinthians 13:13 – “And now faith, hope, and love abide, these three; and the greatest of these is love” (NRSV). Paul also notes that faith and love produce good works, and that hope gives endurance (cf. 1 Thess. 1:2–4); that faith, hope, and love are defensive weapons (cf. 1 Thess. 5:7–9); that faith is active in love (cf. Rom. 5:1–5; Gal. 5:5–6); and that faith and love are the result of hope (cf. Col. 1:4–6). Modern studies of the three theological virtues usually discuss them separately (e.g. Brunner 1956; Pieper 1986; Robinson 2004; Cubillos 2017), whereas ancient commentators stressed their inseparability. Augustine (*Serm.* 359A), for example, in one of his sermons noted:[4]

> Faith does not fail since it has hope to support it. Take away hope, and faith fails. How does someone who does not hope to arrive even move his feet in walking? But if from the two, faith and hope, you take away love, what good does it do to believe, what good does it do to hope? It is not possible to hope for what one does not love. It is love that kindles hope; hope glows with love. But when we have arrived at what we hoped for in faith without seeing it, what faith will be left to praise since *faith is the conviction of things not seen* [Hebr. 11:1]? When we see, it will no longer be called faith. You will see then; you won’t believe. The same is true for hope itself. When the reality is present, you do not hope. For *hope that is seen is not hope* (Rom. 8:24). There it is: when we have arrived, faith is ended, hope is ended. What happens to love? Faith turns to sight and hope to its reality. Now it is sight and reality, not faith and hope. What happens to love? Can it come to an end? No, for if the soul was already aflame with love for what it had not seen, certainly when it sees this it will burn all the brighter. So it was truly said that the greatest of these is love, since faith is succeeded by sight, hope by reality, but love has no successor. It grows, it increases, it is perfected in contemplation.

The importance of the virtues of faith, hope, and love for human personhood is not stressed only in early Christian texts. In 2004, in the field of positive psychology, Christopher Peterson and Martin Seligman (2004) published a landmark cross-cultural list of character strengths and virtues taken from different religious traditions (Confucianism, Taoism, Buddhism, Judeo-Christian, Islam) as well as from ancient and modern philosophy.[5] They distinguish between virtues, character strengths, and situational themes. Virtues are “the core characteristics valued by moral philosophers and religious thinkers: wisdom, courage, humanity, justice, temperance, and transcendence;” character strengths are “the psychological ingredients” that form the routes to displaying virtues; and situational themes refer “to the specific habits that lead people to manifest given character strengths in given situations,” such as the workplace or family (Peterson and Seligman 2004, pp. 13–14). The overall result revealed a surprising amount of similarity across cultures. Six core virtue groups were classified (wisdom and knowledge, humanity, courage, justice, temperance, and transcendence) that are based on 24 character strengths, including the capacity to love and to be loved, leadership, forgiveness and mercy, gratitude, hope, and religiousness and spirituality (Peterson and Seligman 2004, pp. 29–30). According to Peterson and Seligman (2004, p. 13), these virtues and character strengths are no social constructs, but universal predisposed mechanisms that are

[4] English translation of the Latin text is derived from Kovacs (2005, p. 228). Italics in original.

[5] See also http://www.viacharacter.org

"grounded in biology through an evolutionary process that selected for these aspects of excellence as means of solving the important tasks necessary for survival of the species."

Similarly, Deirdre McCloskey (2006, pp. 91–300) in the field of economics argues that the virtues of faith, hope, and love (together with courage, temperance, justice, and prudence) are an integral part of the history of European prosperity, and continue to be essential for the well-functioning of a commercial society. They are classified as soft, "feminine" virtues that complement the overrated strong, "masculine" virtues of courage and prudence in the current world of markets. McCloskey (2006, pp. 168–171) rejects the anti-theistic bias of the French philosopher André Comte-Sponville (1995), who explicitly excludes faith and hope from his list of 18 great virtues since they have God as their object. He argues that courage will suffice in the presence of a danger or an uncertain future. McCloskey herself provides a secular version of faith, hope, and love in order to warrant their transcendent character. Faith is about our awareness of identity, "a backward-looking virtue" (McCloskey 2006, p. 153). Hope, by contrast, is "forward-looking" (McCloskey 2006, p. 160). Love is like "a commitment of the will to the true good of another," and has "the quality of attachment" (McCloskey 2006, p. 91).

When understood transcendently, the virtues of faith, hope, and love mark humans as questing, expecting, and relational beings. In the last decade, three major studies have argued that each trait is inherent in human nature. First, Wesley Wildman (2009) in a wide-ranging study offered a naturalistic interpretation of the human being as *Homo religiosus*. Integrating different academic disciplines, such as molecular biology, evolutionary theory, cognitive neurology, and the scientific study of religion, Wildman (2009, p. xv) basically defended the hypothesis "that religious behaviors, beliefs, and experiences – understood sufficiently broadly – constitute human nature not only historically, culturally, or circumstantially, but also ontologically, essentially, and inescapably." He believes that religion is universal and applies even to atheistic scientists committed to the battle against the myths of religion and superstition. Religion is a commitment to ultimate and existential concerns as "[i]t pertains to the way we bind ourselves (*religio*) to that which has surpassing meaning for us," and, in this sense, "suffuses every aspect of human life" (Wildman 2009, p. xv). Religion is not a cultural product, separate from our genes, but nor is it purely the result of evolutionary adaptation. In evolutionary terms, "religion," according to Wildman (2009, p. 69), "is as an *ad hoc*, complex, and variable assemblage of adapted and exapted genetic traits that constrain culturally colored exploration of a landscape of social and existential possibilities within an ultimate environment defined by the valuational depth of nature itself." This implies that human beings are religiously concerned in any given socio-cultural setting, but it does not require any verdict on the reality of god(s). It simply means that, by nature, we are all "oriented to primordial, ultimate mystery in our experiences, our social practices, our drives and projective impulses, our longings and failures, our malevolence and love" (Wildman 2009, p. 230).

Second, Anthony Scioli and Henry Biller (2009, p. 6) argued that the virtue of hope "is not merely a process by which you arrive at some desired destination," but also "a way of being in the world." Both psychologists insist that hope is a universal emotion, defining it as a "future-directed, four-channel emotion network, constructed from biological, psychological, and social resources" (Scioli and Biller 2009, p. 30). These four channels include mastery, attachment, survival, and spiritual subsystems that operate in semiautonomous fashion at five different levels in the life of every human person: (1) hope blueprints, which are "biologically based motives relating to mastery, attachment, and survival," (2) nature and nurture, consisting of "natural endowments and early nurturing experiences," (3) the hopeful core, including different "kinds of personality dispositions or traits" which emanate from the four-channel emotion network producing goal-related trust, mediated control, relational trust, self-other bonds, survival-oriented trust, terror management, spiritual integrity, and symbolic immortality, (4) the faith system, growing "from the seeds of trust, mediated control, and self-other bonds", and (5) beliefs and behaviors, which are "the manifestations or exterior signs of hope" (Scioli and Biller 2009, pp. 32–38). Scioli and Biller (2009, pp. 41–47) locate the origin of hope in the evolution of man, arguing that the construction of hope developed progressively, from 6,000,000 years ago when the first species possessed the pre-adaptations of hope until 2500 years ago when the grand religious, spiritual, and philosophical systems of the ancients originated. By that time, a form of brain reorganization had occurred that affected the mastery, attachment, and survival systems. According to Scioli and Biller (2009, p. 32), "there is overwhelming evidence that certain brain structures and pathways are primarily associated with these motives," pointing to, *inter alia,* the frontal lobes that allow "for mastery-associated initiative and planning," parts of the right hemisphere, the hormone oxytocin, and the amygdala that allow for "the biology of attachment", and the immune system as well as a complex set of reflexes and the stress-related "fight or flight response" that allow for our survival system.

Finally, Rebekka Klein (2011) described the sociality of the human condition. Acknowledging competing viewpoints in the study of anthropology, Klein (2011, p. 305) refrains from doing interdisciplinary study of anthropology as "[t]he transdisciplinary way of gaining knowledge is rooted in the false premise that there is only *one* correct interpretation of human behaviour, and the best way to find this interpretation is to unify scientific methods and modes."[6] Instead, she prefers to give primacy to philosophical anthropology by using a phenomenological method of multi-perspectivism that allows observers to describe objects from their own limited perspective. As Klein (2011, pp. 1–2) explains,

> Phenomenological criticism is based on the intuition that the unique characteristics of an object of description show themselves precisely in the object's appearance, in its phenomenality to the observer. This applies to experiences in the lifeworld [*Lebenswelt*] as well as to the scientific analysis of an object. As a phenomenon, therefore, an object can never be described independently of the modality of its observation or description. Consequently, there can also be no perspective-free representation of the object in a phenomenological analysis that reduces the various aspects of its appearance to a single, supposedly more

[6] Italics in original.

> objective or more fundamental view. The multitude of appearances of an object is resistant to further analysis and cannot be resolved by interdisciplinary discourse or otherwise. Rather, it is the basic phenomenological task of an inter-disciplinary study to bring its individual perspectives to a point where they acknowledge that their representations are limited, and that they need to be supplemented with other perspectives regarding the phenomenality of their object.

So, Klein (2011, p. 3) urges that we should not seek to answer the question "What is a human being?" by means of empirical methods, but rather initiate a philosophical human self-inquiry by asking "What is human about human beings and their sociality?" She answers this question by offering a wide range of economic, philosophical, and theological perspectives (Klein 2011, pp. 27–301). She finds that human sociality is not found in the difference between human and animal sociality but in the every-day interactivity between human beings through which the humanity (and inhumanity) of human beings is displayed. Because the interactive relationship between human beings is vulnerable and critical, any description of human sociality should acknowledge the ambivalence in terms of "altruism/egoism, reconciliation/hostility, recognition/disrespect, responsibility for/negation of the other" (Klein 2011, p. 307). This anthropological tension is, in fact, acknowledged in theological perspectives, and described in terms of the old and new existence. From the perspective that God is present in the world, the old existence is replaced by the new existence. This entails that human beings become "a neighbour, 'a next one' to God," which makes it possible to explicate "the difference between the humanity and inhumanity of human social life" (Klein 2011, p. 307).

While using different methodologies, Wildman (2009), Scioli and Biller (2009), and Klein (2011) find respectively that we are questing, expecting, and relational beings. In terms of method, Klein's phenomenological analysis and theory of multi-perspectivity allow for the complementarity of these three anthropological accounts. While the interrelationship of faith, hope, and love deserves future study, Scioli and Biller (2009) have indicated that faith is inspired by hope, and Wildman (2009) argued that love is inspired by faith. This aligns with the notion of Franz Foltz and Frederick Foltz (2018, p. 67) that "[f]aith and hope inform and inspire love." Supposing that the virtues of faith, hope, and love are somehow interconnected, we propose to invoke the holistic anthropological concept of *Homo amans* as a prescriptive category referring to man as a questing, expecting, and relational being. Unlike Mill's version of *Homo economicus*, the idea of *Homo amans* is inspired by ancient wisdom that aligns with contemporary scholarship and allows for three of our basic desires: (1) to quest for meaning (faith), (2) to project our desires onto the future (hope), and (3) to relate to other human beings (love):

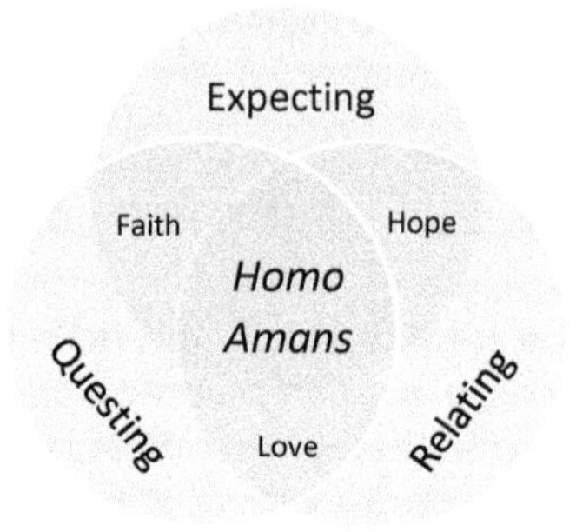

2.4 "The Greatest of These is Love": Exploring Human Relationality

Given the supremacy of love over faith and hope, the remainder of this chapter focuses specifically on our most important virtue. Love is a universal concept. It is present in all world religions (Greenberg 2008, p. xxiii). In the Qu'ran, for example, God is always spoken of as Al-Rahman ("the Compassionate One") and Al-Rahin ("the Merciful One"). Love as an ethics of reciprocity is expressed in the so-called golden rule "do unto others as you would have them do unto you," which has universal support in virtually all societies (Hertzler 1934). Yet this does not mean that love is understood everywhere in the same way. The ancient Greeks, for example, distinguished between *eros*, *philia*, and *agape*. It is often said that these concepts referred to sexual, brotherly, and divine love respectively (e.g. Nygren 1969; Greenberg 2008, p. xxiii), but this does not find support in all ancient sources (Silva 2014a, p. 112, 2014b, p. 606): *eros* is associated with good things, virtues, perseverance and temperance, peace, truth, wisdom, heavenly, divine, and even the source of all virtue (e.g. Philo, *Leg*. 2.55,80,83; *Somn*. 2.40; *Spec*. 2.258; *Virt*. 1.55,62); *philia* is used in reference to political alliances (e.g. Josephus, *Ant*. 7.66; 12.154), seduction (e.g. Sir. 9.8), and the divine-human relationship (John 5:20, 16:27; Philo, *Fug*. 58; *Cont*. 90); and *agape* connotes sexual love (e.g. Prov. 2:4–7).

Semantic ambiguity in the vocabulary of love exposes the need for a sound definition. Yet as Edward Vacek (1994, p. 34) observed, "most philosophical and theological writing, when it speaks of 'love', does not analyze what love is, but rather assumes that it has an evident meaning." Vincent Brümmer (1993, pp. 39–146), being one of the exceptions, distinguishes five attitudinal forms of love, three of which are directed towards beloved persons (exclusive attention, ecstatic union, and passionate suffering) and two of which are directed towards persons in general (need-love and gift-love). Brümmer himself concludes that love is a relationship more than an attitude, arguing that all five attitudinal forms of love are somehow involved in this relationship. The relational nature of love is also reflected in the definition given by Thomas Oord (2010, p. 15): "To love is to act intentionally, in sympathetic response to others (including God), to promote overall well-being." Or, in other words, "loving actions are influenced by the previous actions of others, oneself, and God, and these actions are purposefully executed in the hope of encouraging flourishing" (Oord 2010, p. 15).

Not everyone will agree with Oord's definition. Evolutionary biologists will probably refer to Richard Dawkins' influential thesis (2016, p. 3) that we are blind to our motives because our genes are essentially selfish as they are "programmed" for reproduction:

> [W]e, and all other animals, are machines created by our genes. … [A] predominant quality to be expected in a successful gene is ruthless selfishness. This gene selfishness will usually give rise to selfishness in individual behavior. However, … there are special circumstances in which a gene can achieve its own selfish goals by fostering a limited form of altruism at the level of individual animals. […] Much as we might wish to believe otherwise, universal love and the welfare of the species as a whole are concepts that simply do not make evolutionary sense.

In other words, someone cannot act for the well-being of others without some form of selfish motivation or genetic programming for personal benefit. This makes the intentional act of love and common aim for well-being questionable. Dawkins' theory, however, is not immune to criticism (McGrath 2007). Even our day-to-day experience of people acting benevolently towards others without receiving anything in return challenges Dawkins' theory. This is why Edward Wilson (1975, p. 3) once considered altruism "the central theoretical problem of sociobiology", asking "how … altruism, which by definition reduces personal fitness, [can] possibly evolve by natural selection." One solution that has been proposed is that helping others has personal benefits in the end as it helps a species to survive. As Samuel Bowles and Herbert Gintis (2011, p. 1) explain, "people cooperate not only for self-interested reasons but also because they are genuinely concerned with the well-being of others, try to uphold social norms, and value behaving ethically for its own sake" on the basis that "our ancestors lived in environments … in which groups of individuals who were predisposed to cooperate and uphold ethical norms tended to survive and expand relative to other groups."

For Paul Seabright (2010), this new perspective on human evolution implies that we are cognitively and temperamentally adapted to intimate world cooperation. In the Holocene period, which started about 12,000 years ago, human life became less mobile and was based more on farming. People started to live in less intimate worlds, culminating in more complex social worlds of large-scale states and cities. How did minds, customs, and social technologies adapted to these intimate worlds support cooperation? If humans were to thrive in a more densely populated environment, the circle of cooperation would somehow have to be enlarged. This is how trust in non-intimates became a major issue. The profit in cooperating was dependent on the trustworthiness of others. This makes Seabright wonder how the human species made the transition some 12,000 years ago from "murder that stranger" to "smile at that stranger." Paul Frijters and Gigi Foster (2013) affirm that love is a product of evolution in accordance with elementary desires and basic mental processes, but they also think that this was not a conscious decision. In fact, Frijters and

Foster (2013, p. 88) believe that love is ultimately ego-centric, since the unconscious is prone to believe in reciprocity and thus will "implicitly believe that the entity to which [it is] giving [its] love will reciprocate."

Amidst the confusion about our selfish, cooperative, and altruistic behavior, evolutionary psychologist Dennis Krebs (2012, p. 36) helpfully distinguishes between two types of altruism – "one defined in terms of the consequences of helping behaviors, and the other in terms of the motives and intentions of those who help others." He thinks the former type is biologically selfish, while the latter is not. This makes us partly selfish and partly altruistic by nature. Evidence for the latter was initially provided by social psychologists in the 1970s and 1980s. As Jane Allyn Piliavin and Hong-Wen Charng (1990, p. 27) noted in their literature review of 1990, the "theory and data now being advanced are more compatible with the view that true altruism – acting with the goal of benefitting another – does exist and is a part of human nature." More recently, the findings of neurologists seem to support this conclusion (e.g. Eisenberger 2013; Vrtička 2017). Donald Pfaff (2015) outlined his altruistic brain theory, explaining how neurons in our prefrontal cortex are naturally inclined to make us behave altruistically. For Pfaff (2015, p. 10), "the guiding principle of a healthy human brain is 'First act morally, then ask why'." If people are basically good, he argues, empathy and trust are of enormous practical utility since they are crucial to all sorts of relationships in private and public life. Trust is encouraged by good behavior and this in turn encourages team spirit, as people are willing to rely on each other. When all members of a group hold each other in high regard, their cooperation will produce a positive outcome. Pfaff offers a piece of advice to society on the basis of his altruistic brain theory: remove all obstacles to leadership by women, because "[w]omen's hormones, such as estrogen and oxytocin operating on circuits in the female brain, together with the neural systems they affect, foster prosocial attitudes and good behavior" (Pfaff 2015, p. 264).

For at least three reasons, Pfaff's work is of great significance for economic theory and practice, especially leadership studies. First, it accredits the shift from transactional to (authentic) transformational leadership as being partly motivated by a growing number of behavior studies showing that interest in others motivates us more than self-interest (Bass and Steidlmeier 1999). Second, altruistic leadership theories, such as Servant Leadership (Greenleaf 2002), Responsible Leadership (Pless and Maak 2012) and Spiritual Leadership (Fry 2003), are encouraged to use the notion of trust in rethinking the critical relation between self-love and other-love in terms of cooperation. By way of example, Geoff Moore (2017) recently promoted virtuous leadership in companies and organizations. Distinguishing between internal goods ("goods which we should pursue for their own sake", e.g. love) and external goods ("[goods] which we should pursue for the sake of some other good," e.g. economic success), Moore (2017, p. 59) argues that managers have a specific role to play in upholding the tension between both types of goods in order to establish cooperation between employers and employees. Third, Pfaff's work aligns with McCloskey's notion that love is a feminine virtue. Its findings affirm the importance of moral exemplars, in particular women, because they spark prosocial behavior. As James Van Slyke (2014, p. 476) notes:

> Moral exemplars are persons whose appraisal systems are uniquely attuned to the moral life and are able to know the correct moral action based on intuitive processes running in parallel and linked with other types of evaluation. Over time, these evaluations produce good moral actions that require less and less conscious deliberation and become dispositions towards right moral action. These dispositions become the basis of moral character and generate consistency and reliability in moral action.

Because moral exemplars embody love on a regular and consistent basis, we normally want to imitate them. Thomas Oord (2013, p. 187) suggested that, after determining what criteria should be used, a research program be undertaken to compare the neural systems of moral exemplars with people who did not develop loving characters. In such a program, it would also be interesting to examine if it would make any difference to the results if the (non-)moral exemplars were religious or not. One would expect confessing believers as imitators of their superior moral exemplars (e.g. Jesus, Buddha) to show a more loving character, but the current state of the art cannot confirm that there is a positive correlation between altruism and religion (Habito and Inaba 2008, pp. 4–5).

Our natural inclination to do good, and the very existence of exemplars that embody, *inter alia,* the virtue of love, raises the question of what factors make people develop into such exemplars. Focusing on moral development in early childhood, Robert Emde (2016) assumes virtues to be universal, social, emotion-motivated, polar, and developing over time. Because human behavioral development involves necessary adaptive exchanges within the environment, it must be considered in both its biological and sociocultural context, i.e. "not only from the perspective of continuity, but from the perspective of transformational change; not only from the perspective of successful adaptation and health, but from the perspective of unsuccessful adaptation and disorder" (Emde 2016, p. 71). Key to the formation of the social self in early childhood, according to Emde, are (1) reciprocity (e.g. turn-taking, fairness), (2) empathy (e.g. emotional communication, compassion), and (3) valuation (e.g. the internalization of rules and standards). Each of these dimensions should be supported by parental regulation in order to prevent the moral development of infants from going awry. With regards to this possibility, Emde (2016, p. 83) stresses that future study is needed on why morally virtuous people, at any age, turn "to what most would see as the dark side, and what overcomes such turnings" as well as "the prevention of derailment of individual pathways to what most in a society would consider virtuous."

Emde's study exposes our current ignorance about the specifics of the social circumstances that help people maintain virtue, including love. This applies not only to people of different age-groups, such as children, teenagers, adults, the elderly, etc., but also to people acting in different contexts, such as home, school, work, etc. While Emde stressed the importance of parents acting reciprocally, empathetically, and evaluatively at home in order to encourage virtuous living among their children, Lans Bovenberg (2016) in his inaugural lecture at Tilburg University some years ago argued that education informed by a relational anthropology will create more awareness of citizenship among teenagers. According to Bovenberg, economics is not only about earning money but also about building relationships.

He stresses the importance of finding the right balance in serving one's own needs and those of others. While people will always make mistakes in this process, the overall purpose should be to cooperate in a reciprocal way that eventually gives the best result for all stakeholders involved. In terms of work, Stephen Post and Jill Neimark (2007) encourage organizations to foster a "positive hierarchy," where an ethos of service emanates from the top down and reciprocal behavior is expected, exhorted, acknowledged, and rewarded. These are just examples of how moral development can be supported in the contexts of home, school, and work, but it is to be expected that many more could be discovered for similar and other contexts. One could question, for example, whether companies should offer bonuses to reward their employees for their profit making or their (reciprocal) behavior.

A final thought concerns the future of human relationality in an age of technology. According to Foltz and Foltz (2018, p. 128), the technical revolution reduces loving actions to rational processes and single operations. Yuval Noah Harari (2016, p. 388) warns about dataism that only appraises "the value of human experiences according to their function in data-processing mechanisms." While not necessarily due to technological developments, a 2006 report from the *American Sociology Review* (McPherson et al. 2006) showed that the number of friends for the average American over the period 1985–2004 dropped from 4 to 2. The number of digital friends via networks such as Facebook will have increased, but this is not without negative psychological and relational experiences (Fox and Moreland 2015). These are only some examples of how technology could have negative effects on human relationality, but there are also examples of positive use of technology in this regard. Social neuroscientists, for example, have developed compassion training programs for people lacking empathy, one of which trains people to have more compassion by means of, *inter alia,* simulated video games (Leiberg et al. 2011).

2.5 Discussion

A growing body of evidence across various academic disciplines shows that human beings do not behave in an exclusively selfish way. This means that the concept of *Homo economicus* is in need of serious modification. By way of suggestion, we have introduced the concept of *Homo amans* – a holistic anthropological model that is phenomenologically constituted by the virtues of faith, hope, and love and refers to man as a questing, expecting, and relational being who wants to foster human flourishing. Whether or not *Homo amans* could serve in the future as a complementary model to *Homo economicus* remains to be seen, because several aspects of human relationality in relation to contemporary economics are contested and in need of future study. The following questions might shape a future multidisciplinary dialogue on relational anthropology:

1. How is love best defined, and how does it relate to other virtues in general, as well as faith and hope in particular?

2. Are we naturally predisposed to love, and if so, how does this generate trust?
3. Is there any connection between trust and the virtues of faith, hope, and love, and if so, how are they interconnected?
4. How can the virtue of love develop over a person's life-time, and what factors encourage people to promote well-being in the contexts of home, school, and work?
5. Which areas of the neural system are required to facilitate a person acting intentionally to promote overall well-being?
6. Does gender make any difference to the promotion of well-being in companies and organizations?
7. How is love understood inter-culturally and inter-religiously in relation to global economics?
8. How can technology damage and stimulate human relationality in the future?

References

Arendt, H. 1958. *The Human Condition*. Chicago: The University of Chicago Press.

Bass, B., and P. Steidlmeier. 1999. Ethics, Character, and Authentic Transformational Leadership Behavior. *The Leadership Quarterly* 10 (2): 181–217.

Berger, P.L., and T. Luckmann. 1966. *The Social Construction of Reality: A Treatise in the Sociology of Knowledge*. New York: Doubleday.

Bhaskar, R. 1997. *A Realist Concept of Science*. London: Verso.

Bovenberg, A.L. 2016. *Economieonderwijs in balans: kiezen en samenwerken*. Tilburg: Tilburg University.

———. 2018. Economics as a Discipline of Hope. In *Driven by Hope: Economics and Theology in Dialogue*, ed. S.C. van den Heuvel and P. Nullens, 21–48. Leuven: Peeters.

Bowles, S. 1998. Endogenous Preferences: The Cultural Consequences of Markets and Other Economic Institutions. *Journal of Economic Literature* 36 (1): 75–111.

Bowles, S., and H. Gintis. 1998. Is Equality Passé? *Homo Reciprocans* and the Future of Egalitarian Politics. *Boston Review* 23 (6): 1–27.

———. 2011. *A Cooperative Species: Human Reciprocity and Its Evolution*. Princeton/Woodstock: Princeton University Press.

Brümmer, V. 1993. *The Model of Love: A Study in Philosophical Theology*. Cambridge: Cambridge University Press.

———. 1956. *Faith, Hope, and Love*. Philadelphia: The Westminster Press.

Cohen, D. 2012. *Homo Economicus: Prophète (égaré) des temps nouveaux*. Paris: Michel.

Comte-Sponville, A. 1995. *Petit traité des grandes vertus*. Paris: Presses Universitaires de France.

Cubillos, R.H. 2017. *Faith, Hope, and Love in the Kingdom of God*. Eugene: Pickwick.

Dahrendorf, R. 1958. *Homo Sociologicus: Ein Versuch zur Geschichte, Bedeutung und Kritik der Kategorie der sozialen Rolle*. Cologne/Opladen: Westdeutscher Verlag.

Dawkins, R. 2016. *The Extended Selfish Gene*. Oxford: Oxford University Press.

Devas, C.S. 1883. *Groundwork of Economics*. London: Longmans, Green & Co.

Dinello, N. 1998. Russian Religious Rejections of Money and "*Homo Economicus*": The Self-Identifications of the "Pioneers of a Money Economy" in Post-Soviet Russia. *Sociology of Religion* 59 (1): 45–64.

Doucouliagos, C. 1994. A Note on the Evolution of *Homo Economicus*. *Journal of Economic Issues* 28 (3): 877–883.

Drucker, P. 1939. *The End of Economic Man: The Origins of Totalitarianism*. New York: Day.

Eisenberger, N.I. 2013. Social Ties and Health: A Social Neuroscience Perspective. *Current Opinion in Neurobiology* 23 (3): 407–413.
Elworthy, C. 1993. *Homo Biologicus: An Evolutionary Model for the Human Sciences*. Berlin: Duncker & Humblot.
Emde, R.N. 2016. From a Baby Smiling: Reflections on Virtues in Development. In *Developing the Virtues: Integrating Perspectives*, ed. J. Annas, D. Narvaez, and N.E. Snow, 69–94. New York: Oxford University Press.
Fleming, P. 2017. *The Death of Homo Economicus: Work, Debt and the Myth of Endless Accumulation*. London: Pluto Press.
Foltz, F.A., and F.A. Foltz. 2018. *Faith, Hope, and Love in the Technological Society*. Eugene: Cascade.
Forsythe, R., J.L. Horowitz, N.E. Savin, and M. Sefton. 1994. Fairness in Simple Bargaining Experiments. *Games and Economic Behavior* 7 (3): 346–380.
Fox, J., and J.J. Moreland. 2015. The Dark Side of Social Networking Sites: An Exploration of the Relational and Psychological Stressors Associated with Facebook Use and Affordances. *Computers in Human Behavior* 45 (4): 168–176.
Frank, R.H. 1985. *Choosing the Right Pond: Human Behavior and the Quest for Status*. Oxford: Oxford University Press.
Frijters, P., and G. Foster. 2013. *An Economic Theory of Greed, Love, Groups, and Networks*. Cambridge: Cambridge University Press.
Fry, L.W. 2003. Toward a Theory of Spiritual Leadership. *The Leadership Quarterly* 14 (6): 693–727.
Gintis, H., S. Bowles, R. Boyd, and E. Fehr, eds. 2005. *Moral Sentiments and Material Interests: The Foundations of Cooperation in Economic Life*. Cambridge, MA: MIT Press.
Girgerenzer, G., and H. Brighton. 2009. *Homo heuristicus*: Why Biased Minds Make Better Inferences. *Topics in Cognitive Science*, 1(1), 107–143.
Granovetter, M. 1985. Economic Action and Social Structure: The Problem of Embeddedness. *American Journal of Sociology* 91 (3): 481–510.
Greenberg, Y.K. 2008. *Encyclopedia of Love in World Religions*. Santa Barbara/Denver/Oxford: ABC-CLIO.
Greenleaf, R.K. 2002. *Servant Leadership: A Journey into the Nature of Legitimate Power and Greatness*. New York: Paulist Press.
Habito, R.L.F., and K. Inaba, eds. 2008. *The Practice of Altruism: Caring and Religion in Global Perspective*. Newcastle: Cambridge Scholars Press.
Haidt, J.D. 2003. The Moral Emotions. In *Handbook of Affective Sciences*, ed. R.J. Davidson, K.R. Scherer, and H.H. Goldsmith, 852–870. Oxford: Oxford University Press.
Harari, Y.N. 2016. *Homo Deus: A Brief History of Tomorrow*. London: Secker.
Hengstmengel, J. 2020. *De Homo Economicus: Een familiegeschiedenis*. Amsterdam: Boom.
Hertzler, J.O. 1934. On Golden Rules. *The International Journal of Ethics* 44 (4): 418–436.
Hochwälder, J. 2000. Assumptions about Human Nature: Comparison of Implicit and Explicit Personality Theories. *Psychological Reports* 87 (2): 611–622.
Kirchgässner, G. 2008. *Homo Oeconomicus: The Economic Model of Behaviour and Its Applications in Economics and Other Social Sciences*. New York: Springer.
Klein, R.A. 2011. *Sociality as the Human Condition: Anthropology in Economic, Philosophical, and Theological Perspective*. Transl. M. Sitling. Leiden/Boston: Brill.
Kovacs, J.L. 2005. *1 Corinthians Interpreted by Early Christian Commentators*. Grand Rapids/ Cambridge: Eerdmans.
Krebs, D.L. 2012. How Altruistic by Nature? In *Moving Beyond Self-Interest: Perspectives from Evolutionary Biology, Neuroscience, and the Social Sciences*, ed. S.L. Brown, R.M. Brown, and L.A. Penner, 25–38. Oxford: Oxford University Press.
Kullberg, J.S., and J.D. Singer. 2012. Bringing Neuroscience into Political Science: The Caregiving System and Human Sociopolitical Evolution. In *Moving Beyond Self-Interest: Perspectives from Evolutionary Biology, Neuroscience, and the Social Sciences*, ed. S.L. Brown, R.M. Brown, and L.A. Penner, 246–268. Oxford/New York: Oxford University Press.

Leiberg, S., O. Klimecki, and T. Singer. 2011. Short-term Compassion Training Increases Prosocial Behavior in a Newly Developed Prosocial Game. *PloS One* 6 (3): e17798.
MacIntyre, A. 1981. *After Virtue: A Study in Moral Theory*. Notre Dame: University of Notre Dame Press.
———. 1988. *Whose Justice? Which Rationality?* Notre Dame: University of Notre Dame Press.
McCloskey, D.N. 2006. *The Bourgeois Virtues: Ethics for an Age of Commerce*. Chicago/London: The University of Chicago Press.
———. 2016. *Bourgeois Equality: How Ideas, Not Capital or Institutions, Enriched the World*. Chicago/London: The University of Chicago Press.
McGrath, A. 2007. *Dawkins' God: Genes, Memes, and the Meaning of Life*. Oxford: Blackwell.
McPherson, M., L. Smith-Lovin, and M.E. Brashears. 2006. Social Isolation in America: Changes in Core Discussion Networks over Two Decades. *American Sociology Review* 71 (3): 353–375.
Mill, J.S. 1844. *Essays on Some Unsettled Questions of Political Economy*. London: Parker.
Moore, G. 2017. *Virtue at Work: Ethics for Individuals, Managers, and Organizations*. Oxford: Oxford University Press.
Ng, I.C.L., and L.M. Tseng. 2008. Learning to be Sociable: The Evolution of *Homo Economicus*. *The American Journal of Economics and Sociology* 67 (2): 265–286.
Nussbaum, M.C. 2011. *Creating Capabilities: The Human Development Approach*. Cambridge, MA/London: Harvard University Press.
Nygren, A. 1969 [1938]. *Agape and Eros*. Transl. P.S. Watson. New York: Harper & Row.
O'Boyle, E. 1994. *Homo Socio-Economicus*: Foundational to Social Economics and the Social Economy. *Review of Social Economy*, 52(3), 286–313.
Oord, T.J. 2010. *Defining Love: A Philosophical, Scientific, and Theological Engagement*. Grand Rapids: Brazos.
———. 2013. Types of Love and Types of Exemplars: Implications for Virtue Science. In *Theology and the Science of Moral Action: Virtue Ethics, Exemplarity, and Cognitive Neuroscience*, ed. J.A. Van Slyke et al., 179–190. New York/London: Routledge.
Papadogiannis, Y. 2014. *The Rise and Fall of Homo Economicus: The Myth of the Rational Human and the Chaotic Reality*. North Charleston: CreateSpace.
Pearson, H. 2000. *Homo Economicus* Goes Native. 1859–1945: The Rise and Fall of Primitive Economics. *History of Political* Economy, 32(4), 933–989.
Peterson, C., and M.E.P. Seligman. 2004. *Character Strengths and Virtues: A Handbook and Classification*. Oxford/New York: Oxford University Press.
Pfaff, D.W. 2015. *The Altruistic Brain: How We Are Naturally Good*. New York: Oxford University Press.
Pieper, J. 1986. *Lieben, Hoffen, Glauben*. Munich: Kösel.
Piliavin, J.A., and H.-W. Charng. 1990. Altruism: A Review of Recent Theory and Research. *Annual Review of Sociology* 16: 27–65.
Pless, N.M., and T. Maak. 2012. Responsible Leadership: Pathways to the Future. In *Responsible Leadership*, ed. N.M. Pless and T. Maak, 3–13. Dordrecht: Springer.
Post, S., and J. Neimark. 2007. *Why Good Things Happen to Good People: The Exciting New Research That Proves the Link Between Doing Good and Living a Longer, Healthier, Happier Life*. New York: Broadway.
Raworth, K. 2017. *Doughnut Economics: Seven Ways to Think Like a 21st Century Economist*. White River Junction: Green.
Robinson, E.A. 2004. *These Three: The Theological Virtues of Faith, Hope, and Love*. Eugene: Wipf & Stock.
Rodriguez-Sickert, C. 2009. Homo economicus. In *Handbook of Economics and Ethics*, ed. J. Peil and I. van Staveren, 223–229. Cheltenham/Northampton: Elgar.
Scioli, A., and H.B. Biller. 2009. *Hope in the Age of Anxiety: A Guide to Understanding and Strengthening Our Most Important Virtue*. Oxford/New York: Oxford University Press.
Seabright, P. [2]2010. *The Company of Strangers: A Natural History of Economic Life*. Princeton/Oxford: Princeton University Press.

Sen, A.K. 1982. *Choice, Welfare, and Measurement*. Oxford: Blackwell.
———. 1992. *Inequality Reexamined*. New York/Cambridge, MA: Russell Sage Foundation/Harvard University Press.
———. 1999. *Development as Freedom*. Oxford: Oxford University Press.
Silva, M. 2014a. ἀγαπάω. In *The New International Dictionary of New Testament Theology and Exegesis*, ed. M. Silva, vol. Vol. 1, 103–115. Grand Rapids: Zondervan.
———. 2014b. φιλέω. In *The New International Dictionary of New Testament Theology and Exegesis*, ed. M. Silva, vol. Vol. 4, 605–608. Grand Rapids: Zondervan.
Smith, A. 1759. *The Theory of Moral Sentiments*. London: Millar, Kincaid & Bell.
———. 1776. *An Inquiry into the Nature and Causes of the Wealth of Nations* (2 vols.). London: Strahan & Cadell.
Smith, C. 2010. *What is a Person? Rethinking Humanity, Social Life, and the Moral Good from the Person Up*. Chicago/London: The University of Chicago Press.
———. 2015. *To Flourish or Destruct: A Personalist Theory of Human Goods, Motivations, Failure, and Evil*. Chicago/London: The University of Chicago Press.
Stevenson, L., D.L. Haberman, P.M. Wright, and C. Witt. 2018. *Thirteen Theories of Human Nature*. New York/Oxford: Oxford University Press.
Taylor, C. 1989. *Sources of the Self: The Making of the Modern Identity*. Cambridge, MA: Harvard University Press.
Thaler, R.H. 2000. From *Homo Economicus* to *Homo Sapiens*. *Journal of Economic Perspectives* 14 (1): 133–141.
Torchia, J. 2008. *Exploring Personhood: An Introduction to the Philosophy of Human Nature*. Lanham: Rowman & Littlefield.
Vacek, E.C. 1994. *Love, Human and Divine: The Heart of Christian Ethics*. Washington, DC: Georgetown University Press.
Van Slyke, J.A. 2014. Moral Psychology, Neuroscience, and Virtue: From Moral Judgment to Moral Character. In *Virtues and Their Vices*, ed. K. Timpe and C.A. Boyd, 459–480. Oxford: Oxford University Press.
Vrtička, P. 2017. The Social Neuroscience of Attachment. In *Neuroscience and Social Science: The Missing Link*, ed. A. Ibáñez, L. Sedeño, and A.M. García, 95–120. New York: Springer.
Wildman, W.J. (2009). *Science and Religious Anthropology: A Spiritually Evocative Naturalist Interpretation of Human Life*. Aldershot: Ashgate.
Wilson, E.O. 1975. *Sociobiology: The New Synthesis*. Cambridge, MA/London: Harvard University Press.
Wojtyla, K. 1993. *Person and Community*. Transl. T. Sandok. New York: Lang.

Chapter 3
Natural Goodness

Dennis L. Krebs

Abstract Although the theory of evolution might seem to imply that all animals must be selfish by nature, this is not the case because social animals can propagate their selfish genes in psychologically unselfish ways. To understand the moral aspect of human nature, we must understand the adaptive functions that moral traits served in early human environments. I argue that the central function of morality is to uphold adaptive systems of cooperation. Even though some cooperative strategies are susceptible to exploitation by selfish strategies, there are several ways in which the kind of cooperative behavioral strategies that people consider moral can evolve. Primitive psychological sources of moral behavior, such as moral emotions, and advanced sources, such as perspective-taking and moral reasoning, evolve and develop throughout the life span in a Russian Doll manner. Although the original function of perspective-taking and moral reasoning may have been to help early humans advance their interests in strategic social interactions, these processes may now motivate people to behave in moral ways. We are evolved to be as good as our early ancestors had to be to reap the benefits of sociality and cooperation.

3.1 Introduction

Some eminent evolutionary biologists have asserted that, on the laws of evolution, all animals must be selfish by nature. For example, George Williams (1989) wrote, "there is no encouragement for any belief that an organism can be designed for any purpose other than the most effective pursuit of … self-interest…. [because] evolution is guided by a force that maximizes genetic selfishness" (pp. 195–6). In a similar vein, in *The Selfish Gene*, Dawkins (1989) asserted, "'Nature red in tooth and claw' sums up our modern understanding of natural selection admirably…. Much as we might wish to believe otherwise, universal love and welfare of the species as a whole are concepts that simply do not make evolutionary sense …. Be warned that

D. L. Krebs (✉)
Simon Fraser University, Burnaby, BC, Canada
e-mail: dennis_krebs@sfu.ca

J. van Nes et al. (eds.), *Relational Anthropology for Contemporary Economics*, Ethical Economy 61, https://doi.org/10.1007/978-3-030-84690-9_3

if you wish, as I do, to build a society in which individuals cooperate generously and unselfishly toward a common good, you can expect little help from biological nature" (pp. 3–4).

Claims such as these stem from the assumption that it is appropriate to characterize those who win "survival of the fittest" contests as selfish because they propagate their genes at the expense of those against whom they are competing. It would seem that a mutation that disposed an animal to sacrifice its prospects of surviving and reproducing for the sake of others would not fare well in the process of natural selection. For this reason, so the argument goes, on the laws of evolution, all animals must be selfish by nature.

There is, however, an obvious problem with this conclusion, namely that many animals appear to behave in unselfish ways. Members of many species make sacrifices for their offspring and other relatives. Members of some species join forces to kill prey, and members of other species help one another avoid predators, by for example emitting alarm calls. Many animals collaborate in the building of shelters, dams, and tunnels. Although most people assume that we are the only – or at least the most – altruistic species, we do not even come close to the sacrifices that many social insect species make for their groups. Ants, bees, and termites spend virtually all of their lives gathering food for others, and they willingly sacrifice their lives to defend their colonies.

If biologists such as George Williams and Richard Dawkins were correct in asserting that all traits that evolve through natural selection must be selfish, then evidence that animals behave in altruistic and cooperative ways would constitute a serious challenge to the theory of evolution. Charles Darwin was aware of this challenge, acknowledging that the self-sacrificial altruism of social insects presented "one special difficulty, which at first seemed insuperable, and actually fatal to my whole theory." In a similar vein, Williams (1989) asked, "how could maximizing selfishness produce an organism capable of often advocating, and occasionally practicing, charity toward strangers and even towards animals" (p. 208)?

One of the ways in which skeptical evolutionary theorists have accounted for seemingly altruistic behaviors will seem familiar to many – they have attributed it to social learning and cultural indoctrination. As expressed by Dawkins (1989), "let us try to *teach* generosity and altruism, because we are born selfish…. Our genes may instruct us to be selfish, but we are not necessarily compelled to obey them all our lives" (p. 3). Or, as expressed by Campbell (1978), "in man, genetic competition precludes the evolution of … genetic altruism. The behavioral dispositions that produce … self-sacrificial altruism must instead be products of culturally evolved indoctrination that has had to counter self-serving genetic tendencies." According to Campbell, an important implication of this point is that "man is profoundly ambivalent in his social role – as Freud noted…. The commandments, the proverbs, the religious 'law' represent social evolutionary products directed at inculcating tendencies that are in direct opposition to the 'temptations' representing, for the most part, the dispositional tendencies produced by biological evolution" (pp. 52–3). Campbell and Dawkins are endorsing Original Sin-type models of human nature. Many people find such models appealing: we are born bad, but we can learn to be good.

There is no question that skeptical evolutionary theorists are correct when they assert that we are evolved to behave in sinful, selfish, and immoral ways, and there is no question that they are correct when they assert that we can be taught to be good. However, this is just half the story. We also are evolved to behave in unselfish and moral ways, and we can learn to be bad. In essence, Original Sin models pit nature against nurture, biology against culture, biological evolution against cultural evolution, and genes against environments. However, biology and culture can work together to produce moral traits. I believe that the evidence supports the conclusion that mental mechanisms that dispose us to behave in ways that we consider altruistic, fair, and moral can evolve and have evolved in our species (and in some other species as well) (Krebs 2011). We inherit a capacity to be good. This does not mean that we are entirely good by nature. We are evolved to be good and bad, moral and immoral, virtuous and vicious, depending on the conditions.

3.2 The Nature of Selfishness and Altruism

The first step in explaining how a capacity to be good could evolve is to recognize that genetic selfishness is quite different from the kind of selfishness that we consider bad. The kind of selfishness that is relevant to morality does not pertain to the *propagation of genes;* it pertains to the *motives of individuals*. Several social scientists have pointed out that a great deal of confusion and misunderstanding about human nature has been fomented by scholars who fail to recognize that biologists define selfishness and altruism in qualitatively different ways from the ways in which psychologists and laypeople define these constructs. For example, in response to an assertion by Richard Dawkins that genes that rendered horses susceptible to developing bad teeth and genes that disposed humans to smoke cigarettes would qualify as altruistic if they reduced individuals' prospects of surviving and reproducing, Batson (2000) wrote, "most people interested in the existence of altruism are not thinking about bad teeth in horses or smoking cigarettes; they are thinking about psychological altruism" (p. 208). In a related vein, Sober and Wilson (2000) pointed out that "the automatic assumption that individualism [i.e., selfishness] in evolutionary biology and egoism in the social sciences must reinforce each other is as common as it is mistaken. More care is needed to connect the behaviors that evolved … with the psychological mechanisms that evolved to motivate those behaviors" (p. 205). Expanding on this point, De Waal (2008) explained that although evolutionary accounts of altruism are "built around the principle that all that natural selection can work with are the effects of behavior, not the motivation behind it," they persist in invoking motivational terms:

> The hijacking of motivational terminology by evolutionary biologists has been unhelpful for communication about motivation per se.… It is not for nothing that biologists hammer on the distinction between ultimate and proximate ….ultimate accounts stress return-benefits, i.e., positive consequences for the performer and/or its kin. Inasmuch as these benefits may be quite delayed, however, it is unclear what motivational role, if any, they play (pp. 280–1).

Whether selfish individuals who seek to obtain benefits for themselves without due regard for others fare better biologically and contribute more copies of their genes to future generations than those who behave in more moral ways is an open question. They might, or they might not. There is nothing in the process of natural selection that dictates that individuals who are motivated to behave in ways that we consider bad will prevail in the struggle for existence. Psychologically altruistic individuals motivated to help others as an end in itself, and moral individuals motivated to benefit themselves and others in fair and equitable ways, could be more likely to survive, to produce offspring, and to propagate their genes than individuals who are motivated to advance their own interests without concern for others. Altruistic motives could produce biologically beneficial results. People who genuinely want to help others could fare better biologically than people who are concerned only with themselves. The assumption that all evolved dispositions are selfish is valid only with respect to genetic forms of selfishness in the environments in which they were selected. Inasmuch as moral traits can be genetically selfish (i.e., can increase the biological success of those who emit them), they can evolve.

The question that those who are concerned with human nature should be asking is how *psychologically selfish* strategies, defined in terms of the motivation to advance one's own welfare without concern for others, fared against *psychologically unselfish* strategies in helping early humans propagate their genes (that is to say, achieve genetically selfish effects). Which strategies were selected and evolved to become part of human nature? Did those who were motivated to cooperate, behave fairly, and help others contribute more copies of their genes to future generations than those who were motivated to look out only for themselves?

3.3 The Evolution of Social Strategies

Imagine members of early human groups faced with recurring decisions about whether to behave in selfish or unselfish ways. Evolutionary theorists assume that such choices are guided by genetically influenced strategies, and they seek to understand which strategies produced the most adaptive decisions in early human environments and, therefore, which ones evolved. Although the genes that program evolved strategies were selected hundreds of thousands, even millions, of years ago, evolutionary theorists expect them to guide strategic decision making in modern environments in conditions corresponding to those that regulated them in archaic environments.

3.3.1 *The Adaptive Potential in Cooperative Strategies*

It is easy to see how animals could advance their adaptive interests more effectively by adopting cooperative social strategies than by adopting solitary or selfish strategies. Examples abound in the animal kingdom. We can safely assume that early humans were poorly equipped to survive on their own. A solitary human with small teeth, fingernail claws, devoid of fur to keep warm, and relatively slow afoot would not have lasted long in early environments, just as modern humans would not last long by themselves in the wild today. Although our distant primate ancestors possessed killer ape traits such as large canine teeth and claws, these traits diminished as we evolved because early humans acquired adaptations that enabled them to solve their adaptive problems more effectively in social ways. As expressed by Curry (2016), "humans descended from a long line of social primates; they have spent 50 million years living in social groups…. and two million years making a living as intensely collaborative hunter-gatherers. This has equipped humans with a range of biological – including psychological – adaptations for cooperation" (p. 29). It is easy to see how early humans who inherited genes that induced them to join forces to kill large game and defend their groups, to collaborate in the construction of shelters, to help one another when they were in need, and to coordinate their efforts to mate and rear offspring could have fared better than early humans who inherited genes that induced them to behave in more selfish and immoral ways (Ellis 1998).

There is untold adaptive potential in cooperative social strategies in modern societies. If everyone did his or her share, we would produce significantly more resources than we currently produce, and if everyone took his or her share, we would not have to waste energy competing for them. If no one were disposed to cheat, we wouldn't have to waste resources on crime prevention and the punishment of criminals. Everyone would benefit. So, in view of the tremendous adaptive potential in cooperation, why aren't we more cooperative and moral?

3.3.2 *Obstacles to the Evolution of Cooperation: The Adaptive Potential in Selfish Strategies*

The reason that unconditionally cooperative (purely moral) strategies have not evolved in the human species is because it is in the biological and genetic interest of individuals to maximize their gains and to minimize their costs in exchanges with others, and this creates the temptation to behave selfishly and cheat. As expressed by Rawls (1999) in the opening pages of his classic book, *A Theory of Justice*:

> Although a society is a cooperative venture for mutual advantage, it is typically marked by a conflict as well as by an identity of interests. There is an identity of interests since social cooperation makes possible a better life for all than any would have if each were to live solely by his own efforts. There is a conflict of interests since persons are not indifferent as to how the greater benefits produced by their collaboration are distributed, for in order to pursue their ends they each prefer a larger to a lesser share (p. 4).

Conflicts of interest give rise to moral problems because they tempt us to advance our interests at the expense of others, which undermines cooperative social orders. In the words of Alexander (1985), "if there were not conflicts of interest among people and societies it is difficult to see how concepts of right and wrong, ethics and morality, and selfishness and altruism could ever have arisen." Alexander argues that to understand conflicts of interest fully, we must trace them back to their biological core: "The interests of every individual human (i.e., the directions of its striving) are expected to be toward ensuring the indefinite survival of its genes and their copies, whether these are resident in the individual, its descendants, or its collateral relatives" (p. 3).

Conflicts of interest present obstacles to the evolution of cooperative and fair strategies. For example, it would have been in the interest of early humans who collaborated in hunting large game and defending themselves against predators to conserve their energy, position themselves in ways that diminished their chances of getting injured, let others do the dirty work, and take the lion's share of the spoils. Such cheating is prevalent in the animal kingdom and among modern humans in some situations.

The biological benefits of strategies inducing individuals to behave in cooperative and moral ways hinge on them interacting with other individuals who behave in cooperative and moral ways. The problem is, within populations of individuals inheriting genes that induce them to behave in unconditionally cooperative ways, some individuals inevitably would inherit genes that disposed them to behave in more selfish ways, and unfortunately, unless counteracted effectively, the selfish individuals would come out ahead. The bad guys would take what that the good guys were willing to offer without suffering the costs of giving in return, and the good guys would suffer the costs of giving to the bad guys without reaping the benefits of receiving in return. In the currency of evolution, the selfish individuals would be more likely than the cooperative individuals to survive and propagate selfish offspring like themselves, who would be more likely to propagate additional selfish offspring, and so on, causing an exponential explosion of selfish individuals in the population. It follows that strategies that induce individuals to behave in *unconditionally* cooperative and moral ways are doomed to extinction in groups containing individuals who are willing and able to exploit cooperative individuals by behaving in selfish ways. The only population in which unconditionally cooperative strategies could evolve would be one in which there were no genetic conflicts of interest, such as in a population of clones. In sexually reproducing species such as our own, pure goodness is out of the question.

3.3.3 The Ultimate Irony: Self-Defeating Selfishness

In view of the adaptive superiority of social strategies that induce individuals to behave in selfish ways when competing against strategies that induce them to behave in unconditionally cooperative ways, it might seem that selfish strategies would win all evolutionary contests, rendering all species selfish by nature, as skeptical evolutionary theorists, such as those I quoted above, have claimed. Fortunately, however, this is not the case. Even though strategies that induce individuals to behave in selfish ways can evolve and have evolved in many species, including our own, unconditionally selfish strategies are not optimal in social species that need, or can benefit from, assistance from others. Brown (1984) eloquently explained why.

Imagining a group of cooperative Christian birds dependent for their survival on being groomed by other birds, Brown (1984) considered the ultimate effect of a mutant cheater who reaped the benefits of being groomed without suffering the costs of grooming others in return. As discussed, the cheater would fare better than the cooperative members of the group, propagating offspring who inherited his or her cheating ways, and so on, until the selfish cheaters replaced all of the Christian cooperators. However, Brown points out that this would usher in a tragically self-defeating consequence for the selfish cheaters, because "once grooming birds had become extinct, so eventually would cheaters; one imagines a pathetic final act in which all birds on the stage present to one another heads that none will groom" (Brown 1984). Although it might have been in the biological interest of members of early human groups that collaborated in activities such as hunting prey and defending themselves against predators to do less than their share and take more than their share under some circumstances, this strategy would not have paid off if other members also adopted it or if they got punished for shirking their duties.

The evolution of unconditionally selfish and immoral strategies would be an unmitigated disaster in the human species. No one would help anyone. Everyone would try to cheat everyone else. Unconditional selfishness would inevitably do everyone down because in social species in which individuals are dependent on one another for their welfare, those on whom they are dependent – whether marital partners, friends, or members of their groups – are resources that it is in their interest to preserve and cultivate. Helping those on whom your welfare is dependent is like cultivating resources such as gardens, orchards, and domesticated animals that you can use to advance your welfare down the line. Investing in your group is like investing in public goods such as the common grazing land described by Garrett Hardin in *The Tragedy of the Commons*. Failing to support those on whom you are dependent is like letting your resources go to waste. As expressed by Flack and de Waal (2000):

> Inasmuch as every member [of a group] benefits from a unified, cooperative group, one expects them to care about the society they live in, and to make an effort to improve and strengthen it similar to the way the spider repairs her web, and the beaver maintains the integrity of his dam. Each and every individual has a stake in the quality of the social environment on which its survival depends. In trying to improve this quality for their own purposes, they help many of their group mates at the same time (p. 14).

To summarize, we would expect individuals who inherited genes that disposed them to adopt cooperative moral strategies to fare better than individuals who inherited genes that disposed them to adopt selfish immoral strategies as long as the good guys interacted with other good guys and the bad guys interacted with other bad guys. In addition, we would expect cooperative groups to prevail in competitions against selfish groups – a phenomenon that some theorists believe played a very important role in the evolution of morality. However, within mixed groups, we would expect selfish strategists who exploit cooperative strategists to come out ahead, but only temporarily. If selfish strategists ran cooperative strategists into the ground, they would destroy the resources they needed to advance their welfare, leaving them with no choice but to go it alone or to interact with one another. The solution to this problem – the way in which natural selection solved the problem of selfishness – is to build conditions into cooperative strategies that induce co-operators to interact with co-operators and guard against being exploited by those who are prone to behave selfishly.

3.3.4 Resolving the Conundrum of Cooperation: The Evolution of Conditional Strategies

Evolutionary game theorists have created computer-based simulations of social evolution in which they have pitted a variety of social strategies against one another. In these contests, points equate to replicas, or genetic clones, of winning strategies. The better each strategy does against the other strategies against which it competes, the more copies of itself it contributes to future generations, and the more copies of defeated strategies it knocks out of the population.

"Behave selfishly" is a powerful social strategy – probably the most primitive of all. It doesn't require much brainpower. It is uncomplicated, and it is a daunting foe in social games. One on one, it can't be beaten in single exchanges; the best that other strategies can do is tie it. Pitted against cooperative strategies, behaving selfishly always wins the initial exchange. In one-shot interactions, the best you can do against a selfish opponent is make a selfish move yourself, and tie. For reasons such as these, many evolutionary game theorists assumed that there were no strategies that could defeat purely selfish strategies (and therefore that all animals were selfish by nature), but this changed when some game theorists found that a simple conditionally cooperative strategy, Tit for Tat, could prevail over more selfish strategies in repeated games and evolve under certain conditions.

Tit for Tat contains the decision-rule "on the initial exchange with other players, make a cooperative move, then on the following exchanges, treat them the way they treated you." "If your partner is nice to you, be nice back, but if your partner treats you selfishly, treat him or her selfishly in return." This decision-rule directs players to make a cooperative overture to potential exchange partners and follow it up by reciprocating their decisions. Although the Tit for Tat strategy renders individuals vulnerable to being suckered on the first exchange (causing them to lose to selfish strategies one-on-on), Tit for Tat induces players to cut their losses quickly against those who exploit them, while reaping the benefits of cooperative exchanges with those who treat them right. Tit for Tat can be considered a somewhat moral strategy because it induces individuals to behave altruistically on the first exchange and fairly (quid pro quo) on subsequent exchanges. However, Tit for Tat would not be considered a highly moral strategy by people who believe it is right to forgive those who trespass against us, because Tit for Tat induces people to get even with those who treat them selfishly. In one of the first computer-based simulations of the evolution of social strategies, run by Robert Axelrod and his colleagues at the Institute of Public Policy Studies, University of Michigan in collaboration with the late William Hamilton, from Oxford University, Tit for Tat came out on top, defeating all other strategies against which it competed, including a purely selfish strategy called "All D" (always defect). This outcome excited many evolutionary theorists because it demonstrated that at least one cooperative strategy could defeat purely selfish strategies and evolve, which implied that we could inherit a capacity to behave in moral ways (Axelrod and Hamilton 1981).

At first, it seemed that Tit for Tat would reign supreme over all other strategies. However, follow-up studies revealed that this was not the case. As you might expect, Tit for Tat did well in populations replete with cooperative strategies; however, it did poorly in populations replete with selfish strategies. In addition to being vulnerable to exploitation on the first exchange, the Tit for Tat strategy was susceptible to getting locked into mutually defeating selfish-selfish exchanges. Let's say, for example, that two Tit for Tat strategists are happily enjoying the benefits of cooperative exchanges, but one of them makes a mistake or behaves selfishly in a moment of weakness. Obeying the Tit for Tat decision-rule, the other player returns selfishness with selfishness, which induces the first player to behave selfishly, giving rise to an endless string of self-defeating exchanges – a blood feud. Game theorists came to discover that conditionally cooperative strategies that enable players to break out of such self-defeating exchanges without opening themselves up to ongoing exploitation – strategies such as "Generous Tit for Tat" and "Tit for two Tats" – could defeat Tit for Tat. A hopeful aspect of these findings is that all of the strategies that defeated Tit for Tat were "nicer" than Tit for Tat – that is to say, they were more forgiving and induced players to make more altruistic and cooperative choices (Ridley 1996).

3.3.5 *Paths to the Evolution of Cooperation*

The key to explaining the evolution of goodness lies in explaining how cooperative social strategies that benefit others at immediate costs to actors can pay off genetically in the end, or how such strategies could have evolved even though they were maladaptive. Evolutionary theorists have identified five ways in which conditionally cooperative strategies could evolve. In all five cases, the question to keep in mind is how these strategies help individuals propagate the genes that dispose them to behave in cooperative ways. To begin with, cooperative strategies such as Tit for Tat can evolve when they produce return benefits by inducing recipients to pay donors back (*direct reciprocity*). Second, cooperative strategies can evolve when they produce return benefits indirectly, by inducing third parties who are willing to cooperate to select cooperative individuals as exchange partners (*indirect reciprocity*). Third, cooperative strategies can evolve when individuals suffer the survival costs of helping others in order to increase their chances of propagating their genes by mating (*sexual selection*). Fourth, cooperative strategies can evolve when they increase the biological success of kin who share copies of cooperators' genes (*kin selection*). And finally, cooperative strategies can evolve when they increase the biological welfare of groups that contain members who share copies of cooperators' genes (*group selection*). In all five cases, the immediate costs that individuals suffer from helping others pay off genetically in the end. Inasmuch as conditionally cooperative strategies equate to conditionally moral strategies, they render those who invoke them conditionally good by nature. (Cooperative strategies also can evolve through cultural selection, but I will not discuss this process here.)

3.4 Psychological Sources of Goodness

Biologists focus on the evolution of behavioral strategies; evolutionary psychologists focus on the ways in which the evolved mental mechanisms that give rise to these strategies are designed. Lay people base their attributions of goodness primarily on the psychological sources of behaviors. When we observe others doing good things, we ask ourselves what kinds of motives are driving their behaviors – what they are trying to achieve. To deem a behavior moral, it must be viewed as stemming from a moral motive and being aimed at doing good. For example, if we think that a charitable act stemmed from sympathy for the disadvantaged and was aimed at improving their lot, we would be inclined to consider it moral, but if we thought that it was aimed at establishing dominance, impressing others, or currying favor we would be inclined to consider it selfish.

Mental mechanisms that give rise to love, guilt, gratitude, forgiveness, empathy and other "moral emotions" have evolved in our species. Other animals, especially other primates, display precursors of these emotions. The mental mechanisms that regulate these emotions reside in the older parts of our brains. As our brains evolved, we acquired higher-order mental mechanisms that enabled us to engage in uniquely-human forms of cognition such as perspective-taking and moral reasoning. These mechanisms, which reside in the outer layers of our cerebral cortex, normally become increasingly sophisticated as our brains develop throughout the lifespan. Early-evolved and later-evolved mechanisms participate in the activation and regulation of moral motives.

3.5 Moral Emotions

The function of moral emotions is to motivate individuals to behave in ways that enable them to reap the biological and genetic benefits of cooperation. Early humans who inherited psychological mechanisms that disposed them to experience moral emotions fared better than those who did not inherit these mechanisms. For example, early humans who inherited psychological mechanisms that induced them to love their offspring, siblings, and mates were more likely to propagate their genes through kin selection and sexual selection than those who did not. Groups that contained members who inherited mechanisms that disposed them to experience feelings of solidarity and loyalty fared better than more selfish groups in inter-group conflicts. Moral emotions such as gratitude, guilt, and righteous indignation paid off biologically and genetically by motivating our early ancestors to behave in ways that upheld biologically beneficial systems of social exchange. Feelings of forgiveness motivated early humans to repair broken social relations. A sense of justice evolved because it motivated our ancestors to uphold the cooperative social orders of their groups. Moral emotions are a significant psychological source of goodness.

3.5.1 Empathy

Among the suite of emotions that have been classified as moral, empathy and its cousin, sympathy, have received the most attention from social scientists. Neuroscientists have traced empathic reactions to "mirror neurons." When people observe others performing acts, these mirror neurons fire in exactly the same way as when they perform the acts themselves (Decety 2005). Theory and research on empathy illustrates the ways in which early-evolved and later-evolved mental mechanisms interact to motivate people to do good. As expressed by De Waal (2006), "empathy covers all the ways in which one individual's emotional state affects another's, with simple mechanisms at its core and more complex mechanisms and perspective-taking abilities at its outer layers. Because of the layered nature of the capacities involved, we speak of the Russian doll model, in which higher cognitive levels of empathy build upon a firm, hard-wired basis" (p. 11). Each "layer" gives rise to a different kind of empathic experience, or a different form of empathy. The more recently-evolved and advanced the level, the more altruistic the motives it engenders.

The Evolution of Empathy It seems plausible that the psychological mechanisms that endowed early humans with a capacity for empathy originated though kin selection. Early humans who inherited mechanisms that induced them to share the feelings of their offspring and other blood relatives propagated the genes that guided the creation of these mechanisms by helping those with whom they shared genes. As these mental mechanisms evolved, they came to be activated by individuals other than kin. As expressed by De Waal (2006), "the empathic response is amplified by similarity, familiarity, social closeness, and positive experience with the other.… In human studies subjects empathize with a confederate's pleasure or distress if they perceive the relationship as cooperative." De Waal cites research showing that "seeing the pain of a cooperative confederate activates pain-related brain areas, but seeing the pain of an unfair confederate activates reward-related areas, at least in men." De Waal concludes that, "the empathy mechanism is biased the way evolutionary theory would predict. Empathy is (a) activated in relation to those with whom one has a close or positive relationship, and (b) suppressed, or even turned into Schadenfreude, in relation to strangers and defectors" (p. 16).

It is tempting to view our tendency to empathize with and assist people who share characteristics of our kin as a misfiring of mental mechanisms that evolved through kin selection, and this may, in part, be the case. However, in addition, such "overgeneralizations" probably benefited our early human ancestors by producing several return benefits. Early humans who helped non-kin with whom they empathized may well have been rewarded biologically and genetically by enhancing their reputations, by increasing their chances of mating, by upholding the groups on which they were dependent, by inducing recipients to reciprocate, and so on.

De Waal (2006) asserts that the first type of empathy to evolve, which constitutes the primitive core in humans and some other animals, induces us to experience feelings of *personal distress* when we are exposed to the distress of others – a type of emotional contagion. When we are in this state, we do not differentiate ourselves from those with whom we are empathizing. We are motivated to help others in order to relieve our own feelings of distress, which renders the motivation selfish in nature.

At "the next evolutionary step," which De Waal (2006) labels *cognitive empathy*, "emotional contagion is combined with appraisal of the other's situation and attempts to understand the cause of the other's emotions" (p. 9). Put another way, at this level, individuals attempt to take the perspective of those who are experiencing distress and understand it from their point of view. Cognitive empathy motivates individuals to engage in sympathetic behaviors such as consoling those who have been harmed. De Waal cites evidence demonstrating that consolation is common in humans and apes (and interestingly, in some large-brained birds), but virtually nonexistent in monkeys.

De Waal goes on to suggest that with expanded brain evolution, humans and a few other species acquired increasingly sophisticated perspective-taking abilities, which endowed them with the capacity to experience increasingly other-oriented forms of empathy. According to De Waal (2006), the essential cognitive ability that endows us with a capacity for the highest level of empathy – *empathic perspective taking* – is the ability to distinguish ourselves from others and to understand how others are feeling on their own terms: "For an individual to move beyond being sensitive to others toward an explicit other-orientation requires a shift in perspective. The emotional state induced in oneself by the other now needs to be attributed to the other instead of the self. A heightened self-identity allows a subject to relate to the object's emotional state without losing sight of the actual source of this state" (p. 9). De Waal (2006) cites evidence that apes, humans, elephants, and dolphins are able to recognize themselves in mirrors, that this ability is correlated with perspective-taking abilities in humans, and that animals that possess self-recognition abilities engage in "targeted helping," defined as "help that is fine-tuned to another's specific situation and goals" (p. 9).

Neuroscience research on empathy has supported De Waal's assertion that empathic reactions in humans are produced by an interaction between primitive types of emotional contagion and more advanced forms of cognition. Based on a review of research in the area, the neuroscientist Decety (2005) concluded that "cognitive processes that exert a top-down control on [primitive empathic emotional reactions] are mediated by specific subregions of the prefrontal cortex" that help people distinguish actions that they produce from actions produced by others (p. 153).

The Development of Empathy De Waal accounts for the evolution of empathy in our species in terms of the increasing sophistication of cognitive abilities mediated by the evolution of the brain. The human brain also expands as children develop. Psychologists have advanced models of the development of empathy that are complementary to De Waal's evolutionary model. Consider, for example, the model advanced by Martin Hoffman (2000).

Hoffman (2000) acknowledges that empathy stems from evolved dispositions, then goes on to describe four phases in its growth in children that are defined in large part by the expansion and refinement of perspective-taking abilities. In the first phase, infants experience empathic reactions as "global distress," triggered, for example, by the cries of other infants. In the second phase, infants display egocentric empathic reactions that motivate them to respond to others' distress by engaging in behaviors that make them (but not those with whom they are empathizing) feel better. For example, they might hug their teddy bear. In the third phase, children's empathic reactions are evoked by interpretations of the situations that others experience, and children make more finely tuned emotional attributions, realizing that others' thoughts and feelings may differ from their own. In the final, most advanced, phase (not discussed by De Waal), those who develop sophisticated perspective-taking abilities acquire the ability to understand that others' reactions are affected by life experiences that go beyond the immediate situations at hand. Such people are able to experience empathy for disadvantaged groups or classes of people that they have never observed directly.

3.5.2 *Empathy and Altruism*

Empathizing with others in distress motivates us to help them – there is no question about that. However, there is some question about the extent to which such helping behaviors are aimed at relieving the suffering of victims, as opposed to improving the welfare of recipients, and therefore how altruistic they are. Daniel Batson, from the University of Kansas, has investigated this issue most extensively. Batson

(1991, 1998) launched his research program on what he called "the empathy-altruism hypothesis" by demonstrating that we may react in two quite different ways when we are exposed to the suffering of others. First, in concert with De Waal and Hoffman, Batson suggested that we may experience *personal distress* that we can allay in a variety of ways, such as looking away, leaving the scene, or helping the suffering person. Batson conceded that when we help others in order to relieve feelings of personal distress, our behavior is selfish in nature. However, argued Batson (2000), observing others who are feeling bad also may evoke "an other-oriented emotional response…[such as] empathy, sympathy, compassion, etc." (which he labeled *empathic concern*) that engenders "a motivational state with the … goal of increasing another's welfare" (pp. 207–8). Batson argued that empathic concern motivates us to help others as an end in itself, as opposed to helping them instrumentally in order to relieve our own vicariously experienced personal distress or to achieve other selfish goals.

Batson reasoned that if, as cynics claim, people who empathize with victims help them in order to reduce their personal distress (that is to say, if the goal they are attempting to achieve is to make themselves feel better), then they should not help victims when they are able to reduce their personal distress in less costly ways, such as leaving the scene. Batson and his colleagues designed experiments to test this hypothesis and found that participants who empathized with victims (but not participants who did not empathize with them) chose to help them even when given opportunities to reduce their distress in other ways. Batson concluded that empathy (but not personal distress) engenders altruistic motives.

However, Batson's findings did not satisfy some of his more cynical colleagues, who argued that the participants in Batson's experiments who seemed to be behaving altruistically could have been attempting to achieve selfish goals other than reducing their personal distress. For example, they could have been trying to avoid feeling guilty; they could have been trying to improve their mood; they could have been trying to make a good impression on the experimenter, and so on. Batson and his colleagues conducted some 30 experiments that evaluated the possibility that participants who experienced empathy with victims helped them in order to advance their own interests. Consider three examples. To evaluate the cynical claim that people help those with whom they empathize in order to gain social approval or to avoid disapproval, Batson and his colleagues determined whether people who empathized with victims were more likely to help in public than they were to help in private. To evaluate the claim that those who empathize with victims help them in order to avoid self-censure and guilt, Batson and his colleagues determined whether participants they had induced to empathize helped victims when they were offered personally and socially acceptable reasons and justifications for not helping. To evaluate the claim that those in empathic states help others in order to feel good about themselves, Batson and his colleagues assessed the mood of empathizing participants after they learned that third parties helped victims.

Batson and his colleagues were remarkably successful at disconfirming competing hypotheses and demonstrating that people choose to help those with whom they empathize even when they are prevented from using their helping behaviors to achieve selfish goals, and even when they are offered more direct and less costly ways of achieving selfish goals than helping others. These investigators also found that when people who empathized with others in need were prevented from helping them, they felt bad. Citing a review of the literature on prosocial behavior by the psychologists Piliavin and Charng (1990), Batson (1998) concluded that a "paradigm shift" is occurring in psychology "away from the earlier position that behavior that appears to be altruistic must, under closer scrutiny, be revealed as reflecting egoistic motives. Rather, theory and data now being advanced are more compatible with the view that true altruism – acting with the goal of benefiting another – does exist and is a part of human nature" (p. 27). Natural goodness.

It is important to note that Batson and his colleagues did not claim that people do not ever help others for selfish reasons. Even in Batson's research, participants who were not induced to empathize with victims helped others in order to pursue selfish goals such as reducing their personal distress, gaining social approval, and improving their mood. Batson claimed only that a particular set of mental mechanisms – those that mediate advanced levels of empathy – engender altruistic motives. Note also that it is not possible to prove conclusively that participants in Batson's studies who empathized with victims were not driven to help them by some hidden selfish motive activated by Batson's methods of evoking empathy. And finally, note that Batson acknowledged that empathy does not always engender moral motives; it can also motivate people to behave in immoral (e.g., nepotistic and unjust) ways.

3.6 The Evolution and Development of Moral Reasoning

The Russian Doll model that De Waal invoked to explain the evolution of empathy can also be invoked to account for the evolution of moral reasoning. Moral reasoning probably originated as a tool used by early humans to advance their interests in strategic interactions with members of their groups. "You should be good to me because it will pay off for you in the end ...." As humans evolved larger brains, their capacity to invoke increasingly sophisticated forms of moral reasoning would have increased in much the same manner it does in children as they develop. According to cognitive-developmental theorists such as Kohlberg (1984), moral reasoning is the central source of goodness in people. The better we become at moral reasoning, the greater our capacity to make fair and impartial moral decisions, and the more highly developed our sense of justice. However, viewing moral reasoning as a tool that evolved to help early humans advance their biological and genetic interests raises questions about its status as a source of goodness.

Do people use moral reasoning to reach impartial moral decisions, or do they use it to advance their own selfish interests? On the one hand, there is a great deal of evidence that most people are inclined to process information in ways that favor them, their relatives, and members of their in-groups (Pyszczynski and Greenberg 1987). For example, people tend to hold others to higher moral standards than they apply to themselves, and people are more likely to argue that others should sacrifice their interests for their sake than that they should sacrifice their interests for others' sake. People tend to overestimate how much they deserve (their rights) and underestimate how much they owe (their duties), while underestimating how much others deserve and overestimating how much others owe (Greenberg and Cohen 1982). People tend to overvalue the contributions that they make to others, while undervaluing the contributions that others make to them. And people often use moral judgments to justify their immoral acts and to deflect responsibility onto others (Haidt 2001), diminishing their transgressions and excusing their misdeeds, while exaggerating the blameworthiness of their adversaries' immoral behavior (Krebs and Laird 1998).

Fortunately, however, there are several antidotes to self-serving biases in moral judgment. To begin with, people may constrain their self-serving biases in order to achieve the long-term benefits of moral strategies. In *The descent of man*, Charles Darwin (1874) suggested that early humans' capacity to reason enabled them to understand that it is in their long-term interest to forgo immediate gratification in order to uphold the interests of their communities and to figure out which customs are best equipped to help them improve their welfare: "As the reasoning powers and foresight of the members [of early human groups] became improved, each man would soon learn from experience that if he aided his fellow-men, he would commonly receive aid in return" (p. 127). On this line of thought, the capacity to reason facilitated the evolution of morality by enabling early humans to figure out that investing in their groups and behaving in moral ways paid off better than more selfish alternatives in the end – a form of enlightened self-interest.

In a similar vein, people may constrain their self-serving biases during the process of moral negotiations with others in order to avoid stalemates and reach win-win deals, and in addition, people may persuade themselves to abide by moral rules and principles in the process of attempting to persuade others. As expressed by Singer (1981), "ethical reasoning, once begun, pushes against our initially limited ethical horizons, leading us always toward a more universal point of view." "If I claim that what I do is right, while what you do is wrong, I must give some reason other than the fact that my action benefits me (or my kin, or my village) while your action benefits you (or your kin or your village)" (pp. 118–9). In a similar vein, Bloom (2004) asserted "once a creature is smart enough, impartiality – and an appreciation of moral codes such as the Golden Rule – will emerge as a consequence of this smartness" (p. 139). In a book entitled *The Better Angels of our Nature*, Pinker (2011) adduced a great deal of evidence in support of the conclusion that advances in our ability to reason accompanied by cultural developments such as mass media have mediated significant increases in the goodness of the human race over the past several thousand years.

3.7 Summary

Evolutionary theorists who have concluded that, on the laws of evolution, we (and all other animals) must be selfish by nature are not referring to the kind of selfishness that we consider immoral. The question that arises from an evolutionary analysis of morality is how behavioral strategies that we consider moral fared against behavioral strategies that we consider immoral. Did early human ancestors who treated their fellows right fare better than those who wronged them?

To understand the evolution of goodness, we must understand the adaptive functions that moral traits served in early human environments. Along with many other theorists, I argue that the central function of morality was (and still is) to uphold systems of cooperation that advanced the adaptive interests of members of groups. In large part, moral behaviors equate to cooperative behaviors. Evolutionary theorists have explained how a variety of conditionally cooperative strategies could evolve. Such strategies render us conditionally good (and conditionally bad) by nature.

A suite of psychological mechanisms has evolved to motivate us to behave in cooperative and moral ways. It is helpful to view these mechanisms in a Russian doll manner, with those that give rise to primitive emotions such as love and empathy at the core and those that give rise to higher-order cognitive processes such as perspective-taking and moral reasoning in the outer layers. Although perspective-taking and moral reasoning abilities probably originally evolved to help early humans prevail over members of their groups in strategic social interactions, there are several ways in which they can produce impartial moral judgments. Perspective-taking and moral reasoning abilities normally increase in sophistication as we develop, and they affect the ways in which we experience moral emotions, which increases our capacity for goodness. Cultural changes that render us increasingly civilized contribute to this process. Although we have not yet reached the summit of the mountain of goodness – indeed, it could be argued that we have a long way to go – we have made a great deal of progress.

References

Alexander, R.D. 1985. A Biological Interpretation of Moral Systems. *Zygon* 20: 3–20.

Axelrod, R., and W.D. Hamilton. 1981. The Evolution of Cooperation. *Science* 211: 1390–1396.

Batson, C.D. 1991. *The Altruism Question: Toward a Social-psychological Answer*. Hillsdale: Erlbaum.

———. [4]1998. Altruism and Prosocial Behavior. In *The Handbook of Social Psychology*, ed. D.T. Gilbert, S.T. Fiske, and G. Lindzey, 282–315. Boston: McGraw-Hill.

———. 2000. Unto Others: A Service… and a Disservice. *Journal of Consciousness Studies* 7: 207–210.

Bloom, P. 2004. *Descartes' Baby: How the Science of Child Development Explains What Makes us Human*. New York: Basic Books.

Brown, R. 1984. *Social Psychology*. 2nd ed. New York: The Free Press.

Campbell, D. 1978. On the Genetics of Altruism and the Counterhedonic Components of Human Nature. In *Altruism, Sympathy, and Helping*, ed. L. Wispe, 39–58. New York: Academic Press.
Curry, O.S. 2016. Morality as Cooperation: A Problem-centered Approach. In *The evolution of Morality*, ed. T.K. Shackelford and R.D. Hansen, 27–52. Cham: Springer.
Darwin, C. 1874. *The Descent of Man and Selection in Relation to Sex*. New York: Rand, McNally & Co.
Dawkins, R. 1989. *The Selfish Gene*. Oxford: Oxford University Press.
de Waal, F.B.M. 2006. *Primates and Philosophers: How Morality Evolved*. Princeton: Princeton University Press.
———. 2008. Putting the Altruism Back in Altruism. *Annual Review of Psychology* 59: 279–300.
Decety, J. 2005. Perspective Taking as the Royal Avenue to Empathy. In *Other Minds: How Humans Bridge the Divide between Self and Other*, ed. B.F. Malle and S.D. Hodges, 143–157. New York: Guilford Press.
Ellis, B.J. 1998. The Partner-specific Investment Inventory: An Evolutionary Approach to Individual Differences in Investment. *Journal of Personality* 66: 383–442.
Flack, J.C., and F.B.M. de Waal. 2000. 'Any Animal Whatever': Darwinian Building Blocks of Morality in Monkeys and Apes. *Journal of Consciousness Studies* 7: 1–29.
Greenberg, J., and R.L. Cohen. 1982. *Equity and Justice in Social Behavior*. New York: Academic Press.
Haidt, J. 2001. The Emotional Dog and its Rational Tail: A Social Intuitionist Approach to Moral Judgment. *Psychological Review* 108: 814–834.
Hoffman, M. 2000. *Empathy and Moral Development: Implications for Caring and Justice*. Cambridge: Cambridge University Press.
Kohlberg, L. 1984. *Essays in Moral Development: The Psychology of Moral Development*. Vol. Vol 2. New York: Harper & Row.
Krebs, D.L. 2011. *The Origins of Morality: An Evolutionary Account*. New York: Oxford University Press.
Krebs, D.L., and P. Laird. 1998. Judging Yourself as You Judge Others: Perspective-taking, Moral Development, and Exculpation. *Journal of Adult Development* 5: 1–12.
Piliavin, J.A., and H.-W. Charng. 1990. Altruism: A Review of Recent Theory and Research. *Annual Review of Sociology* 16: 27–65.
Pinker, S. 2011. *The Better Angels of our Nature*. New York: Viking.
Pyszczynski, T., and J. Greenberg. 1987. Toward an Integration of Cognitive and Motivational Perspectives on Social Inference: A Biased Hypothesis-testing Model. *Advances in Experimental Social Psychology* 20: 297–340.
Rawls, J. [2]1999. *A Theory of Justice*. Cambridge, MA: Harvard University Press.
Ridley, M. 1996. *The Origins or Virtue: Human Instincts and the Evolution of Cooperation*. New York: Viking.
Singer, P. 1981. *The Expanding Circle: Ethics and Sociobiology*. New York: Farrar, Straus & Giroux.
Sober, E., and D.S. Wilson. 2000. Summary of Unto Others: The Evolution and Psychology of Unselfish Behavior. In *Evolutionary Origins of Morality: Cross-disciplinary Perspectives*, ed. L.D. Katz, 185–206. Thorverton: Imprint Academic.
Williams, G.C. 1989. A Sociobiological Expansion of "Evolution and Ethics.". In *Evolution and Ethics*, ed. J.G. Paradis and G.C. Williams, 179–214. Princeton: Princeton University Press.

Chapter 4
Homo Amans: A Personalist Response

James Beauregard

Abstract The *Homo amans* project has called for a re-examination of the notion of persons as *Homo economicus*, an outdated notion that does not fully account for the whole human person. The authors have proposed the concept of *Homo amans* as a model for considering the nature of persons and their role in the economic sphere. This essay responds to the authors' initial challenge from the perspective of the philosophy of personalism, specifically in the areas of philosophical anthropology, the virtues, some aspects of contemporary neuroscience, and how these might be brought into dialogue with economic theory.

4.1 Introduction

I am grateful to Patrick Nullens and Jermo van Nes for their invitation to participate in the project, "*Homo Amans*: A Relational Anthropology for Work and Economics." This project seeks to develop an adequate philosophical anthropology that sees the human person "as phenomenologically constituted by the virtues of faith, hope, and love…since multidisciplinary yet complementary study has shown that human persons are questing, expecting, and relational beings" (Nullens and Van Nes, Chap. 2, p. 9, this volume). This is captured in the phrase '*Homo amans*.' Nullens and Van Nes attempt to bring this anthropology into conversation with the discipline of economics as a viable alternative to the limited and outdated notion of human beings as *Homo economicus*.

Rather than an attempt to summarize the discussion paper and the project (the other essays in this book have already admirably done so), this essay turns to the key questions the authors put forward at the end of the paper. These act as a *de facto* summary of their work as well as a plan for future development:

J. Beauregard (✉)
Rivier University, Nashua, NH, USA
e-mail: jbeauregard@rivier.edu

J. van Nes et al. (eds.), *Relational Anthropology for Contemporary Economics*, Ethical Economy 61, https://doi.org/10.1007/978-3-030-84690-9_4

1. How is love best defined, and how does it relate to other virtues in general, as well as faith and hope in particular?
2. Are we naturally predisposed to love, and if so, how does this generate trust?
3. Is there any connection between trust and the virtues of faith, hope, and love, and if so, how are they interconnected?
4. How can the virtue of love develop over a person's life-time, and what factors encourage people to promote well-being in the contexts of home, school, and work?
5. Which areas of the neural system are required to facilitate a person acting intentionally to promote overall well-being?
6. Does gender make any difference to the promotion of well-being in companies and organizations?
7. How is love understood inter-culturally and inter-religiously in relation to global economics?
8. How can technology damage and stimulate human relationality in the future? (Nullens and Van Nes, Chap. 2, pp. 24–25, this volume)[1]

In reading the paper, I discern three continuous and intertwined threads. *First*, philosophical anthropology, our notion of the human person, *second*, virtue ethics as a valuable and necessary aspect of personhood, *third,* the field of economics and how it might be transformed by a vision of the human person as *Homo amans.*

It is this author's opinion that the first of these three threads, philosophical anthropology, is the foundational and most vital feature. If we get persons right, that is, if we can develop a robust and adequate notion of what it means to be a human person, then the outline for the two subsequent threads is already present. In what follows, then, we will consider first and foremost the vision of the human person, and then make some final comments on how such a vision might move into and inform the discipline of economics.

4.2 Philosophical Anthropology: What Is at Stake?

Nullens and Van Nes are fundamentally correct in asserting that the vision of person that has long survived in economic theory, that of *Homo economicus,* is badly outdated and in need of reformulation. In addition, it is not only that particular and utilitarian vision of *person* that is outdated, the *philosophical presuppositions* about persons, society, and economics are not only outdated, but fundamentally in error. *Homo economicus* does not provide an accurate description of who we are, either then or now. Those presuppositions move from the particular world view of the modern era and in doing so embrace, to a greater or lesser degree of consciousness, a certain scientific world view that is truncated and incomplete.

[1] See the "Discussion" section immediately prior as well.

All political questions and all economic questions are, ultimately, *ethical questions*, since they are directed at some good, including the question of how the good life is to be lived individually and in community. How we understand persons is the first step in raising these larger sociopolitical questions – anthropology and ethics are distinct but deeply interwoven. Our notion of person delimits what is and is not possible in the larger societal framework. Getting anthropology right, then, is the essential first step in addressing all social questions, including, here, the question of economics.

Philosophical anthropology is almost as old as human thought itself. The question arises early in the history of western philosophy.[2] While the earliest Greek philosopher asked questions of nature, they considered themselves very much a part of that natural world. Socrates began to ask questions of virtue and the soul, and it was Plato and his student Aristotle who gave direct attention to questions of philosophical anthropology. The Christian tradition continued to raise these questions, and did so in a new way in light of the life, death, and resurrection of Jesus of Nazareth. Many of our contemporary notions of personhood were first formulated during the patristic period of Christianity, as early believers sought to understand how God, in light of Christian revelation, could be both one and three. Their essential answer was to conceptualize *three persons and one God*. Initially they made use of the Greek Platonic tradition (consider Plato, Plotinus, and Augustine), and at the height of the Middle Ages, the work of Aristotle (for example, in Albert the Great and his student, Thomas Aquinas).[3] Questions about personhood continued to be asked as the West moved forward form the Christian synthesis of the Middle Ages into the early modern era, and into the profound changes in human thought that occurred during and in response to the scientific revolution). It was, however, in the move to a scientific paradigm, that the question of personhood became progressively fragmented, as science adopted a physicalist vision of the universe, first evident in physics and chemistry, and later in nineteenth century biology. We live now in an era that has been called both post-modern and post-Christian. The term "post-" can be quite misleading, as it does not really describe a complete rupture with modern thought, but developed out of it and in reaction to it. We live now in an era frequently marked by fragmentation – social, spiritual, intellectual, moral, in which grand narratives have been rejected and relativism is a common presence.[4]

Given this intellectual, cultural, and spiritual environment, is it even possible today to articulate a robust and comprehensive philosophical anthropology, one that is capable of responding to the eight questions that Nullens and Van Nes propose at the end of *Homo amans*? In response to this question, I will argue below that the

---

[2] This is not to say that questions of person did not emerge in Eastern tradition or that they are not vital and relevant today. I am confining my comments here to the western philosophical tradition; no devaluation of Eastern philosophical traditions is intended, and in fact, Eastern traditions will emerge later in this paper in a consideration of persons, virtue ethics and technology.

[3] The development of Greek philosophy, and its transmission into early Christianity has been extensively studied. For an overview see, for example, Guthrie (1975); Copleston (1993a, b).

[4] A classic text in this regard is Lyotard (1979).

answer is, and must be, *yes*. If such a response is not possible, then we can have no guidance in thinking about persons, about ethics and about human activity in the world, including the authors' questions about economics. There is in fact a contemporary philosophical vision, one with ancient roots in both East and West, that can respond to these fundamental human questions – the philosophy of personalism.

4.3 Personalism

In what follows, as a response to the question about persons, I will outline a particular tradition within the broader philosophy of personalism, Integral Personalism, that is capable of bearing fruit both anthropologically and in the field of economics.

In the first instance, personalism can be broadly defined as "any philosophy that considers personality the supreme value and the key to the measuring of reality" (Buford n.d.). Personalism has also been defined as "a 'current' or a broader 'worldview,' since it represents more than one school or one doctrine while at the same time the most important forms of personalism do display some central and essential commonalities. Most important of the latter is the general affirmation of the centrality of the person for philosophical thought" (Williams and Bengtsson 2020). There are a number of characteristics common to personalist thought, evident in numerous personalist philosophers including a fundamental distinction between persons and animals and the rest of the natural world, the dignity of the human person, persons as possessing an interior/subjective life (persons as conscious subjects rather than merely objects), the realities of freedom and self-determination, and the social/relational nature of human persons (Williams and Bengtsson 2020).[5]

Within this broader personalist framework I will focus on one specific current of personalism, that of Integral Personalism, as a personalist response capable of providing a sound philosophical anthropology capable of addressing the fundamental anthropological, ethical and economic questions facing humanity today.

[5] Williams & Bengtsson delve into these characteristics in detail in their *Stanford Encyclopedia of Philosophy* article. These aspects will be presented and developed below in the section on Integral Personalism.

4.4 Integral Personalism: Philosophical Anthropology[6]

Integral Personalism is the name of the philosophical position developed by Spanish philosopher Juan Manuel Burgos (1961–), which seeks to bring into conversation the best elements of both ancient and modern philosophical tradition.[7]

4.4.1 Philosophical Anthropology

Burgos has argued that an adequate contemporary philosophical anthropology ought to contain the following features:

1. *Explanation and Understanding:* Philosophical anthropology seeks to move beyond description to a deeper level of explanation and understanding. It must ask the fundamental human questions – What is the meaning of life? What is the meaning of death? What is love?
2. *Metaphysical or ontological perspective:* Anthropology must move beyond the early modern reductionist conceptions of persons arising from phenomenalism, from the notion that we are merely the bundle of our conscious experiences, as Hume believed, and recognize the continuity and permanence of identity and personhood rooted in being.
3. *Integration:* It must offer us a comprehensive notion of personhood that stands against attempts at reductionism or fragmentation, and that takes into account all dimensions of person: physical, psychological, spiritual, cognitive, affective, dynamism, and that is able to draw upon all of the hard sciences as well as the human sciences – sociology, psychology, economics, history, philosophy, theology, etc.

[6] While I will be focusing on one particular personalist strand of thought (Integral Personalism), it is important to note that there are multiple personalist currents in existence today, including *Anglo-American Personalism* (representative philosophers include, in the United States, Borden Parker Bowne, Edgar Sheffield Brightman, Peter A. Bertocci, Martin Luther King Jr., Thomas Buford, Randall Auxier, James McLaughlin; in England Michael Polanyi, Austin Farrer, John Macmurray, Richard T. Allen, Charles Conti, Simon Smith;) *Phenomenological Personalism* (Max Scheler, Dietrich von Hildebrand, Edith Stein, Viktor Frankl, Josef Seifert); *Communitarian Personalism* (Emmanuel Mounier); *Dialogical Personalism* (Martin Buber, Emanuel Lévinas, Romano Guardini), *Classical Ontological Personalism* (Jacques Maritain). Authors working in the Integral Personalist Tradition today include Elio Sgreccia, Elias Bermeo, Xosé Manuel Dominguez, Rosa Zapién, J.L. Cañas, James Beauregard, Sergio Lozano, Alfonso López Quintas, Denis Larrivee, Gregorz Holub, Raquel Vera.

[7] The majority of Burgos' work has not yet been translated into English, but a notable exception is Burgos (2018). The reader is referred there for a detailed explication of his thought. His major work on philosophical anthropology is *Antropología: una guía para la existencia* (2013). It is currently in the process of translation into English. I will refer when possible to English language translations to his work; translations from the Spanish-language editions are my own.

4. *Scientific character:* Philosophical anthropology in particular, and the human sciences in general must reclaim their character as sciences, broadly understood as investigation, as the search for knowledge, each discipline according to its methods and content, and each discipline recognizing its limitations and boundaries, rather than the common position of scientism, the belief that only the hard sciences provide valid knowledge. Science is far broader than physics, chemistry, and biology.
5. *Experiential character:* A robust anthropology must analyze and take into account the whole of human experience, not merely the sensory/perceptual aspects recognized in the biological sciences. Our experience of the world includes the experience of ourselves and our own subjectivity, and involves sensation and perception, but also cognition and affectivity, understanding and the organization of knowledge that allows for its transmission to others, e.g. in a communal process of scholarship (Burgos 2013, pp. 18–9).

4.4.2 Integral Personalism – Structure

4.4.2.1 The Structural Centrality of Person

In keeping with the personalist tradition in general, Integral Personalism places the person at the structural center of thought. It is the notion of person that is the central vision that bears fruit in anthropology and in ethics. While this may at first appear an obvious philosophical move in personalist thought, the history of the concept of person belies this. In Aristotelian thought, for example, persons were not thought of in and of themselves but rather in relation to something else – the animal kingdom. To begin with a concept of person that is derived directly from persons is a relatively recent move in philosophical thought (Burgos 2018, pp. 204–5).

4.4.2.2 Personalist Categories

This notion brings us to a central point in Integral Personalism, and one that can flow out into economic theory, with which this project is explicitly concerned. As noted above, Aristotle the biologist sought to categorize living things by kingdom and species. He conceptualized human beings as part of the animal kingdom, that is, as a type of animal, with many features in common with other animals. The species distinction, that which differentiated human beings from other members of the animal kingdom, was the human capacity for rationality – we are *rational animals*. Along with this, Aristotle refined the notion of substance that was carried forward in western thought – Boethius' individual substance of a rational nature, Aquinas thought on substance. The notion lived in the scholastically trained Descartes, and continues to manifest itself in various ways in contemporary thought; it underlies, for instance, notions of a mind body dualism, mind-body medicine, etc. There remains a notion present that a human being is composed of distinct and separable parts that need to be linked together in some way. Dualism stood at the foundation of Greek thought, and has accompanied us on the journey, influencing our fundamental vision of persons at every turn.

The philosophy of persons often continues to experience a category problem, a consequence of the Greek ballast of organic and animal categories applied directly to human beings (Burgos 2007, pp. 58–64). In other words, a critical conceptual problem in the philosophy of person has been the making of what Gilbert Ryle termed a category mistake – the application of one category of thought onto something which is a poor or incomplete fit. The inevitable consequence is that once this transfer is made, some aspects of persons are highlighted, while others are obscured by the very category in use (Ryle 2002, p. 19ff).[8] An example would be the classical Aristotelian definition of human beings as rational animals. As long as we are placed in the category of the animal kingdom, it is difficult to recognize aspects of human persons that are univocal to us, such as freedom and our capacity for self-determination.

This is a critical point to consider in the philosophy of person – does the use of terms drawn from biological and animal categories directly and completely apply in the same manner when they are applied to persons? The term instinct has been used of both human beings and animals, but there is a crucial difference – animals *must* follow their instincts, while human beings *may* follow theirs. The category of instinct does not allow for the reality of human freedom, for the reality that we can freely choose to act against instinct when we decide there is a higher purpose to be served. The "instinct" for self-preservation exists in all living things. Yet, when Maximillian Kolbe offered to take the place of another prisoner chosen for execution in the Auschwitz concentration camp, he overrode his own instinct for self-preservation, knowing with certainty that he would die as a result.[9] These actions and experiences do not exist in the animal kingdom, and to apply animal categories to human beings typically obscures what is most univocal about us – Freedom, self-determination, self-sacrifice for a higher good, love, etc.

[8] Ryle includes in this concept the polysemic character of words. When we speak of human "mind" and animal "mind" does the word "mind" *mean the same thing?* We have direct access to our own minds, and by report of the minds of other persons, and we see the obvious similarities. We do not, however, have direct access to the "minds" of animals, though when this is discussed, there is often an implicit assumption that the word "mind" means exactly the same thing both the human and the animal sphere, rather than recognizing that we are to some extent speaking metaphorically.

[9] There had been an escape from Auschwitz and as a result ten prisoners were chosen to be executed. Kolbe, a Polish Roman Catholic priest, offered to take the place of one of them. He died by lethal injection August 14th, 1941. He was canonized by Pope John Paul II on October 10, 1942. https://blog.franciscanmedia.org/sam/martyr-of-auschwitz. Accessed 3/20/20.

4.4.2.3 Personalist Method

If the *Homo amans* project is to consider the virtues of faith, hope, and love, and furthermore to consider trust, empirical scientific methods will be of only the most limited utility. A methodology is needed that can capture the fullness of what it means to be a person. Integral personalism has developed a method of investigation (Integral Experience) that gives proper place to the typically empirically studied aspects of human knowledge (sensation and perception) but is broader in perspective. Briefly, knowledge begins with experience, in keeping with both the hard sciences and empirical philosophy (Locke, Hume, etc.). Our experience, though, is integral. It is not merely blind sensation and the integration of percepts through neural processes. Integral Experience recognizes that our most fundamental contact with the world, our direct experience of the world and ourselves, also has, from the outset, cognitive and affective aspects. In other words, human experience has an intellectual-affective-sensitive structure from its origin. This is our most direct contact with the world and ourselves, an originary experience upon which knowledge at more complex levels is based. We explore and process our experience, seeking for example stable or universal categories to help us understand our experience, and we also reflect critically on our experience in a more systematic way that allows us to share our knowledge with others. Human experience extends far beyond the sensory and perceptual, and it has characteristics unique to us as persons (Burgos 2016, pp. 41–79).[10]

4.4.2.4 Personalism and the Transformation of Society

There are few public intellectuals today who are philosophers dedicated to meaningful social change (*Homo amans* presents a noteworthy exception to this statement). Personalist thought in its twentieth century European expression, beginning with the work of Emmanuel Mounier and arising, as it did, between the two world wars, sought to directly influence society since "Every human being is called, by means of his action, to influence and modify the world which surrounds him" (Burgos 2018, p. 212). In the specific case of personalist philosophy, the philosopher "promotes a philosophy that vindicates the very special dignity of the person with respect to everything that exists" (Burgos 2018, p. 212).

[10] This book chapter provides an overview of Integral Experience as an epistemological model. For a more comprehensive treatment, see Burgos (2016).

4.4.2.5 The Three-Dimensional Structure of the Person

I have alluded above to the necessity of getting the model of persons right before one proceeds to consider human action and the transformation of society. Integral Personalism offers this model of person:[11]

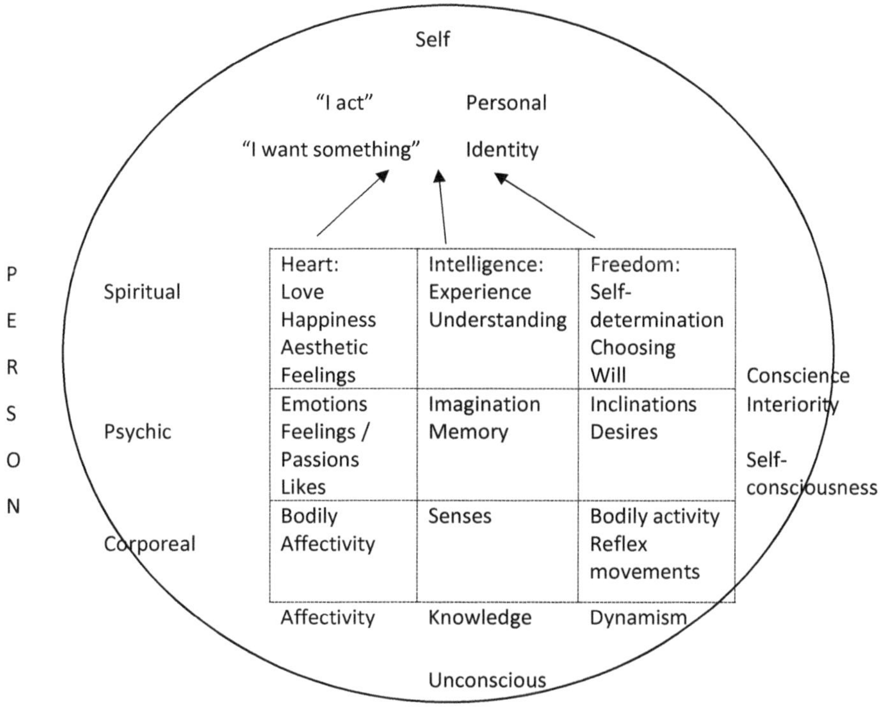

A brief explanation of certain aspects of this diagram can clarify the nature of the person as conceptualized in this anthropological model.

The first thing to point out about this anthropology is that is it *dynamic*. A person is a unity, and a dynamic unity, a being who thinks, feels, and acts. "Person" is both noun and a verb. Dynamism is what characterizes our nature; we are relational beings, in relation to ourselves and to others, social by nature and living in community. To be a person is to be with.

A second aspect of this model is that persons are considered *ontologically prior* to relation. Some accounts of person view us as being created *by* relationships, that is, there is no person considered present until one is in relation with others. This view, however, overlooks a most fundamental reality. There is someone there to start with. Relationships are not creative in this sense, but formative. We are born

[11] Figure by Juan Manuel Burgos. Used by permission.
From an earlier diagram by Mollenido (2006). Also used by permission.

into a relational world, and we grow and develop in this same world. Personhood is ontologically prior to relation, including all forms of human social relations.[12] This can be conceptualized by comparison with a well-known statement from the religious domain: "Grace builds on nature." In order for grace to be active in us, there must first be a structure, a person in whom it can act. So with persons vis a vis relationships.

A third point to consider is that *a person is a unity*. This is depicted in the diagram above through the dotted lines inside the diagram. In the three-by-three matrix above, each of the nine individual areas is conceived as an aspect of the whole person, not a distinct, separable part. Persons are not bundles of distinct actions or activities, they are persons, unified and active in all aspects of their being and activity.

Fourth, there are *three levels* of person to consider, body, psyche, and spirit. Our corporeality is an essential aspect of our personhood – it is more than mere organism; it is the locus of our psyche and spirit. The body has not only a physical and organic meaning, but a personal one.

Fifth, the term "spirit" here is not used in an exclusively religious sense, but more broadly to include all aspects of persons that exist beyond the physical aspects of corporeality and the psychological processes of conscious life. Love, aesthetic experience, moral experience are spiritual aspects of the person.

Sixth, *knowledge and affectivity* are distinct but equally important aspects of the person. The history of philosophy has tended to downgrade affectivity, viewing it as something that has the ongoing potential to interfere with our rational capacities, seeing affect as an enemy of reason. To do this is to fail to see human affectivity as an integral aspect of our being, ever present and ever operative in our actions and our knowing.

Seventh, and lastly, this is an anthropology that is anti-reductive in nature. It stands in its structure against two trends of our technological and scientific age: gradualism and functionalism. *Gradualism* suggests that we become persons, in a slow process of development, typically sometime after the very beginning of life. Many points have been arbitrarily named down through the centuries as the moment of personhood, and with more specificity in recent years – 14 days, at the time of implantation in the uterus, a certain number of weeks after conception, when measurable EEG activity is present in a fetus, at the point of viability outside the uterus, in children when certain aspects of personal activity are objectively observable. *Functionalism* points to this last, "personal activity," that is, a person is defined as a

[12] This is a point of contrast within in the personalist tradition as some view person as ontologically prior to relation (as Integral Personalism does) while other personalist traditions, such as aspects of the Anglo-American tradition, view relationship as ontologically prior to and creative of person. Dialogical personalism, for example, while it recognizes the spiritual aspects of persons in relation, tends to see relationships as first creative of persons, then formative. See, e.g. Buber (1996). In Buber's case, relation and ontological priority can be debated, given that his focus is on the I-You relation and relationality in general, hence, "there is no I as such but only the I of the basic word I-You" (p. 54), and "Man becomes an I through a You" (p. 80).

person when certain functions, arbitrarily assigned, become objectively observable or measurable. The necessary corollary of this view is that when such functions are no longer evident, person is no longer present. A person is, rather, a unity, not a collection of functions. There are probably relatively few moments in our lives when every aspect of person is evident. When we sleep many aspects of personhood are absent. And yet, we do not typically assert that a sleeping person is not a person. Functionalism becomes a prominent concern, for example, at the end of life, in cases of dementia and in the criteria for death. The broader question of who counts as a person will pervade a personalist view of economics as well.

4.4.3 Integral Personalism – Key Anthropological Features

Here I will touch briefly on some of the critical features of personalist anthropology which can be of assistance in approaching economic concerns.

4.4.3.1 Human Freedom

If we focus on the material or the organic, as the empirical sciences do, we are forced to reach a conclusion of determinism. Physical reality is subject to the law of cause and effect, and biological life to the law of stimulus and response. In fact, there is a long history of argument, going all the way back to Democritus in ancient Greece, that, for these reasons, human beings have no free will. There is, however, a fundamental flaw in the presuppositions that underlie arguments against free will – the belief that we are exclusively material beings, living organisms to be sure, but subject to deterministic laws. To assert this is to ignore the spiritual aspects of persons evident in the diagram above. There is much about us that is simply not explainable from the perspectives of matter and organism. Love, freedom, and self-determination, the moral life, many of our human social emotions, make no sense from an organismic perspective. Happiness is not a physical or a biological concept, but a human one.

4.4.3.2 Good and Evil: Ethics

I mentioned above that if we are to understand the fullness of persons, we must approach anthropology in categories specific to persons, abandoning the Greek ballast of animal views of persons, but also contemporary neuroscientific views of persons that also view us in purely biological categories. All ethical thinking presupposes freedom, and the hard sciences give us no way to conceive of freedom. Beings driven solely by instinct do not live the moral life, they live an organic one. An animal that kills its prey is not acting in an ethical manner – it is following instinct and the self-preservative drive of hunger. Moral experience, the experience of good and evil, is a category specific to persons. Postmodern relativism has often made this difficult to see. If we accept that there are no longer any grand narratives, and that all aspects of all cultures are relative and deserving of equal respect, then we effectively blind ourselves to the reality of good and evil. Pure relativism is quite rare – many of us are relativists in some areas but ethical absolutists in other areas. Here in the United States, for example, we have seen doping scandals in sports, baseball and cycling being but two examples; Lance Armstrong was stripped of his seven *Tour de France* titles for this reason. Our sense of fairness and justice, which emerges in the deep sense that cheating in these arenas is wrong, suggests a moral sense within us that extends beyond relativism. "Do good, avoid evil" is the most fundamental precept of the moral life. This can only be fulfilled in freedom, with free will, and specifically, by persons.[13]

4.4.3.3 The Primacy of Action and Love

Augustine introduced the concept of love into philosophical thought. Nullens and Van Nes also bring it into the center of their discussion of *Homo amans*. An integral vision of person recognizes the nature and activity of love as it pervades our personhood and our relationships with others at many levels. If persons are dynamic beings, rather than static ones, then love stands at the foundation of many of our most important actions; "personalism emphasizes the primacy of love as the guiding factor in human activity and as a decisive thematic action, which gives meaning to life in the context of interpersonal relations" (Burgos 2018, p. 229). In light of the *Homo amans* project, it is necessary to consider how love can inform economic thought, moving away from the utilitarian self-interest of *Homo economicus* and toward a different conception of persons. What would happen in theoretical and practical economics if we took seriously Wojtyła's personalistic norm: "A person is an entity of a sort to which the only proper and adequate way to relate is love" (Wojtyła 1993, p. 41).

4.5 Philosophical Anthropology: Love and the Virtues

In light of what has been presented here, how might we understand love from within a personalist perspective? To begin with, love can be seen as *a dynamic activity of the whole person, encompassing both affectivity and knowledge, and impacting every aspect of the person, body, psyche, and spirit.*

[13] On good and evil as a category specific to persons, see Burgos (2018, pp. 220–1).

4.5.1 Phenomenology of Love

As Nullens and Van Nes make explicit mention of the phenomenological method in their paper, it may be helpful to turn to one personalist philosopher who has given us a detailed phenomenology of love: Dietrich von Hildebrand.[14] In his work *The Nature of Love,* von Hildebrand (a student of Edmund Husserl also influenced by the phenomenological work of Max Scheler) wrote of love most essentially as a value response: "The self-giving and commitment proper to every kind of love…is necessarily based on the fact that the beloved person stands before me as beautiful, precious, as objectively worth of being loved. *Love exists as a value response*" (von Hildebrand 2009, p. 17). Von Hildebrand notes four characteristics of values:

(i) They have the ability to *bestow delight* upon us
(ii) They *address themselves to us* in specific ways, making us aware of them and imposing an obligation to respond
(iii) They call forth from us an *appropriate* response
(iv) The value response called forth in us by values has a character of *transcendence and submission* to the value, of abandoning ourselves to the value before us (von Hildebrand 1953, p. 32ff).[15]

That which we see as valuable delights us, reaches out to us, and elicits a response from us, that is, we are affected by value. As noted above, we must think of persons in categories specific to persons, that is, we must move directly from experience as persons and not draw upon categories outside personhood to attempt to understand ourselves – to fall into such a category error is to blind ourselves to that which is uniquely human and belongs to persons.

Love is a polysemic word.[16] It is the love between persons as persons that is perhaps the supreme category specific to persons, pointing to capacities and actions unique to us. Love is expressed in the free gift of self to another, and a life lived in the practice of the virtues is one that makes such a gift possible.

---

[14] Dietrich von Hildebrand (1889–1977) was a member of the early Göttingen circle of Husserl's students and a contemporary of Adolf Reinach, Edith Stein, Romano Guardini, Roman Ingarden and others. Von Hildebrand's work is being intensively studied, and his works appearing in new translation, through The Hildebrand Project, centered at Franciscan University, Steubenville, Ohio, http://www.hildebrandproject.org

[15] Furthermore, he identifies value as one of three categories of importance: the merely subjectively satisfying, the objectively good for the person and the important in itself (=value).

[16] On the polysemic nature of the word *love,* see Pieper (2012, pp. 145–62).

4.5.2 *Love and Ethics*

Anthropology is distinct from, but has a deep connection to ethics. To get persons right makes it possible to get ethics right. In light of persons as integral, dynamic beings, the word "person" is both a noun and a verb. To be a person is to be acting, to engage with oneself and with the world, and to do so with all of our personhood – body, psyche, and spirit, embracing our knowledge and affectivity. In addition, the virtues of faith, hope, and love are dispositions and activities of the whole person, manifested by the whole person in relation to other persons and to the community. Love is the gift of self to the other, and the receiving of that same gift. The virtues can be seen as manifestations of love, united by it and directing us toward the good.

Here, we can see how the vision of persons outlined above is entwined with *Homo amans* as person and as an ethical being. A person is a unity. An ethical vision that seeks both the individual and the common good can be an activity of the whole person, and the virtuous life is an integral life directed toward these goods. Love is the foundation and the unifying force of this type of life. St. John of the Cross, in his work *The Spiritual Canticle,* depicts each of the virtues as flowers woven into a garland: "all the virtues and gifts the soul (and God within her) acquires are like a garland of various flowers within her."[17] John further notes that the weaving of the garland of the virtues is not a matter of acquiring one particular virtue individually and then adding it in, but rather that the garland is "made at the same time," that is, the virtues are acquired not individually or sequentially, but concurrently – to grow in love is also to grow in faith and in hope. It is, again, an activity of the whole person, enacted in community.

4.6 *Homo Amans* and Neuroscience: What Might the Relationship Be?

The *Homo amans* project makes frequent reference to neuroscience and how it might interface with the project, touching specifically on the domains of social neuroscience, neuroscience and morality, including decision-making neuroscience, and biological bases of altruism.

Approaching this question as a clinical neuropsychologist, I would offer several considerations with regard to what role neuroscience in general might play in the *Homo amans* project.

[17] St. John of the Cross (1991, p. 592, stanza 30, no. 6).

4.6.1 The Worldview of Neuroscience

My first comment is a word of caution. The scientific world view, in terms of the hard sciences and the empirical method, can only offer limited help at the level of conception. Neuroscience is structured conceptually in the same manner as biology and the other empirical sciences. This mean that at the theoretical level at least, there are assumptions of materialism and determinism operative that do not allow for the existence of free will, and so cannot serve as a basis for thinking about *amans*, which entails freedom and choice.

A second caution is that neuroscience must be approached at its cutting edge if it is to make any significant contribution to philosophy in general and the *Homo amans* project in particular. The era of examining specific discrete brain regions – for example, Broca's Area in the frontal lobes for expressive language or the primary occipital cortex for vision, effectively came to an end with the arrival of functional neuroimaging in the 1990's. This allowed for an examination *in vivo* of some of the things happening in the brain during different aspects of thought. The current neuroscience understanding of the brain is to view it as a connectome, that is, the entire network of connectivity between each of the brain's 80–100 billion neurons. The neuroscience technique of diffusion tensor imaging, for example, is able to highlight axonal pathways in the brain and illustrate connectivity in ways that did not yet exist even a few decades ago. It is now possible to visualize the human brain as a complex matrix of connections and interactions across many regions. The understanding of a variety of neuropsychiatric diseases is being transformed by this level of understanding.[18]

The recent field of neuroeconomics defined as "a research program founded on the thesis that cognitive and neurobiological data constitute evidence for answering economic questions," provides a case in point (Clarke 2014, p. 195). It has been brought into dialogue with Confirmation Theory (Clarke 2014, p. 195), and as a resource to enrich contemporary economic models (Fumagalli 2017, pp. 210–20). Decision making has been a particular point of interest at the intersection of neuroscience and economics.[19] The intersection and utility of neuroscience has also been challenged (McMaster and Novarese 2016, pp. 963–83).

[18] For an overview of this level of understanding of the human brain, see for example, Sporns (2012). To speak of brain regions exclusively is, today, to speak an outdated language.

[19] See for example, Mudrick et al. (2019, pp. 67–86); Hamoway and Conigliaro (2016, pp. 27–9).

4.6.2 *Neuroscience: Normative or Informative for* Homo Amans?

Given these cautions, neuroscience can provide a great deal of useful information that can be useful to the *Homo amans* project, but should not be looked to at a normative or theoretical level. Areas of neuroscience that could provide useful information to the project would certainly include social neuroscience, as well as developmental neuroscience and the neuroscientific aspects of both psychiatry and neurology. Neuroscience, in this sense, can help flesh out understanding of human persons, but it is important not to adopt the materialist or deterministic underpinnings of the empirical methods of neuroscience.[20]

In addition, the data neuroscience provides must be correctly understood. Functional neuroimaging data (fMRI), for example, is not a depiction of the actual process of thought; thus, claims that functional neuroimaging may someday be able to engage in "mind reading" are overblown, science fiction rather than fact. FMRI measures energy use by neurons as we engage in various cognitive or emotional activities, the point being that the more active neurons are, the more energy they use. It is important not to confuse the purely physical with more complex processes. Uncertainties about the nature and reliability of neuroimaging data is evidenced, for example, in the fact that it is typically not accepted as evidence in legal proceedings, because it can be misleading. If a defense attorney points to a neuroimaging scan, for example, and indicates a specific place or lesion in the brain, and then argues that this is the *reason* that their client committed the act for which they are on trial (and thus should be held less than fully accountable), it must be said in response that many others may have virtually identical lesions observable on neuroimaging who do not commit similar crimes. Furthermore, it is important to separate out the data of neuroscience from the hype about it. Mirror neurons provide a perfect case study for this. The discovery of mirror neurons occurred first in monkeys, and, from this, leaps were made to their *possible* role in humans. Realistically, mirror neurons appear to activate in response to observed action and may play a role in intention detection. However, once they were on the scene, many claims about them were made without adequate empirical justification. They have been implicated as being involved in such far flung issues as Schizophrenia, hypnosis, sexual orientation, smoking, music appreciation, obesity, degree of male erection, psychopathy, business leadership, love, mass hysteria, substance abuse, and self-awareness in other

[20] On the preeminence of the empirical perspective in neuroscience, see, for example, Gazzaniga et al. (2009, p. 4), where the authors write, "Philosophy can add perspective, but is it right? Only scientific method can move a topic along on sure footing."

mammalian species. New findings in neuroscience can become fads, but in time the expectations prove overblown.[21]

Another caution about neuroscience data arises in the context of models of decision making developed in neuroscience that are taken over into neuroeconomics. Much of the contemporary literature on decision making from a neurobiological perspective has arisen from several now classic studies by the American neuroscientist Benjamin Libet.

These studies point to the stark and necessary distinction between neuroscience data and the *interpretation* of that data, a distinction that often goes unnoticed. Libet conducted studies of what were termed conscious intentions to act. For example, experimental subjects were asked to view an analogue clock with a circulating dot in the place of the second hand, while being monitored by surface EEG. They were asked to press a bar at some point in the rotation of the dot. Subjects were later asked when they were first conscious of their intention to press the bar. In a consistent and replicated finding, EEG activity was recorded prior to the subject's reported conscious intention to act, by several hundred milliseconds. The finding has been replicated more than once. Difficulty has arisen, though, in discussion of what the data actually meant (the interpretive aspect). Some have argued that given that our conscious intention to act is preceded by frontal neural activity we do not have free will, but rather, our brains make decisions for us prior to our conscious awareness. Some have supported this conclusions while others have rejected it.

The debate continues.

An additional issue not often attended to in these debates is the nature of language itself. Empirical experiments require operational definitions of the matter under study – the language must be as specific and as concrete as possible in order to be measured accurately. But this is only one aspect of human speech. Experimental conditions are, by design, as literal and concrete as possible. Once the data is collected, though, it must be interpreted. It is here that neuroscientists make a leap, often unnoticed, from literal to metaphorical speech. While experimental conditions are carefully laid out in the methodology section of research articles, and data are scrupulously reported, the interpretation and reporting of the meaning of such data is a different cognitive and linguistic process altogether. Here scientists often move to metaphorical speech without identifying the shift, and it is here we run into a common problem – scientists are not philosophers. Their training is in science, not in philosophy, the philosophy of language or in logic. For example, while EEG parameters are well-defined, terms such as "free will," "voluntary," "consciousness," "unconscious" and "intention" typically are not. An assumption is made that we all agree on the meanings of those terms, and also that they mean the same thing

[21] For an overview of how mirror neurons were discovered and the many things in which they have been implicated, see Hickok (2014). The areas mentioned above for mirror neurons are from a much longer list on pages 24–5 of this book. Eric Racine has done extensive research on public perceptions of neuroscience, and perceptions of neuroimaging in particular. See Racine (2010), esp. Chapter 5, "Public Understanding of Neuroscience Innovation and Emerging Interpretations of Neuroscience Research," 97–119.

across species.[22] This has been an unspoken and often unrecognized source of confusion in the discussion of Libet's findings since the 1980's. When examining decision-making models, whether in neuroscience or in economics, our use of language, and the move from the concrete and literal to the metaphorical should always be considered.[23]

4.6.3 Anthropology

Neuroscience can, at most, provide us with a partial anthropology, and this limitation places boundaries on what is essential a philosophical/theological project. The field of neuroscience, a child of the discipline of biology, follows biology's empirical methods and presuppositions, operating in the world of the organic. That which is specifically and univocally personal (what I have outlined above as the level of spirit) cannot be accessed by empirical methodology in the way that matter and organism can. In order for *Homo amans* to provide a comprehensive and robust philosophical anthropology, it is the data of the human sciences that must hold sway, drawing as needed on the hard sciences, but keeping them in their proper context, and recognizing their conceptual (empirical, physicalist and deterministic) limitations.

4.6.4 Ethics

Ethics is not an empirical science: it is a human science. In the world of *Homo amans*, it is the disciplines of philosophy and theology that must be drawn upon to develop an ethical vision (including by the field of economics, which aims at certain goods). This is not to say that neuroscience has no role to play. It can, and has, informed us about the neural networks underlying processes of decision making, and human moral life has become subject to neuroscientific study. Moral enhancement is a field of neuroscientific endeavor. It can tell us about brain areas and networks active during certain types of tasks, but it cannot tell us what is or is not moral, nor can it direct us to what goods we ought to seek. Neuroscience studies the world as it *is*; ethics studies the world, and the person, as we *ought* to be.

---

[22] Libet himself does not define such terms in his work. See, for example, his discussion of the implications of his experimental findings, Libet (2002, pp. 291–9). The bibliography to this article lists many of Libet's now-classic experimental studies.

[23] For a detailed discussion of the different aspects of language employed in science and in conversational speech, see Beauregard (2019).

4.7 Philosophical Anthropology, Ethics and Economics

The *Homo amans* project asks if a new philosophical anthropology, that of *Homo amans*, grounded in faith, hope, and love, can become a viable substitute for *Homo economicus*. If the life of the virtues, intertwined and lived, can inform economic theory, it will be important for economic theory to integrate two fundamental concepts: human dignity and the common good. *Homo amans* has articulated three principle virtues – faith, hope, and love. It is important that these virtues are not thought of as distinct, but as interrelated virtues, and related to the other virtues as well, including the classic cardinal virtues of prudence, justice, temperance, and fortitude. This catalogue of virtues, and the many subordinate virtues related to them, can serve as a guide for economic thought in light of a robust anthropology that gives attention to human dignity and the common good.

Human dignity is a much-debated topic today. Some have argued that it is essential, some, in contrast, that it does not exist. Some years ago the bioethicist Ruth Macklin argued that human dignity is a "useless concept" that ought to be replaced with the more concrete notions of respect and autonomy (Macklin 2003, pp. 1419–20). Human dignity was on the minds of many in the post-World War II era, when the nature and extent of the violations of persons received widespread attention. This was the era in which the world saw the creation of documents like the United Nations *Universal Declaration of Human Rights* and, in which respect for the dignity the human person was integrated into numerous bioethical documents.

A common denominator to the question of dignity is that it is typically referenced, but not defined. There seems to be an assumption that everyone knows what dignity is, but as soon as one tries to define it, words often fail. This ought to be addressed in light of the current project.

Dignity is, first, a question of the whole, integral person. It is question of fundamental value. Recognition of dignity is the recognition that there is something precious, unique, unrepeatable, deeply valuable about each human person. As Kant asserted, each of has a dignity, not a price. Furthermore, the question of dignity is not a question of definition or ascription – we do not assign dignity to persons, we recognize that dignity is present and inherent. Perhaps a fundamental reason that the post-World War II era was the time that saw the creation of illuminating documents on human dignity and human rights is that the world, as a community, was forced to reckon with the concept of dignity by having witnessed its profound violation across the decades and in time of war. Events like those witnessed across Europe from 1939 to 1945 forced us to ask why the Nazi concentration camps were so deep a violation of persons and the dignity of persons.

Never since, has the entire human community been brought face to face in the same way with the questions of persons, violations, and dignity. This is perhaps a reason why the notion of dignity has receded, and in particular, why the question of dignity is sometimes opposed outright in first world countries. Dignity is a "useless concept" only when one's own dignity is not subject to violation or annihilation. By its violation, the presence and nature of dignity is thrown into sharp relief. It is borne within us, not conferred – or withdrawn – by the state or any other organization. Human persons are bearers of dignity.

Furthermore, the question of dignity is one that science cannot help us answer, especially an empirical science grounded in physicalist views. If dignity is to be recognized and understood, it will happen from a direct examination of the human person that reveals all the uniqueness and preciousness of what it means to be human, to be a person.

The common good is the second concept to be considered in a contemporary economic vision, if such a vision wishes to give pride of place to persons rather than capital. The personalist philosopher Jacques Maritain reflected on the question of the common good in the mid-twentieth century. At the outset, he stated that we desire to live in community because we are social by nature, and also because it is necessary for our flourishing as persons (Maritain 1966, p. 47).

How, then, can we bring these thoughts about persons into the economic sphere? I want to suggest that such a discussion can be centered around the notion of human dignity. Economic decisions, like political ones, are fundamentally moral decisions, as they affect the individual and the common good. The personalistic norm is a norm that can be brought into economic theory. Life in community promotes the good of the individual, and includes many aspects, including public services, sound economic functioning, law and governance, customs, institutions, culture (Maritain 1966, p. 52). At the same time, the common good is more than the sum total of individual goods. In Maritain's words, it is "the good *human* life of the multitude, of a multitude of persons; it is their communion in good living. It is therefore common to both *the whole and the parts into which it flows back and which, in turn, must benefit from it.*"

Economics is, at its foundation, a moral activity, given that it aims at some good. Different economic theories have identified different goods to be sought. An economic theory that looks to the good of both persons and the community, that grounds itself in a notion of person, would be an ethical activity that takes into account the nature and activity of the whole person, individually and in community, and this common good as well.

There are already theoretical models of how this can be accomplished. As an example, consider a document that weaves together the themes that have been mentioned here – the dignity of persons, the common good, the virtues and the question of economics. In 1986, the United States National Conference of Catholic Bishops published *Economic Justice for All: Pastoral Letter on Catholic Social Teaching and the U.S. Economy* (National Conference of Catholic Bishops 1986).[24]

In this document, the U.S. Bishops clearly stated that they were not offering an economic "blueprint," nor a particular economic theory. Their purpose, rather, was to "discover what our economic life must serve, what standards it must meet" (National Conference of Catholic Bishops 1986, p. vii). They present, rather, six

[24] A chapter-length work does not allow the author to delve into these principles in detail. They are presented here in their basic outline, and are developed within the document itself. http://www.usccb.org/upload/economic_justice_for_all.pdf

overarching themes that are in consonance with what *Homo amans* has investigated, and that can provide guidance for economic considerations:

(v) Every economic decision and institution must be judged in light of whether it protects or undermines the dignity of the human person.
(vi) Human dignity can be realized and protected only in community.
(vii) All people have a right to participate in the economic life of society.
(viii) All members of society have a special obligation to the poor and vulnerable.
(ix) Human rights are the minimum conditions for life in community.
(x) Society as a whole, acting through public and private institutions, has the moral responsibility to enhance human dignity and protect human rights (National Conference of Catholic Bishops 1986, pp. viii–ix).

Recognizing that economic questions are fundamentally moral questions, they then identify a series of moral norms in relation to economic activity. It is here that the consonance with *Homo amans* becomes even more explicit:

1. "The commandments to love God with all one's heart and to love one's neighbor as oneself are the heart and soul of Christian morality" (National Conference of Catholic Bishops 1986, p. 16).
2. "Commutative justice calls for fundamental fairness in all agreements and exchanges between individuals or private social groups" (National Conference of Catholic Bishops 1986, p. 17).
3. "Distributive justice requires that the allocation of income, wealth, and power in society be evaluated in light of its effects on persons whose basic material needs are unmet" (National Conference of Catholic Bishops 1986, p. 17).
4. "Social justice implies that persons have an obligation to be active and productive participants in the life of society and that society has a duty to enable them to participate in this way" (National Conference of Catholic Bishops 1986, p. 17).
5. "Basic justice demands the establishment of minimum levels of participation in the life of the human community for all persons."
6. "Basic justice demands the establishment of minimum levels of participation in the life of the human community for all persons" (National Conference of Catholic Bishops 1986, p. 18).
7. "The common good demands justice for all, the protection of the human rights of all" (National Conference of Catholic Bishops 1986, p. 20).
8. "The obligation to provide justice for all means that the poor have the single most urgent economic claim on the conscience of the nation" (National Conference of Catholic Bishops 1986, p. 20).
9. "The fulfillment of the basic needs of the poor is of the highest priority" (National Conference of Catholic Bishops 1986, p. 21).
10. "Increasing active participation in economic life by those who are presently excluded or vulnerable is a high social priority" (National Conference of Catholic Bishops 1986, p. 21).

11. "The investment of wealth, talent, and human energy should be specially directed to benefit those who are poor or economically insecure" (National Conference of Catholic Bishops 1986, p. 21).
12. "Economic and social policies as well as the organization of the work world should be continually evaluated in light of their impact on the strength and stability of family life" (National Conference of Catholic Bishops 1986, p. 22).

Love, faith, hope, justice, and a pervasive notion of both the individual and the common good are all evident in this response to the economic realities of the 1980s. One can argue that they have ongoing relevance today as the fundamental economic issues addressed in the letter have become more pressing. On March 26, 2020, the New York Times reported in relation to the COVID-19 pandemic that applications for unemployment benefits had substantially increased, reporting over three million people filing, compared to 200,000 just three weeks earlier (Casselman et al. 2020).

In the national and international picture, the economic struggles that began at the end of the last decade have fueled populist movements of the right across the western world. This author suggests that the principles articulated above can provide food for thought in addressing the larger questions of economics in light of the human person.

In light of all of the above, brief responses to seven of the questions the authors raised are presented here:

Question 1. How is love best defined, and how does it relate to other virtues in general, as well as faith and hope in particular?

Love is a dynamic activity of the whole, integrated person, an action of self-donation in which we transcend ourselves. Love is integral to all the virtues, and can be conceived of as a manifestation of the specific virtues.[25]

Question 2. Are we naturally predisposed to love, and if so, how does this generate trust?

The nature of the human person, as described here, answers "yes." We are naturally disposed toward self-transcendence, to relationship, and it is the life of the virtues, love first of all, that stands at the root of our mutuality, in which trust is born.

Question 3. Is there any connection between trust and the virtues of faith, hope, and love, and if so, how are they interconnected?

All of the virtues are interconnected; we cannot develop one virtue without other virtues being included in the process. They form a crown of personhood that guide us in the way we think and act, that help form our predispositions and attitudes. To encourage one virtue is to encourage virtuous living in general, so in the process, all the virtues grow.

Question 4. How can the virtue of love develop over a person's life-time, and what factors encourage people to promote well-being in the contexts of home, school, and work?

---

[25] See, for example, Pieper (2012).

Virtues are not a matter of one-trial learning. They develop slowly, through observation of virtuous persons, guidance by them, and our own actions. They eventually become stable dispositions and habits of action.

Question 5. Which areas of the neural system are required to facilitate a person acting intentionally to promote overall well-being?

The inevitable answer from contemporary neuroscience must be, our entire connectome, the whole human brain in all its connectivity and interaction, from individual neurons to local and to far flung networks that subserve all of our human activity. We must, however, be cautious in looking too exclusively to the brain, a single though important organ, to find answers to questions like this one. It is the whole person who intends, the whole person who acts, the whole person who loves, has faith in and hopes for. Human flourishing and human excellence and happiness are the results of the integrated functioning of the whole human person. It is the role and responsibility of the state, and of its economic systems, to promote this well-being

Question 6. Does gender make any difference to the promotion of well-being in companies and organizations?

While the issue of gender was not addressed in this essay, the answer to this question may be a qualified yes. Men and women are different, to be sure, but this difference ought not to blind us to our fundamental equality in personhood and dignity. Notions of gender have been addressed across the human sciences. Recent neuroscientific research has been more mixed when it comes to identifying gender difference, and the validity of the notion of male and female brains has been called into question.[26] It is likely that we would do better, in terms of workplace-related issues, to give thoughtful consideration to the gender roles that exist in any given society, and the often unconscious expectations and disparities they create about men and women in the workplace.

Question 7. How can technology damage and stimulate human relationality in the future?

Technology can help us connect to others, but it can also isolate us. There is no substitute for in-person, human connection. Technology is a place where virtue ethics can play a central role, as demonstrated by the philosopher Shannon Vallor, in her book *Technology and the Virtues*, a comparative philosophical study of virtue ethics across three global traditions: the classical virtue tradition

[26] See, for example, Rippon (2019). Rippon, herself a neuroscientist, surveys the several centuries of research on the human brain, especially on assumed differences between the brains of men and women, and concludes that many of the "findings" of the neurosciences of the past are heavily marked by biased presuppositions that have not been verified in contemporary research. She alerts the reader throughout the book to the existence and enduring power of neuromyths, false beliefs about the brain, disproven by neuroscience, that often take on a life of their own, for example, the myth that we use only 10% of our brains. This belief was disproven the first time a functional neuroimaging study was completed.

of the West, beginning with Aristotle, Confucian ethics and Buddhist ethics. Drawing on this comparative study, she articulates a catalogue of virtues and argues that they can be instrumental in coping with the reality of increasingly rapid technological change across societies (Vallor 2016).[27]

4.8 Conclusion

The model of *Homo amans* presented by Nullens and Van Nes address many problems that need to be addressed in both philosophical anthropology generally and the specific discipline of economics in its historical context. The model of *Homo economicus* is laden with numerous presuppositions, as highlighted by the authors, and its reductionism is a severe limitation. They have created the model of *Homo amans* as an alternative to the limitations of earlier economic models and visions of persons.

This essay has presented an anthropological vision which presents the human person as a dynamic unity, active, and capable of learning and living the virtues, including the key virtues of faith, hope, and love. Some of the strengths and limitations of neuroscience were also examined as this field has been identified as a contributor to economic theory. An economic vision consistent with the *Homo amans* project was presented.

References

Beauregard, J. 2019. *Philosophical Neuroethics: A Personalist Approach, vol. 1: Foundations*. Wilmington: Vernon Press.

Buber, M. 1996. *I and Thou*. Transl. W. Kaufmann. New York: Simon & Schuster.

Buford, T.O. n.d. Personalism. In the *Internet Encyclopedia of Philosophy*. http://www.iep.utm.edu/personal/. Accessed 19 Mar 2020.

Burgos, J.M. 2007. *Repensar la naturaleza humana*. Pamplona: EUNSA.

———. [5]2013. *Antropología: una guía para la existencia*. Madrid: Palabra.

———. 2016. Integral Experience: A New Proposal on the Beginning of Knowledge. Transl. J. Beauregard. In *In the Sphere of the Personal: New Perspectives in the Philosophy of Persons*, ed. J. Beauregard and S. Smith, 41–58. Wilmington: Vernon Press.

———. 2018. *An Introduction to Personalism*. Transl. R. T. Allen. Washington, DC: The Catholic University of America Press.

Casselman, B., P. Cohen, and T. Hsu. 2020. It's a Wreck: 3.3 Million File Unemployment Claims as Economy Comes Apart, The New York Times, https://www.nytimes.com/2020/03/26/business/economy/coronavirus-unemployment-claims.html?searchResultPosition=6. Accessed 26 Mar 2020.

Clarke, C. 2014. Neuroeconomics and Confirmation Theory. *Philosophy of Science* 81: 195–215.

[27] She names (on page 120, as principal virtues, additional subsidiary virtues): honesty, self-control, humility, justice, courage, empathy, care, civility, flexibility, perspective, magnanimity, and technomoral wisdom (prudence).

Copleston, F. 1993a. *A History of Philosophy, vol. 1, Greece and Rome: From the Pre-Socratics to Plotinus*. New York: Doubleday.
———. 1993b. *A History of Philosophy, vol. 2, Medieval Philosophy: From Augustine to Duns Scotus*. New York: Doubleday.
Fumagalli, R. 2017. On the Neural Enrichment of Economic Models: Recasting the Challenge. *Biology and Philosophy* 32: 210–220.
Gazzaniga, M.S., R.B. Ivry, and G.R. Mangun. [3]2009. *Cognitive Neuroscience: The Biology of the Mind*. New York: Norton.
Guthrie, W.K.C. 1975. *The Greek Philosophers: From Thales to Aristotle*. New York: Harper & Row.
Hamoway, C., and C. Conigliaro. 2016. Using Neuroeconomics to Help Client Make the Right Financial Decisions. *Journal of Financial Planning* 29 (11): 27–29.
Hickok, G. 2014. *The Myth of Mirror Neurons*. New York: Norton.
John of the Cross. (1991). Collected works. Washington, DC: ICS Publications,
Libet, B. 2002. The Timing of Mental Events: Libet's Experimental Findings and Their Implications. *Consciousness and Cognition* 11: 291–299.
Lyotard, J.-F. 1979. *The Postmodern Condition: A Report on Knowledge*. Transl. G. Bennington and B. Massumi. Minneapolis: University of Minnesota Press.
Macklin, R. (2003). Dignity is a useless concept. BMJ (20-27 December), 327: 14190–1420.
Maritain, J. 1966. *The Person and the Common Good.* Transl. J.J. Fitzgerald. Notre Dame: University of Notre Dame Press.
McMaster, R., and M. Novarese. 2016. Neuroeconomics: Infeasible and Underdetermined. *Journal of Economic Issues* 50 (4): 963–983.
Mollenido, K. 2006. *El diagrama de la persona según Burgos y su aplicación en la psicoterapia.* Instituto de Ciencias de la Familia, Universidad Galileo, Guatemala. Used by permission.
Mudrick, L., D.J. Levy, J. Gavenas, and U. Maoz. 2019. Studying Volition with Actions that Matter: Combining the Fields of Neuroeconomics and the Neuroscience of Volition. *Psychology of Consciousness: Theory, Research and Practice* 7 (1): 67–86.
National Conference of Catholic Bishops, United States of America. 1986. *Economic Justice for All: Pastoral Letter on Catholic Social Teaching and the U.S. Economy*. Washington, DC: United States Conference of Catholic Bishops. http://www.usccb.org/upload/economic_justice_for_all.pdf.
Pieper, J. 2012. *Faith, Hope, Love*. San Francisco: Ignatius Press.
Racine, E. 2010. *Pragmatic Neuroethics: Improving Treatment and Understanding of the Mind–Brain*. Cambridge, MA: MIT Press.
Rippon, G. 2019. *The Gendered Brain: The New Neuroscience that Shatters the Myth of the Female Brain*. London: The Bodley Head.
Ryle, G. 2002. *The Concept of Mind*. Chicago: The University of Chicago Press.
Sporns, O. 2012. *Discovering the Human Connectome*. Cambridge, MA: MIT Press.
Vallor, S. 2016. *Technology and the Virtues: A Philosophical Guide to a Future Worth Wanting*. Oxford: Oxford University Press.
von Hildebrand, D. 1953. *Christian Ethics*. New York: McKay.
———. 2009. *The Nature of Love*. Transl. J.F. Crosby and J.H. Crosby. South Bend: St. Augustine's Press.
Williams, T.D., and J.O. Bengtsson. 2020. Personalism. In *The Stanford Encyclopedia of Philosophy*, ed. E.N. Zalta. https://plato.stanford.edu/archives/spr2020/entries/personalism/.
Wojtyła, K. 1993. *Love and Responsibility*. Transl. H.T. Willetts. San Francisco: Ignatius Press.

Chapter 5
God's Work in the World: The Deep Compatibility of Real Liberalism with Any Abrahamic Religion

Deirdre Nansen McCloskey

Abstract I propose, in brief, an intimate, perhaps desirable, but anyway necessary, connection between free will in Abrahamic theology and free action in liberal ideology. The economy, its work, its consumption, even its banking, are not inconsistent with a Christian life if achieved by free will. That is to say, contrary to a century-long supposition among theologians and their enemies, belief in a just and loving God does not entail socialism. The Christian gospels and many a Christian theologian attack wealth, surprisingly harshly by the standards of the rest of the world's religious canon. It is not surprising, therefore, that in the nineteenth century, a bourgeois but Christian Europe invented the idea of socialism. But statism is by no means necessary for a Christian community. I gesture here towards a much longer case made earlier and recently by me and other Christian admirers of commercially tested betterment. The great liberal era was brief, from 1776 to 1848. It established freedom of religion. But freedom is freedom is freedom. A free-willed person should be, in God's eyes, free from human interference in religion and behavior and business.

I propose in brief an intimate, perhaps desirable, but anyway necessary, connection between free will in Abrahamic theology and free action in liberal ideology. The economy, its work, its consumption, even its banking, are not inconsistent, with a Christian life if achieved by free will. That is to say, contrary to a century-long supposition among theologians and their enemies, belief in a just and loving God does not entail socialism.

The Christian gospels and many a Christian theologian attack wealth, surprisingly harshly by the standards of the rest of the world's religious canon. It is not

Parts of this essay are previously published in McCloskey (2010, 2013, 2019).

D. N. McCloskey (✉)
University of Illinois Chicago, Chicago, IL, USA
e-mail: deirdre2@uic.edu

J. van Nes et al. (eds.), *Relational Anthropology for Contemporary Economics*, Ethical Economy 61, https://doi.org/10.1007/978-3-030-84690-9_5

surprising, therefore, that in the nineteenth century, a bourgeois but Christian Europe invented the idea of socialism. Marx and Engels wrote fiercely about it in 1848: "Nothing is easier than to give Christian asceticism a Socialist tinge. Has not Christianity declaimed against private property. . . ? Christian Socialism is but the holy water with which the priest consecrates the heart-burnings of the aristocrat" (Marx and Engels [1848] 1988, p. 77). The co-founder of the Catholic Worker movement, the French peasant and priest Peter Maurin, used to wander the streets of America in the early twentieth century declaring, "The world would be better off/ if people tried to become better./ And people would become better/ if they stopped trying to be better off" (Ellsberg 1983, p. xxv). Do good by doing poorly.

In 1919, Paul Tillich, then a 33-year old Protestant pastor in Germany, wrote with his friend Carl Richard Wegener an "Answer to an Inquiry of the Protestant Consistory of Brandenburg" (1919):

> The spirit of Christian love accuses a social order which consciously and in principle is built upon economic and political egoism, and it demands a new order in which the feeling of community is the foundation of the social structure. It accuses the deliberate egoism of an economy . . . in which each is the enemy of the other, because his advantage is conditioned by the disadvantage or ruin of the other, and it demands an economy of solidarity of all, and of joy in work rather than in profit (Tillich [1919] 1971).

The economy in this view is a zero sum game. As the economist and theologian the late Robert Nelson puts it, "If the private pursuit of self-interest was long seen in Christianity as a sign of the continuing presence of sin in the world – a reminder of the fallen condition of humanity since the transgression of Adam and Eve in the garden – a blessing for a market economy has appeared to many people as the religious equivalent of approving of sin."

I gesture here towards a much longer case made early and late by me and other Christian admirers of commercially tested betterment (McCloskey 2016, 2019, and esp. 2006).

First, political economy.

The "real liberalism" in my title is the liberalism of, for instance, John Stuart Mill and of the Blessed Adam Smith. I do not intend to dismiss merely by choice of terminology the "liberalism" of the United States, which is leftish, or that of Latin America, which is rightish. It might be a good plan by the U.S. "liberal" left to make public universities free at Federal expense, bestowing therefore a large subsidy (as an economist is duty bound to point out) on rich parents with college-ready children. Or it might be a good plan by the Latin "liberal" right to support militaries devoted to suppressing domestic dissent (as an admirer of liberty is duty bound to point out). Perhaps you can discern that I don't agree with either plan. But opposing or supporting them is not the direct purpose of returning here to the original and non-Western-hemisphere meaning of "liberal." (Opposing both left and right plans, though, is on the cards.)

We need now, as much as in 1776, to have a prominent word for the political position that is wary of state power, whether exercised by left or right. In the Netherlands and other reasonably well-run polities the state is not always the enemy of the people. But we are framing principles for actual humans, not angelic Swedish bureaucrats. It is surely ethically irresponsible to assume that we have easily available a government of angels. As James Madison remarked in 1788

> If men were angels, no government would be necessary. If angels were to govern men, neither external nor internal controls on government would be necessary. In framing a government which is to be administered by men over men, the great difficulty lies in this: you must first enable the government to control the governed; and in the next place oblige it to control itself (Madison 1788)

The question is *quis custodiet ipsos custodies?* Who guards the very guardians? We do, of course. And we need to watch them closely. After all, the guardians are armed.

In the world at large, which a Christian admitting the fallen character of humans is duty bound to note, there are very many exceptionally bad guardians, murdering journalists and dismembering them, say, or running phony elections in which the present government gets 95 percent of the vote. The liberal and well-managed countries, in which the monopoly of coercion is exercised with reasonable justice and competence, under suitable guarding of the guardians, are startlingly rare in human experience. Before 1800 there were a handful of them, ever, anywhere, locally.

Nowadays, look at the 176 countries in the world ranked in 2016 by Transparency International for its Corruption Perceptions Index, ranging from Denmark and New Zealand at the top to Zimbabwe and North Korea at the bottom. Suppose, generously, that we reckon the top 30 or so to be reasonably honest – worthy, say, of fresh infusions of taxpayer dollars, and, anyway, worthy of a degree of trust in their politicians and guardians (Transparency International, 2017). Portugal in 2016 was the marginal case of the 30, ranked 29th. Italy, by contrast, though in many ways liberal, or indeed anarchistic, was ranked at 60th out of the 176, just below Romania, which is highly corrupt, and Cuba, which is highly illiberal, and just above Saudi Arabia, which is both. Despite many upstanding Italian judges, prosecutors, and police, no wise Italian (of which there appear to be too few) wants to give the extant government more power.

The prime minister in liberal Spain (ranked 41st) arranged to build a hugely expensive high-speed train from Madrid to his small home city. It wouldn't happen in Denmark or New Zealand, though in some U.S. states quite similar corruptions do occur. In my own state of Illinois, for instance, a proposed third airport for Chicago was corruptly sited. In the state I grew up in, Massachusetts, a corrupt Big Dig in Boston buried a highway, making richer the rich friends of the politicians. (I focus here on self-interested corruption alone, setting aside economic incompetence without notable venality, such as the half-built high-speed rail between San Francisco and Los Angeles.) The United States overall ranks 18th. But some of its constituent states and cities would rank much lower. The politicians and guardians in such places lack full integrity or competence, as for example the city government of Chicago covering up torture and murder of African-Americans by the police.

Ask, then: What percent of the world's population was governed in 2016 by the better governments, taking countries as a whole and following the relaxed, better-than-Portugal standard, such as Japan (20th) or France (23rd)? What is the weight of present-day human experience with honest and competent government? Answer: 10 percent. That is, fully 90 percent of the world's population suffered in 2016 under governments agreed on all sides to be disgracefully corrupt and incompetent, and mostly illiberal, being notably worse than Portugal's.

And of course, in a fallen world, even the competent governments are not omnicompetent. The presumption, often unspoken, leading to fresh proposals for governmental regulation is that the government is wise. One will hear of numerous failings in the voluntary, non-governmental sphere. (The importance of which, by the way, no economist has demonstrated, not ever in the century of economic policy past.) But the question is whether the government can do better than some proffered "monopoly" or "externality," considering that governments are not of the angels.

We need to revive for present use a word for the anti-statism that for a century or so characterized much of Western and then Eastern thought, such as that of Henry David Thoreau in 1849: "I heartily accept the motto, 'That government is best which governs least'; and I should like to see it acted up to more rapidly and systematically." Thomas Paine had written in the liberal birth year of 1776, "Government, even in its best state, is but a necessary evil; in its worst state, an intolerable one" (Paine [1776] 2004, p. 47). Better keep the power to coerce modest, said the liberals coming into their own in the late eighteenth century. Old Adam Smith recommended in the same revolutionary year of 1776 "the obvious and simple system of natural liberty," by which he meant "the liberal plan of [social] equality, [economic] liberty, and [legal] justice." It is liberty from literal human tyranny (Greek *tyrannos,* "master"), as also in the free evolution of language or art or science. It entails not equality of result – an unattainable goal if people have differing gifts of prophesy and speech and height and soccer-playing ability and desirable entrepreneurship – but equality of permission and approval from other people. Let my people go.

In its fitful development after the eighteenth century in northwestern Europe such a liberalism – from Latin *liber,* long understood by the slave-holding ancients as in the words of *The Oxford Latin Dictionary* "possessing the social and legal status of a free man (as opp. to slave)," and then *libertas* as "the civil status of a free man, freedom"–came to mean the theory of a society consisting *entirely,* if ideally, of free people (Glare 1982, pp. 1023, 1025). No slaves at all. No masters. No priests. (Liberalism is Protestant – or Early Church, before the western church took on a reinvention of the Roman Empire). Equality of status. No pushing people around by physical coercion. Sweet talking. Persuasive. Rhetorical. Voluntary. Minimally violent. Humane. Tolerant. Unenvious. Accepting of difference. No racism enforced by the state. No imperialism. No unnecessary taxes. No domination of women by men. No casting couch. No beating of children. No messing with other people's stuff or persons.

Liberalism is not anarchism, though we liberals look with sisterly affection on such anarchists as Mikhail Bakunin, Prince Kropotkin, Emma Goldman, and Murray Rothbard. Considering, though, that we are *not* anarchists, it does not suffice to dispose of real liberalism, as did the New Liberals in the 1880s in Britain and the Progressives in the U.S. in the 1900s, and many of our good government-loving friends nowadays on the left and right along the usual spectrum, by remarking irritably that "after all, government must have *some* role."

A government of course "has a role"– as my progressive and conservative friends put it to me, predictably, relentlessly. George Romney, the automaker and conventional 1950s Republican, opposing the liberal 1.0 (I am an Abrahamic liberal, version 2.0, if you care) and conservative Barry Goldwater in 1964, declared, "Markets don't just happen," that there must be "some role for government" (quoted in Schultz (2015, p. 77). True, governments sometimes support markets, though they more usually tax, obstruct, outlaw, or monopolize them. And contrary to Romney's assertion most markets do in fact "just happen," because people find them mutually beneficial, with or without governmental action. Markets just happen, to take the extreme case, inside jails and prisoner-of-war camps, with no governmental action to enforce the deals made. Markets just happened among pre-contact Australian aborigines buying their boomerangs from better-skilled hands hundreds of miles distant (Radford 1945; Berndt and Berndt 1964, pp. 302–5).

Yes, government should have some role. The political question is how much. The government, declared Max Weber in 1919, can, with justice, claim "the monopoly of the legitimate use of physical constraint/ force/ violence/ coercion" ("*das Monopol legitimen physischen Zwanges*") (Weber 1919, p. 310). Good. Such a monopoly is to be preferred to oligopolies of gangs, surely. Liberalism merely recommends that the monopoly be exercised gingerly. Very gingerly. It recommends a maximum liberty to pursue your own project, free of taxing or interference for "social" purposes, if your project does not use your own or the government's physical coercion to interfere with other people's projects.

Real liberalism is a noble vision, suited to free men and women. Contrary to the charge of anti-liberals, it is not destructive of community (Deneen 2018; McCloskey 2018). Rather the contrary. It is a vision of free cooperation, as against regimented obedience.

The left "liberalism" as understood in the U.S., and pretty much only there, is in the classical sense "illiberal." It recommends massive use of coercion of one class of citizens to achieve capabilities for another class, and the massive use of coercion to regulate all classes by our masters in the government. The ends are said to be "social," from which we understand the sweet-sounding word "socialism," helping the poor or invading Iraq, separating toddlers from their mothers at the southern border, protecting doctors from competition.

At the scale of such social projects as pursued in, say, France, with 55 percent of the nation's production funneled through *l'Élat*, one might as well name it 55 percent "socialist." American left "liberals" such as Paul Krugman wax wrath if one applies the word to their proposals, but there does not seem to be a difference in kind between 55 percent and 100 percent (and there *is* between 10 percent and 35 percent), especially considering that even a communist economy uses prices a little, pushing the percentage below 100, and even the 45 percent remnant not spent by the government in France is tightly regulated, by populist-statist demand and by regulatory capture. The composition of bread has been regulated in Paris since the Middle Ages (with, it must be admitted, satisfactory results). Rents in Paris have been frozen since 1914 (with not so satisfactory results). Henry Kissinger, a war criminal but a witty man, calls France "the only successful communist country."

The real liberal David Boas of the real liberal (not "conservative" or "right wing") Cato Institute notes that it is a question whether a modern nation like the U.S. is more or less free than it was in 1776, or as Boas notes, 1919. On the one hand, more and more people have been freed from private and some public enslavements of, for example, poor men and chattel slaves still in 1776, or women and gay men and southern Blacks still in 1919. But on the other hand, and especially since 1919, public enslavement to the will of the government has radically increased. The cowboy comedian Will Rogers used to say in the 1920s, when the share in national product of taxes spent by government at all levels was about 10 percent, "Just be glad you don't get the government you pay for." Nowadays on TV, the congresspeople (representing a government at all levels that takes over 30 percent) are interviewed in front of a statue in the Capitol Rotunda of the same eloquent cowboy. One wonders why Will doesn't topple over when he hears the present extent of socialized expenditure and bureaucratic regulation, and the proposals to do more, emulating France.

The New Liberal/Statist/Progressive has believed in a particular theory of the economy. She has believed down to the present that the economy is above all *easy* to administer, and that therefore intentional action by wise folk having no business or technical experience does the trick, quite easily. The woman of system, to quote Smith again, "seems to imagine that [s]he can arrange [by governmental coercion] the different members of a great society with as much ease as the hand arranges the different pieces upon a chess-board. [She] does not consider that . . . every single piece has a principle of motion of its own."[1] People are motivated in varying proportions by prudence, temperance, courage, justice, faith, hope, and love, together with the corresponding vices. By way of such principles of motion, you and I pursue our endlessly diverse projects, knitting and model railroading. Let them do it. Such a modern liberal plan fits well a society in which people are taken to be free and equal and increasingly competent, unlike the stolid peasants or helpless proletarians of conservative theorizing always, or progressive theorizing since 1848.

The social/socialist plan is to pass a law seizing, say, two percent of financial wealth for governmental projects, which is to say a third or so of the annual yield on non-human capital. Problem solved, says the woman of system, if our masters (including the very woman in charge) are thus enabled to spend an immense sum as they wish rather than as we wish. The woman of system here does not appear to believe that the allocation of capital between its human and non-human forms will be distorted by reducing the return to one of them by a third. She does not believe that knowledge of what we should do and how to do it is distributed locally among

[1] 4.2.2.17, pp. 233–234.

the people, accessible only by unregulated markets. And above all she does not believe it is unethical to coerce people.

In fact, people, she believes, get better housing and the eight-hour day from governmental plans and compulsions, such as the Wagner Act facilitating excellent industrial unions, or rent controls providing wonderfully cheaper housing, or an entrepreneurial government coming up with brilliant ideas (Mazzucato 2013).[2] John R. Commons (1862–1945) of the University of Wisconsin was the American sage of such statism, described at length in the Irish poet Michael O'Siadhail's astounding epic in 2018, of which Quintet 2, still more astoundingly, sings accurately of, believe it or not, economics and its intellectual history. Says O'Siadhail [oh-sheel, by the way] of Professor Commons: "Empiricist, you purged the harsh / And gilded age with labour law / And compensation, chose to side / With plans to practice price controls; Protectionism too you saw / As trammeling a too-free trade" (O'Siadhail 2018, p. 129).

Betterment, the statist says, especially if she is a labor lawyer or a labor historian inspired by Commons, or a senator inspired by Thomas Piketty, had little or nothing to do with private agreements in commerce directed by profits earned both by producers and consumers, and yielding, therefore, a working class enriched 3000 percent since 1800. A working class 30 times better off than its ancestors, the liberal claims in response to the statist faith, could get beyond houses without central heating or 12-hour working days without rest. "Don't be silly," the statist retorts to such a liberal account of enrichment. "We New Liberals and Continental socialists came in the nineteenth century to see 'intentionality' [to use again the word favored in New-Liberal public theology] as crucial to making a just society – easily done in law though a struggle in politics. After intentional struggles on the picket line and intentional votes in Parliament, the just and rich society was finally achieved. None of your mythical invisible hand about it!" The just and rich society did not occur, she is saying, through enrichment from creative trade and innovation, allowed to better ourselves and others by free exchange, down in the farmers' market or the auto dealership – but by pure hearts and coercive regulations.

A weak reply (among many weak replies) to liberalism's stand against coercion supposes that the government is composed of ethical philosopher-monarchs, who can therefore be trusted to run a government kindly, giving us wisely the monarch-chosen stuff out of taxes – the taxes gently, sweetly, democratically extracted from the stuff we make. Says the liberal then: Maybe it's roughly true in Sweden or New Zealand; but not in the U.S. When the Commissioner of the U.S. Food and Drug Administration, Margaret Hamburg, retired in 2015, she was introduced on National Public Radio as having regulated fully a fifth of the American economy (Hamburg 2015). The statistic is startling, but accurate (Walker and Nardinelli 2016). Food. Drugs. Was Ms. Hamburg a Wonder Woman – a wholly ethical and wholly wise philosopher queen? It seems unlikely, though I am sure she is very

[2] The idea is old, even in the United States. "You gotta go down and join the union," as I sang in my socialist youth.

nice. Therefore the early-stage cancer treatment that works in Berlin, may not be accessible to you in HoustonJ, because the useful treatment still awaits a certified finding by the FDA, affirming that the drug or medical appliance or procedure has "efficacy," tested unethically by "gold standard" double-blind experiments guided by meaningless tests of statistical significance, and going far beyond the original brief of the FDA to test merely for safety, not for an elusive efficacy, efficacy anyway regularly modified in the clinic by discoveries by doctors trying out the drug or appliance off-label.[3] That last was the history of Rogaine (minoxidil), originally an FDA-restricted heart drug, now an over-the-counter treatment for male-pattern baldness –"over-the-counter" because the politicians responded to the middle-aged men demanding that it be made easily and cheaply available, despite the FDA.

"Freedom," the Latin-French "liberty," is often extended to equality of result, Roosevelt's "freedom from want." But we already have words for such "freedoms"–namely, adequate comfort, great wealth, considerable power, physical abilities, central heating, subsidies from taxes. To use the freedom-word to mean all these other good things, such as in the economist Amartya Sen's and the philosopher Martha Nussbaum's vocabulary of "capabilities," confuses the issue (Sen 1985, 1999; Nussbaum and Sen 1993). Capabilities are very good. We should work to assure that every person on the planet has them, chiefly if not only by letting a free economy enrich ordinary people, as it has regularly done by that 3000 percent. Smith declared, when a nascent science of economics was shifting attention away from the glory of the king toward the flourishing of the people, that "no society can surely be flourishing and happy, of which the far greater part of the members are poor and miserable" (Smith 1776, I.viii.36, p. 96). That's the humane part of humane liberalism, expressed in its goal of higher real income per head, and greater flourishing of the heads, especially the poor ones. But developing such good things is not itself "freedom," unless we want to smoosh into the one word all good things under the sun.[4]

To put it another way, Smith and I do claim emphatically that economic, or indeed ethical, development is the consequence of freedom, the "obvious and simple plan of natural liberty." But development – contrary to the title of one of Sen's book – is not the *same thing* as freedom. A cause is not the same thing as its consequence. No one would deny that it's good to be developed to the extent of being adequately rich. In 1937, Beatrice Kaufman advised a friend, "I've been poor and I've been rich. Rich is better!"[5] Yup. Yet we still need a word for a distinct "freedom

[3] On the FDA see Briggeman (2015) and Bhidé (2017, p. 28), and on development of drugs for early-stage cancer see Budish et al. (2015). On the meaninglessness of tests of statistical significance see Ziliak and McCloskey (2008) and the statement of the American Statistical Association in Wasserstein and Lazar (2016, pp. 131–3). On corruption of the procedures at the FDA, see Piller and You (2018).

[4] In 2018 I discovered that Tom Palmer had reasoned before 2009 in the same way I am here, to the same conclusion (Palmer 2009, pp. 32, 35–6).

[5] Quoted in Lyons (1937).

from physical constraint by others humans." The constraint in political terms is called "tyranny," its opposite "liberty/freedom." We need to watch out for masterful tyranny by kings and bureaucrats and husbands and priests, and its consequences in poverty. And beyond money and poverty, we need to watch out for the consequences of tyrannical unfreedom in preventing other sorts of human flourishing, such as a spiritual one. Tyranny is bad for the human soul. Nowadays, as much as in 1776 or 1789 or 1848, we need to watch out for the tyranny of the king, husband, slave owner, chief, village elder, priest, bureaucrat, police. Watch and beware. To do so, we need a word for it, avoiding a smooshing that makes it difficult to watch, and which indeed excuses tyrannical coercion.

So much for a sketch of the political economy of liberty. Consider then, with, I am afraid, markedly less authority or competence, theology – leading, if combined with the political economy, to a new and truly liberal public theology.

We are God's creatures. God therefore owns us, by an analogy with Lockean mixing of labor with unappropriated land, or by an analogy with the ownership of children by parents. But He, or rather She, chooses to make us free, not slaves. She wants us to be free adults, not perpetual children. We Jews and Christians say at Passover/Easter that She brought us out of slavery in Egypt and then, by Christ's sacrifice, out of death. We Jews or Moslems say that a child undergoes a bar/bat mitzvah or instruction in the Holy Koran to become an adult, a *mukallaf* – in modern English a "responsible" person (Haskell 1999).

The core of Christian theology, I need hardly say, is free will. God does not want us to be Her pets, but individuals with autonomy ("self-governance"), able to choose evil as well as good, and living therefore in a real world in which the Lisbon earthquake of 1755 can happen. If we lived in Eden, it would not be so. But, as free adults in a real world governed by natural and social laws, we chose, as Eve in the tale chose, and Adam, too, chose by the persuadable will of a free man.

Now the central theme of my argument: The uber-liberal "Austrian" economics, which speaks of free will as "human action." It is free will. Putting the two together, I am afraid, will annoy both my Austrian economist friends, who are mainly atheists, and my progressive Anglican friends, who are mainly socialists. But I can't help it, because human action and free will *are* the same. As against the Marxism I espoused at age 16, or the Samuelsonian Chicago-School economics I came to teach ten years later, real choice is involved in both a Christian life and in the system of commercially tested betterment misleadingly labeled "capitalism." It is an unhappy fact that orthodox, non-liberal public theology nowadays wants the government and God to treat us like obedient pets, not free wills. It is an equally unhappy fact that orthodox, non-Austrian economics nowadays views people as entirely reactive, like pigeons maximizing utility under a constraint, or like grass seeking light and water optimally.

No. God made us in the *imago Dei/Deae.* Free.

Christian and leftish communitarians celebrate what they consider interdependence, which they think is the furthest thing from independence. Oh, no. The *in*dependence of the individual in a liberal economy lets people converse and exchange freely – and results in the great *inter*dependence of modern life. It gives us by the grace of liberty our shoes, TVs, books, whatever come from the voluntary paid work of thousands of people worldwide. Listen yet again to Smith:

> The woollen-coat,. . . . is the produce of the joint labour of a great multitude of workmen. [and workwomen, dear!] The shepherd, the sorter of the wool, the wool-comber or carder, the dyer, the scribbler, the spinner, the weaver, the fuller, the dresser, with many others, must all join their different arts in order to complete even this homely production. How many merchants and carriers, besides, must have been employed in transporting the materials from some of those workmen to others who often live in a very distant part of the country! . . . . Let us consider only what a variety of labour is requisite in order to form that very simple machine, the shears with which the shepherd clips the wool. . . . the workmen who attend the furnace, the mill-wright, the forger, the smith, must all of them join their different arts in order to produce them.

Cooperation, that is, does not by any means always require intentional direct action on the model of the good Samaritan, and especially not the coercive action of a taxing and regulating state. As Smith also said, cooperation in society often results even if the good done was, as Smith noted elsewhere, "no part of his intention." When Jesus' fishermen sold their catch – the abundant one He arranged for them, for example – they intended only to help their own families. But thousands ate. The unintended consequence of specialization and trade is a social miracle analogous to the divine miracle of loaves and fishes.

The Smithian point is something Donald Trump, for example, doesn't get, because like his opponents on the left he thinks of the economy as a battle, not as cooperation. Indeed, he puts the "dependence" of nationalism ahead of everything: he wants a slavish dependence of the individual *imago Dei* on The Leader, who in the Nuremberg rally usurps the place of G-d.

In saying that we should "keep away from believers who are living in idleness," St. Paul is not here recommending a life of work, work, work ignoring the sacred. A young lawyer working a 70-hour a week should not draw comfort from Paul's words, unless indeed the lawyer's work is infused with the Holy Spirit. Paul is warning instead against a particular type of *un*worldly excess, a laying down of tools in expectation of the Second Coming. He appears to have heard that some of the Thessalonians were withdrawing from the world to prepare for the end days, which they thought in 53 C.E. were coming any day now.

The early Christians were of course not the last to form such expectations. Readers of a certain age will remember the Johnstown cult. Such millenarianism breaks out repeatedly, as it did in the 35 million copies sold of the first of the Rapture books. "I must work the works of Him who sent Me while it is day; the night is coming when no one can work. As long as I am in the world, I am the light of the world" (John 9:4–5). By a mechanism that the sociologist of religion Rodney Stark has described in historical detail, cult-formation is natural in any religion that emphasizes a distinction between the sacred and the profane, the Lord's work and the world's work (Stark 2001). The Church of Faith, as Stark calls it, grows restive under the rule of the Church of Power. The holy ones repeatedly break off from the world and form cults in expectation of Christ's coming. One sees a similar joyous expectation, of the *First* Coming of the Lord, in the Jewish Hassidim. And if they believe the time is late and the End is Near they stop working, as St. Paul complained. One of these cults is called Protestantism, and some of the Radical Reformation such as the Anabaptists in the sixteenth century, were willing, on account of imminent salvation, to go to the stake singing hymns.

Thus earlier, in the eleventh century in southern France, the Albigensians, or Cathars – the Greek *katharos* means "pure" – would in their last days withdraw from Satan's world to enter God's kingdom as "Perfects," as they called themselves. The believing Cathars who were short of perfection would go about their worldly business until their end days. As St. Paul said, "work with quietness and eat your own [earned] bread." But when the Cathars were called to perfection – and many were called from the elite of Languedoc society during the twelfth and thirteenth centuries – they gave away all their goods and followed Jesus. Stark notes that in European history, or for that matter in Islamic or Jewish history, such purifying moves did not usually come as an upwelling from the poor and oppressed. The cults tended to be led and staffed on the contrary by the rich, or more exactly the formerly rich, such as St. Francis of Assisi. Compare Lord Buddha. The riches of Mammon (the word means in Aramaic simply "wealth") were spurned in the name of purity. No need to work. Just pray.

The Church of Power did not look kindly on the Cathars. And their anticipation of the priesthood of all believers. The ironically misnamed Pope Innocent III arranged in 1209 a crusade of northern knights, led by Simon de Montfort, in which fully 200,000 withdrawers from the world were sent out of it prematurely. The Inquisition of later notoriety was invented by the papacy in 1284 to deal with the persistent remnant of Cathars. So the Church of Power has always been suspicious of what it regards as *excessive* withdrawal from God's beloved world of work. Augustine, who was not exactly easy going about worldly pleasures, nonetheless was harsh, with fire and sword, against the holier-than-thou Donatists.

The social science of worldly goods called economics could be expected to have a similar attitude, right? *Not* working is bad. Stay in the world. Pump up the economy.

But economics doesn't. On the contrary, economists view withdrawal from the world, a refusal to work (because what is the point of work if Christ is coming soon?), as what they call "leisure." "Leisure" in economic analysis is anything but paid work. The economist views volunteer "work," visiting the sick or feeding the poor or just sitting there praying in expectation of the End Times, as something you do, literally, in your spare time. Work or pray. No worries: your call, or calling. Whatever.

What's St. Paul's complaining about, then? He goes on to remind the Thessalonians that when he was visiting them, he himself worked "night and day." In a verse that sounds to an economist like a lesson in the budget constraint he declares, "Anyone unwilling to work should not eat." The economist would put it a little differently: "Anyone unwilling to work," she would say, "will not *in fact* eat, unless he has support from outside the marketplace. But no blame attaches," says the non-Christian economist. "It's his choice. Whatever."

Notice that the economist is not *angry* at the idle person. That's the force of the Valley-girl "whatever" that one feels comes after most refusals by economists to think seriously about ethics. The idler "chooses leisure," or, in the case that he does *not* have that support from a mother or a charitable person, he "chooses" starvation. St. Catherine of Siena (1347–1380) starved herself to death at age 33, the age that Jesus died, by refusing to eat anything but the communion host. The French mystic Simone Weil followed St. Catherine, starving herself to death during the Second World War, age 34. An economist is likely to analyze such behavior as a mere choice, like choosing between chocolate and vanilla ice cream, and leave it at that. Whatever.

St. Paul, with some theologians such as Aquinas and up to the present, would have taken a less neutral view of Catherine and Simone. Such radical withdrawing from the world strikes some Christians as spiritual pride (McCloskey 2006). I am proud that I am so humble, and Satan swoops down at the last minute to claim my soul. An old *New Yorker* cartoon shows two monks walking in the cloister, one saying to the other, "But I *am* holier than thou." (And the Devil swoops in at the last minute and takes his soul, for the sin of pride that he is not proud.)

What, then, is the theological gripe against the holier than thou? Why isn't withdrawal from the world orthodox (in Greek the word means "upright opinion")? What's not upright about withdrawing from the world?

The answer I would give is that the world's work in Christianity is *dignified.* If Christianity is to be, in Nietzsche's sneering characterization, a slave religion – we Christians embrace the characterization with satisfaction – it cannot downgrade what slaves do, that is, work. Paul, in requiring that people work if they are to eat, was standing against the ethos of a slave and patriarchal society in which dignified people, such as non-slaves and non-women and free male citizens of Rome, like Paul, specifically did *not* work "night and day," or at all. St. Benedict's Rule, in about the 530rd year of the Christian era at Monte Cassino, uses the same word for work in the fields and the "work of God." The monastic formula was *laborare est orare*, to work is to pray. Work in the world is a form of prayer, if done with God in mind: "Idleness is the enemy of the soul," said Benedict (Verheyen 1949, chap. XLVIII). This work-praising tendency in Christianity made it easy for urban monks in the high Middle Ages, such as Aquinas, to justify the urban work of say, merchants, as creative work, like God's.

The obligation to self-development is the obligation to use God's gifts. The Christian version is reformulated in 1673 by Joseph Pufendorf of Leipzig, Heidelberg, and Lund thus:

> It seems superfluous to invent an obligation of self-love. Yet. . . . man is not born for himself alone; the end for which he has been endowed by his Creator with such excellent gifts is that he may celebrate His glory and be a fit member of human society. He is therefore bound so to conduct himself as not to permit the Creator's gifts to perish for lack of use. . . . (Pufendorf [1673] 1991, Bk. I, Chp. 5, p. 46).

Thus Comus, tempting the Lady in John Milton's poem of 1634, argues that from niggardliness in using God's gifts "Th'All-giver would be unthanked, would be unpraised/ Not half his riches known . . ./ And we should . . . live like Nature's bastards, not her sons."

The liberal Christian tradition of the urban friars, such as Francis and Dominic and Aquinas, recommended *working* on God's gifts. "Albert the Great and [his student, St.] Thomas," writes Lester K. Little, "brought about the emancipation of Christian merchants." They were not commending unlimited greed, but a purposeful buying low and selling high. "The honest merchant, for all these writers, was a man deserving of the profit he made, for they considered it as payment for his labor (*quasi stipendium laboris*)" (Little 1978, p. 178). Profit paid for alertness. This is the virtue of the liberal man, in Aquinas's words: "by reason of his not being a lover of money, it follows that a man readily makes use of it, whether for himself, or for the good of others, or for God's glory" (Aquinas, c. 1270, IIa IIae, q. 117, art. 6). The miser keeps his pile. The liberal man spends it for the three levels of ethics, self (for lessons in the cello, so as "not to permit the Creator's gifts to perish for lack of use"), for others (in Jesus of Nazareth's formulation of the Golden Rule), for the transcendent answer to the question "so what," *quo vadis*?

One wonders where the work-praising came from, because in the Greek and Roman world any work except war-making and speech-making was so very undignified, and the collection of feudal rents by the genteel was precisely why they did not work at anything but war and courtesy. After Adam's curse, of course, a human was to earn his bread by the sweat of his brow. Yet Judaism praised work – "Seest thou a man diligent in his work? He shall stand before kings." Maimonides wrote in the early thirteenth century "One who make his mind up to study Torah and not to work but to live on charity profanes the name of God, brings the Torah into contempt, extinguishes the light of religion, brings evil upon himself, and deprives himself of the life hereafter."[6] It sounds like Paul scolding the Thessalonians. The Christians of course go further than the Jews, praising diligence or the Muslim's listening to an inspired merchant of Mecca. *God himself*, in the form of God's only begotten son, became in the words of the Creed "truly human." God was a carpenter, the Christians say, and not merely metaphorically as among Jews and Muslims, a maker of the world, but literally in the sweat of his brow. That is the startling Christian story.

But wherever it came from historically, God appears to want it. He wants us to live and choose in his created world, though not, since the Fall, in the Edenic part. To put it economically, God wants us to face scarcity. He wants it, not because He is a trickster who is amused by seeing us struggle with disease and the law of gravity in our pain-filled and finite lives. He so loves us that, after Eden, he wants *us* to have the dignity of choice. That is what free will means. Denys Munby said to me once, "In Heaven there is no scarcity and in Hell there is no choice." In the created world there are both. The dignity of free will would be meaningless if a choice of one good, such as apples, did not have what the economists call an "opportunity cost"

[6] Maimonides, *Mishnah Torah*, c. 1200, quoted in Sacks (2002, p. 95).

in, say, oranges. If we could have all the apples and oranges we wanted, "living in idleness," as Paul put it, with no "budget constraint," no "scarcity," we would live as overfed pet cats, not as human beings. If we have free will, and *therefore necessarily face scarcity*, we live truly in the image of God.

Scarcity is necessary for *human* virtues. Humility, said Aquinas, answers among the Christian virtues to the pagan virtue of Great-Souledness that Aristotle the pagan teacher of aristocrats admired so much. To be humble is to temper one's passions in pursuing as Aquinas put it "*boni ardui*," goods difficult of achievement. To be great-souled, which in turn is part of the cardinal virtue of Courage, is to keep working towards such goods nonetheless.[7] No one would need to be courageous or prudent or great-souled or humble if goods were *faciles* rather than *ardui*.

The virtue of Temperance, again, is not about mortification of the flesh, at any rate in Christian thinkers like Aquinas (there were others, descendants of the Desert Fathers, who had another idea). On the contrary, this side of Christianity says, we should admire the moderate yet relishing use of a world charged with the grandeur of God. It is the message of the Aquinian side of Christian thought that we should *not* withdraw from the world. On the contrary, as Jesus was, we should be truly, and laboriously, and gloriously human. As the economists say, too, though they omit the Christian claim that working is praying.

The economist Frank Knight, in an anti-clerical fury, mistook the Christian morality of charity for a call to common ownership, the extreme of loving Solidarity, and attacked it as unworkable. (It is said that the only time the University of Chicago has actually refunded money to a student was to a Jesuit who took Knight's course on "the history of economic thought" and discovered that it was in fact a sustained and not especially well-informed attack on the Catholic Church.) Knight wrote a book with T. W. Merriam in 1945 called *The Economic Order and Religion* which mysteriously asserts that Christian love destroys "the material and social basis of life," and is "fantastically impossible," and is "incompatible with the requirements of everyday life," and entails an "ideal . . . [which is] not merely opposed to civilization and progress but is an impossible one." Under Christian love "continuing social life is patently impossible" and "a high civilization could hardly be maintained long, . . to say nothing of progress" (Knight and Merriam 1945, pp. 29, 30, 31, 46).

It develops that Knight and Merriam are arguing that social life in a large group *with thoroughgoing ownership in common* is impossible. *That* is what they believe Christian love entails.[8] Their source is always the Gospels, never the elaborate compromises with economic reality of other Christian writers, such as Paul or Aquinas or Luther, or the 38th article of the Anglicans: "The riches and goods of Christians are not common, as touching the right, title, and possession of the same, as certain Anabaptists do falsely boast."

But, yes: social life without private property *is* impossible, at any rate in large groups. So said Pope Leo XIII in 1891 in *Rerum Novarum*, re-echoed by Pius XI in

[7] IIa IIae, q. 161, a. 1, quoted in Pope (2002, p. 311).

[8] See for example Knight and Merriam (1945, p. 48).

1931, John XXIII in 1961 and 1963, by Paul VI in 1967 and 1971, and by John Paul II in 1981 and 1991.[9] These men were not nineteenth-century liberals – especially, as Michael Novak explains, not in the harsh, Continental sense, the "old liberals" of Jan Gresshof's satiric poem of the 1930s (Novak 1989). They celebrated private property – when used with regard to soul and community. They were nothing like the Sermon-on-the-Mount socialists that Knight and Merriam attack.

Thus Leo: "private possessions are clearly in accord with nature" (15), following his hero, Aquinas.[10] "The law of nature , . . by the practice of all ages, has consecrated private possession as something best adapted to man's nature and to peaceful and tranquil living together" (17). "The fundamental principle of Socialism which would make all possessions public property is to be utterly rejected because it injures the very one's whom it seeks to help" (23). "The right of private property must be regarded as sacred" (65). "If incentives to ingenuity and skill in individual persons were to be abolished, the very fountains of wealth would necessarily dry up; and the equality conjured up by the Socialist imagination would, in reality, be nothing but uniform wretchedness and meanness for one and all, without distinction" (22).

Nick Hornby's comic novel *How to Be Good* (2001) shows the difficulties of To Each According to His Need, Regardless of His Property Acquired by Effort Directed at Supplying Goods and Services That Other People Are Willing Themselves to Expend The Effort to Acquire ("Thank you for your service"). A graceful generosity that works just fine within a family works poorly within a large group of adult strangers. In Hornby's book the husband of the narrator goes mad and starts giving away his and his wife's money and his children's superfluous toys. He and his guru are going to write a book:

> "'How to Be Good', we're going to call it. It's about how we should all live our lives. You know, suggestions. Like taking in the homeless, and giving away your money, and what to do about things like property ownership and, I don't know, the Third World and so on."
>
> "So" [replies his annoyed wife, a hard-working GP in the National Health Service] "this book's aimed at high-ranking employees of the IMF?" (Hornby 2001, p. 210).

It's a version of the Sermon on the Mount, from which many people have concluded that Jesus was of course a socialist. "The love-gospel," writes Knight and Merriam, "condemning all self-assertion as sin. . . would destroy all values" (Knight and Merriam 1945, p. 50). Knight and Merriam are correct if they mean, as they appear to, that Love *without other and balancing virtues* is a sin. Knight's understanding of Christianity appears to have derived from his childhood experience in a frontier Protestant sect, the Campbellites (evolved now into a less fierce Church of Christ and Disciples of Christ), and theirs is what he took to be the core teaching of Christianity: "No creed but the Bible. No ethic but love."

---

[9] These are Pius: *Quadragesimo Anno*; John: *Mater et Magistra* and *Pacem in Terris*; Paul: *Populorum Progressio* and *Octogesima adveniens*; and John Paul: *Laborem Exercens* and *Centesimus Annus*. Michael Novak is my guide here (1989, chapt. 6–8).

[10] Leo XIII. 1891. *Rerum Novarum,* paragraph numbers given. See Aquinas *Summa Theologiae*, c. 1270, IIa IIae, Q 66, quoted and discussed in Fleischacker (2004, p. 35 and n40).

But Love without Prudence, Justice, Temperance, and the rest is not Christian orthodoxy – for example the orthodoxy of Aquinas or of Leo XIII. Leo in fact was a close student of Aquinas, and in 1889 elevated him to dogma within the Church. And, yes, such a single-virtue ethic would *not* be ethical in a fallen world. Economists would call the actual orthodoxy a "second-best" argument, as against the first best of "if any man will sue thee at the law, and take away thy coat, let him have thy cloak also." Given that people are imperfect, the Christian, or indeed any economist would say, we need to make allowances, and hire lawyers. Otherwise everyone will live by stealing each other's coats, with a resulting failure to produce coats in the first place, and a descent into poverty for everyone but the thief.

St. Paul himself said so, in his earliest extant letter (1 Tim. 3: 8–11):

> Neither did we eat any man's bread for naught; but wrought with labor and travail night and day, that we might not be chargeable to any of you . . . .to make ourselves an example unto you to follow us. . . . We commanded you that if any would not work, neither should he eat. For we hear that there are some . . . among you disorderly, working not at all.

Or to put it more positively, as Michael Novak did, "one must think clearly about what actually does work – in a sinful world – to achieve the liberation of peoples and persons" (Novak 1989, p. xvi). "In the right of property," wrote even the blessed Pope John XXIII in 1961, "the exercise of liberty finds both a safeguard and a stimulus."[11] Frank Knight couldn't have put it better.

Charity is not socialism. Generosity is not a system at all. It is of a person, then two, then a few. God arranges such encounters, a Christian might say. But humans want them, too, the gift-economy of grace above material concerns. So the great Quaker and economist Kenneth Boulding said. To make them into a system, *How to Be Good*, is to cancel their virtue. The heroine and narrator of Hornby's novel sees that Erasmus began all editions of his *Adages* from 1508 onwards with "Between friends all things are common," remarking that "If only it were so fixed in men's minds as it is frequent on everybody's lips, most of the evils of our lives would promptly be removed. . . . Nothing was ever said by a pagan philosopher which comes closer to the mind of Christ" as the proposed socialism of goods in Plato's *Republic*.[12] Such is the first best. But Erasmus notes, sadly, "how Christians dislike this common ownership of Plato's, how in fact they cast stones at it." Many of his 4150 proverbs collected from classical and Christian sources recommend attention to Prudence and work, if not quite with the insistence of, say, proverbs he might have collected in his native Dutch. We are mostly not friends, but strangers, and even in the Society of Friends property was not held in common. Knight and Merriam are not really undermining Christian orthodoxy and Christian ethics. They are misunderstanding it.

One owes Love to a family first. Property, with the virtue of justice, protects the beloved family. If any would not work, neither should he eat. Work, depending on temperance and prudence, is desirable to create and to acquire the property. So is

[11] From the encyclical *Mater et Magistra,* 1961, quoted in Novak (1989, p. xxii).

[12] Erasmus, *Adages,* 1500–1533, 1508 onwards I i 1 (Barker 2001, p. 29).

prudent stewardship in managing it, though the lilies of the field toil not. For societies of humans, she realizes, not lilies and families, the right prescription is bourgeois virtue. True, she cannot quite get rid of the notion that "maybe the desire for nice evenings with people I know and love is essentially bourgeois, reprehensible – depraved, even" (Hornby 2001, p. 218). Such is the agony of the left US "liberal."

It is a matter of Christian ethics.

Ethics has three levels, the good for self, the good for others, and the good for the transcendent purpose of a life. The good for self is the prudence by which you self-cultivate, learning to play the cello, say, or practicing centering prayer. Self-denial is not automatically virtuous. (How many self-denying mothers does it take to change a lightbulb? None: I'll just sit here in the dark.)

The good for a transcendent purpose is the faith, hope, and love to pursue an answer to the question "So what?" The family, science, art, the football club, God give the answers that humans seek.

The middle level is attention to the good for others. The late first-century BCE Jewish sage Hillel of Babylon put it negatively yet reflexively: "Do not do unto others what you would not want done unto yourself." It's masculine, a guy-liberalism, a gospel of justice, roughly the so-called Non-Aggression Axiom as articulated by libertarians since the word "libertarian" was redirected in the 1950s to a (then) right-wing liberalism. Matt Kibbe puts it well in the title of his 2014 best seller, Don't Hurt People and Don't Take Their Stuff: A Libertarian Manifesto.

On the other hand, the early first-century CE Jewish sage Jesus of Nazareth put it positively: "Do unto others as you would have them do unto you." It's gal-liberalism, a gospel of love, placing upon us an ethical responsibility to do more than pass by on the other side. Be a good Samaritan. Be nice.

In treating others, a humane libertarianism attends to both Golden Rules. The one corrects a busybody and coercive pushing around. The other corrects an inhumane and soul-destroying selfishness. Together they are the other-ethics of modern liberalism. What we do not need is the reactionary version, the old spoof of the Golden Rule, namely, "Those who have the gold, rule." Nor do we need to follow the Florida football player on the eve of the Florida-Florida State game, "I follow the Good Book: 'Do unto others before they do it unto you.'" Neither is non-aggressive or nice.

The Golden Rule in either formulation, note, is radically egalitarian. In the Abrahamic religions you are to treat every human soul the way you would wish to be treated. You are to honor your one God and keep His day holy, but the rest of the Ten Commandments are about treating other humans as you would wish to be treated in matters such as truth telling or adultery. By contrast, in the theism of the Hindus or in the civic religion of the Confucians you are to treat the Brahman or the emperor as superior souls. An Untouchable or a peasant or a woman or a younger son is not to expect equal, reciprocal treatment. Of course, it was not until the bourgeois societies of late eighteenth-century Europe that anyone but an early Christian radical or a late Muslim saint thought to carry out in any large society the sweetly other-regarding theory of Abrahamic egalitarianism. Until Tom Paine or Adam Smith, a duchess was still a duchess, a sultan still a sultan, King Herod still Great.

It is liberalism, a fulfillment at last of the Abrahamic equality of souls, that brings us human flourishing and human virtue, as God wishes for Her creations.

To this the Christian statist has a series of worries, replies, indignant objections.

For one thing, she says, work is not free. We are "wage slaves." The claim was in fact the defense of actual slavery offered by Southern apologists before the Civil War in the United States. The Northern factory workers, they said, were virtual slaves. The leftish usage and its politics echo down to the present, as in *The Concise Oxford Dictionary* of 1999, in which "wage slave" is defined coolly as "a person who is wholly dependent on income from employment," with the notation "informal" – but not "ironic" or "jocular" or, better, "economically illiterate" (Pearsall 1999, p. 1610). Thus Judy Pearsall, the editor of the *Concise Oxford*, who lives, it may be, in a nice semidetached in London NW6 and drives an old Volvo, is a "slave." You yourself are probably a slave. I certainly am a slave. We are all "slaves" – though all of us are paid in proportion to the traded value of goods and services we produce for others and none of us owes *unpaid* service to any boss (except, as Higgs and I would observe, to the state through taxation or draft, an actual slavery admired by most of the left and much of the right). Such progressive or conservative terminology of "wage slavery" is like calling an exchange of harsh words "verbal rape." We need terms for the physical violence entailed in actual slavery and in actual rape, or for that matter in actual taxation backed by the wide powers of the IRS to do violence. We should not cheapen them by applying them to our middle-class guilt in NW6 or Morningside Heights.

One finds Oscar Wilde in 1891 declaring that "socialism [about which he knew only the contents of a lecture he had just heard by George Bernard Shaw] would relieve us from that sordid necessity of living for others," by which he means charity but also paid work: "An individual who has to make things for the use of others, and with reference to their wants and their wishes, does not work with interest, and consequently cannot put into his work what is best in him" (Wilde [1891] 1930, pp. 257, 270).[13] Even the owner of property is not exempt, Wilde continues, because property "involves endless claims upon one, endless attention to business, endless bother" (Wilde [1891] 1930, p. 259). Think of it. Worker or capitalist or landlords, we are all "slaves" to supplying things for others. Frightful.

In that highly metaphorical and imprecise sense, we are indeed "enslaved," and to our mutual good. After Hegel, many intellectuals have declared that capitalism makes people work for others, and makes the worker therefore an "object," not a "subject." So it was said by Marx and Heidegger and Sartre, since "being for others" is "inauthentic." If I adopt a social role, such as selling you a deep-fried Mars bar from my fish-and-chips shop in Edinburgh, I am treating you as an object, and you, when you hand over your money, are treating me the same. As the philosopher Roger Scruton puts it, to follow such a Kantian obedience to ethical law with respect

[13] The editor, Hesketh Pearson, remarks that Wilde had been inspired by Shaw's lecture, "without bothering himself much about economics" (p. xii). The astoundingly scholarly Wikipedia entry for "wage slavery," by the way, gives arguments from people like Noam Chomsky against my views, and those by people like Robert Nozick in favor of them.

to others "launches us down that path towards the 'bourgeois' order on which finicky intellectuals are so reluctant to tread" (Scruton 1994, p. 468).

Or they say things like, "All right, a 3,000% increasing in material goods and services since 1800 – but humans do not live by bread alone." Yes, certainly. If economic growth, as many conservatives and some socialists argue, corrupts the human soul, I will join them in attacking it. What benefit is it to someone who gains the world but loses her immortal soul? But the counter argument was the burden of *The Bourgeois Virtues: Ethics for an Age of Commerce*, the most theological of the trilogy. "Consumerism," for example, is a common worry. But it has an answer, chiefly that it does not corrupt and is not new and is anyway a worry only for the rich, who are always with us.

Or they say that inequality is worrisome. Or that monopolies are prevalent and corrupt the government. Or that the 1980s Me Decade was a bad 'un. Or, or, or. They all have answers that ought to satisfy a Christian or Jew or Muslim, and did before the theologians and their enemies became confused and immune to the evidence on innovism and its sad opposite in statism. The liberal era was brief, from 1776 to 1848. It established freedom of religion. But freedom is freedom is freedom. A free-willed person, in God's eyes, should be free from human interference in religion and behavior and business.

References

Aquinas, T. 1267–1273. *Summa Theologica*. Transl. Fathers of the English Dominican Province.

Barker, W.W., ed. 2001. *The Adages of Erasmus*. Toronto: University of Toronto Press.

Berndt, R.M., and C.H. Berndt. 1964. *The World of the First Australians*. Sydney: Smith.

Bhidé, A. 2017. Constraining Knowledge: Traditions and Rules that Limit Medical Innovation. *Critical Review* 29 (1): 1–33.

Briggeman, J. 2015. *Searching for Justification of the Policy of Pre-Market Approval of Pharmaceuticals*. PhD diss. George Mason University.

Budish, E., B.N. Roin, and H. Williams. 2015. Do Firms Underinvest in Long-term Research? Evidence from Cancer Clinical Trials. *American Economic Review* 105 (7): 2044–2085.

Deneen, P.J. 2018. *Why Liberalism Failed*. New Haven: Yale University Press.

Ellsberg, R. 1983. Introduction. In *Dorothy Day: Selected Writings*, ed. Robert Ellsberg, xv–xli. New York: Orbis.

Fleischacker, S. 2004. *A Short History of Distributive Justice*. Cambridge, MA: Harvard University Press.

Glare, P.G.W., ed. 1982. *Oxford Latin Dictionary*. Oxford University Press.

Hamburg, M. 2015. Margaret Hamburg Ends Six-Year Run as FDA Commissioner. Interview by Robert Siegel. All Things Considered, National Public Radio, April 1. www.npr.org/2015/04/01/396871346/margaret–hamburg–ends–six–year–run–as–fda–commissioner.

Haskell, T.L. 1999. Responsibility, Convention, and the Role of Ideas in History. In *Ideas, Ideologies, and Social Movements: The United States Experience since 1800*, ed. P.A. Coclanis and S. Bruchey, 1–27. Columbia: University of South Carolina Press.

Hornby, N. 2001. *How to Be Good*. London: Penguin.

Knight, F., and T.W. Merriam. 1945. *The Economic Order and Religion*. New York: Harper & Brothers.

Little, L.K. 1978. *Religious Poverty and the Profit Economy in Medieval Europe*. Ithaca: Cornell University Press.
Lyons, L. 1937. The Post's New Yorker. *The Washington Post*, May 12, 1937.
Madison, J. 1788. *The Federalist*, No. 51. February 6, 1788.
Marx, K., and F. Engels [1848] 1988. *The Communist Manifesto*. Transl. F.L. Bender. Norton Critical Edition. New York: Norton.
Mazzucato, M. 2013. *The Entrepreneurial State: Debunking Public vs. Private Sector Myths*. New York: Anthem Press.
McCloskey, D.N. 2006. Humility and Truth. *Anglican Theological Review* 88: 181–196.
———. 2010. Life in the Market is Good for You. In *Accepting the Invisible Hand: Market-Based Approaches to Social-Economic Problems*, ed. Mark D. White, 139–168. New York: Palgrave Macmillan.
———. 2013. *Working in the World: An Economist's Sermon*. November 27. https://www.abc.net.au/religion/working–in–the–world–an–economists–sermon/10099498.
———. 2016. *Bourgeois Equality: How Ideas, Not Capital or Institutions, Enriched the World*. Chicago: The University of Chicago Press.
———. 2018. Why the Enemies of Liberalism Fail. [A review essay on Patrick Deneen, *Why Liberalism Failed*]. *Modern Age*: 15–23.
———. 2019. *Why Liberalism Works: How True Liberal Values Produce a Freer, More Equal, Prosperous World for All*. New Haven: Yale University Press.
Novak, M. ^{2}1989. *Catholic Social Thought and Liberal Institutions: Freedom with Justice*. New Brunswick: Transaction.
Nussbaum, M., and A. Sen. 1993. *The Quality of Life*. Oxford: Oxford University Press.
O'Siadhail, M. 2018. *The Five Quintets*. Waco: Baylor University Press.
Paine, T. [1776] 2004. *Common Sense*. Broadview Press.
Palmer, T. 2009. *Realizing Freedom: Libertarian Theory, History, and Practice*. Washington, DC: Cato Institute.
Pearsall, J., ed. 1999. *The Concise Oxford Dictionary*. Oxford: Oxford University Press.
Piller, C., and J. You. 2018. Hidden Conflicts? An Investigation Finds a Pattern of After-the-Fact Compensation by Pharma to Those Advising the U.S. Government on Drug Approvals. *Science* 36: 17–23.
Pope, S.J., ed. 2002. *The Ethics of Aquinas*. Washington, DC: Georgetown University Press.
Pufendorf, S. [1673] 1991. *On the Duty of Man and Citizen According to Natural Law*. Cambridge: Cambridge University Press.
Radford, R.A. 1945. The Economic Organisation of a P.O.W. Camp. *Economia* (New Series) 12 (48): 189–201.
Sacks, J. 2002. *The Dignity of Difference: How to Avoid the Clash of Civilizations*. London: Continuum.
Schultz, K.M. 2015. *Buckley and Mailer: The Difficult Friendship that Shaped the Sixties*. New York: Norton.
Scruton, R. 1994. *Modern Philosophy: An Introduction and Survey*. London: Sinclair-Stevenson.
Sen, A. 1985. *Commodities and Capabilities*. New York: Elsevier Science Publishing.
———. 1999. *Development as Freedom*. Oxford: Oxford University Press.
Smith, A. [1776] 1981. *An Inquiry into the Nature and Causes of the Wealth of Nations*, ed. R.H. Campbell, A.S. Skinner, and W.B. Todd. 2 vols. Indianapolis: Liberty Classics.
Stark, R. 2001. *One True God: Historical Consequences of Monotheism*. Princeton: Princeton University Press.
Tillich, P. [1919] 1971. Answer to an Inquiry of the Protestant Consistory of Brandenburg. Transl. J.L. Adams. *Metanoia: An Independent Journal of Radical Lutheranism*, 3(3), 10–12.9.16.
Verheyen, B., transl. 1949. *The Holy Rule of St. Benedict*. Atchison: St. Benedict's Abbey.
Walker, S., and C. Nardinelli (2016). Consumer Expenditure on FDA Regulated Products: 20 Cents of Every Dollar. *FDA Voice*.

Wasserstein, R.L., and N.A. Lazar. 2016. The ASA's Statement on p-Values: Context, Process and Purpose. *American Statistician* 70 (2): 129–133.

Weber, M. [1919] 1994. The Profession and Vocation of Politics. In *Weber: Political Writings*, ed. and transl. P. Lassman and R. Speirs, 309–369. Cambridge: Cambridge University Press.

Wilde, O. [1891] 1930. The Soul of Man under Socialism. In *Wilde, Plays, Prose Writings, and Poems*, ed. H. Pearson, 257–288. London: Dent.

Ziliak, S., and D.N. McCloskey. 2008. *The Cult of Statistical Significance: How the Standard Error Costs Us Jobs, Justice and Lives*. Ann Arbor: University of Michigan Press.

Chapter 6
What Is the Nature of Christian Love? *Homo Amans* and Revolutionary Altruism

Rebekka A. Klein

Abstract The attempt to explore human beings transdisciplinarily as beings of love can contribute to a more realistic anthropology, with an increased practical relevance for science and research. On the other hand, with its holistic orientation towards the whole person, it leads to an improper standardization of scientific research results. In order to avoid the problems associated with the holistic study of man as *Homo amans*, this article therefore reverses the perspective. Fundamentally, the nature of love is not discussed anthropologically on the basis of an examination of human nature and its altruism or egoism, but on the basis of the phenomenon of love in its ambivalence. Following Kierkegaard's phenomenology of love, the article shows that love cannot be clearly distinguished from selfish acts without the reference of interpersonal relationships with a "third party." In the Christian perspective, God is such a "third party," who makes our fellow human beings recognizable to us as neighbors of God and enables us to behave in the spirit of love. Christian love of neighbor is therefore an example of the revolutionary, socially transformative dynamics of love.

6.1 Introduction

> *"A person can flourish only by seeking the common good, by seeking the good for oneself and others."*
>
> *"Economics should foster the human well-being."*

These quotes from the outline of the *Homo amans* project are significant for the aspirations and hopes that our society and culture ascribe to science in the present day. They remind us that science and ethics are subject to intense questioning these days in terms of their usefulness and real-world orientation. This questioning of science as a whole represents a major trend in society and politics as well as in the

R. A. Klein (✉)
Ruhr-Universität Bochum, Bochum, Germany
e-mail: rebekka.klein@rub.de

J. van Nes et al. (eds.), *Relational Anthropology for Contemporary Economics*, Ethical Economy 61, https://doi.org/10.1007/978-3-030-84690-9_6

contemporary philosophy of science. In this respect, it is no longer regarded as sufficient for scientific knowledge and interdisciplinary research to seek the truth or find out facts and figures concerning a certain subject or question of theory. Rather, the two processes are brought together to make a substantial contribution to solving the real-world problems of our society (Mittelstraß 1982; Klein 2017). One slogan that is very well known in this context is "science into society," which is currently very common in the design of new research projects and proposals in so-called hard sciences.

In order to contribute to solving real-world problems – which can be said to be the main goal of scientific research in the twenty-first century – it is suggested that science should take a more holistic perspective, not submerging itself in the production of academic and scholarly knowledge, but rather it should develop concrete insights, which can actually be proven to be orientational and useful in our everyday lives (Nowotny 1997, 1999; Nowotny et al. 2001). A viable way to achieve this goal, which has evolved in recent decades, is to pursue science in a transdisciplinary manner, i.e., by integrating different scholarly and disciplinary approaches, methods, and perspectives into a more comprehensive and unifying scientific endeavor (Hirsch-Hadorn et al. 2008; Mittelstraß 2003). The rationale behind this trend is the idea that science *has* the power to influence and transform real life but that it can only *actualize* this power when it becomes holistic again – as with premodern scientific knowledge practices, for example. Consequently, a trend has also resurfaced towards the antique and premodern traditions of wisdom and knowledge.

Likewise, the *Homo amans* project seeks to develop the idea that science should serve the common good of society and help to solve real-world problems. In the outline of the Project it is argued that economics must foster human flourishing instead of merely finding out the truth about human nature (as it is). What is implied here is that science has to prove the anthropological, psychological, societal and political usefulness, pragmatic and ethical impact of its insights, rather than merely safeguarding the correct methodological fabrication of scientific facts. Thus, transdisciplinary and holistic research prospects also represent a shift towards greater commitment from scientists to ethical and social change, and also to political and societal interests. A political interest which could be seen to lie behind this focus on human flourishing in current science, especially in economics and ethics, is the concern that people should not be broken by the wheels of late-modern capitalist working conditions; becoming mentally or physically sick from exhaustion, for example. Thus, the focus on human well-being as the latest goal to be served by the economy represents a political resource, transforming contemporary society for the better. A concrete example of the increasing relevance of this issue can be seen in the public discussion of the retirement of German politician Andrea Nahles in June 2019 who gave up her leading position in the social democratic party after severe infighting. Responding to this incident, a journalist from the German newspaper DIE ZEIT claimed that the exercise of power in politics, which was formerly a domain of masculine virtues and cold-blooded heroism, should become more humane and solidary (Peitz 2019).

A second point of reference in explaining society's current interest in human flourishing is the attempt to interpret it as a response to the nihilisms of late modernity. As theologian Miroslav Volf has argued in his book on this topic, there are two nihilisms in late modernity which reinforce each other: the passive nihilism of fundamentalists and the active nihilism of libertarians (Volf 2015, p. 200f). Both have in common an unsustainable end for our lives. The passive nihilism of religious world-deniers and world-destroyers offers a life with strong values and a transcendent foundation which imbues the order of life with "weight" and meaning. This is illustrated, for example, in the attractiveness for young Westerners of terrorist organizations such as the Islamic State. Here, such a strict and stable order of meaning can be a welcome alternative to the active nihilism practiced in market-driven globalization movements of late modernity. The latter have given rise to a character type which Volf calls "free spirits," i.e. consumerists for whom nothing matters with any sort of profundity, or who lack a constancy of meaning. Their nihilism consists in the willingness to fight "for the pleasures and comforts of their way of life" (Volf 2015, p. 201) making the realm of values ultimately arbitrary and insignificant. According to Volf, the plea for human flourishing in the present is therefore to be seen as an attempt to find a third way which – as he suggests – is the great challenge of our time (Volf 2015, p. 201).

Thus, current endeavors to reorient science and research towards human well-being as a whole, stand on the horizon of a broader development in late modern culture. A number of consequences follow from this reorientation of science which can be summarized as follows: firstly, pressure to solve overall societal problems and to present an all-inclusive solution to them means that scientists are motivated to develop an integrative and overly harmonious picture of human society which tends to make the solutions they are studying more plausible and approachable. Consequently, they are inclined to disregard the fractures and ambivalences of certain phenomena or theories under investigation, for in giving attention to such fractures they would make their own account more vulnerable and less efficient. Secondly, transdisciplinary research projects ultimately create transformative knowledge rather than picturing and reproducing the world as it is. As convincing as this endeavor may be in times of postmodernist relativism, constructivism, and perspectivist visions of truth, it nonetheless shifts the focus of science away from objectivity and independence of real-world matters, and reshapes its work into a kind of service enterprise (which is, I believe, problematic in the long run). Thirdly, scientists who take a transdisciplinary perspective and attempt to solve real-world problems of a holistic nature are in danger of becoming "do-gooders" (*Weltverbesserer*, in German) when participating in the scientific process. This means that they might leave the "cool mood" of science and philosophy and become over-engaged campaigners.

Let us now turn to the *Homo amans* project. The initiators of this project would probably resist my emphasis on the major shift from investigating human nature (as it is) to studying human flourishing (as it can be advanced by society and science). They would certainly argue that such predestined flourishing refers directly to human nature (as it is) and is not to be separated from it. This is rational because they argue from an approach of virtue ethics. In this approach, flourishing and the nature of human beings are essentially the same thing. Hence, human beings always become what they should be, and the study of human nature is the study of human beings' final destiny.

Now, my aim in this regard is not to downgrade or devalue the perspective of the initiators of the *Homo amans* project in any way. Rather, I want to create a productive contrast, applying my own approach and experience (Klein 2011) from a transdisciplinary perspective in order to shed some light on aspects which may not have been given enough attention in the outline of the *Homo amans* project. This means that my goal is to challenge and, ultimately, complement the project's perspective, as well as to describe and to explore the limits and problems inherent in the argument that is presented here.

My discussion is divided into two main parts as follows: sections two and three of my chapter critique and respond to the *Homo amans* model as given in the initiators' outline. I will focus on the opposition of *Homo economicus* and *Homo amans*, critically exploring the holistic nature of anthropological models in general. Finally, I will contrast the understanding of the virtue of love in *Homo amans,* taking a phenomenological approach that encompasses ambivalence as well as the failure of human love. The second main part of the paper will then develop and elaborate upon my own understanding of the nature of love. It will effectively present a reversal of perspective by, firstly, seeking to understand the nature of love and then questioning the nature of human beings on the basis of this understanding. I will argue that this is exactly the right order of thought if we truly want to adopt a Christian perspective on the topic. In section four, this thesis is elaborated further by following the thought of the Danish philosopher and theologian Søren Kierkegaard and his argument that a (self-)critique of love is the key to love's flourishing. Although Kierkegaard regards love as a reality of human life and not as a purely fantastical idea that belongs to some Christian people, he strongly resists the opinion that love could be exercised as a virtue of human nature itself. He defends the view that Christian love is not among the capabilities of human beings and should not be identified with the nature of human being. Instead, he argues that love is made possible by a relationship to the other as a child of God, and that it is God as a "middle term" in this relationship who liberates human beings from their narcissism and selfishness. I will provide some support for this position and, finally, I will try to give my own answer to the question of the true nature of Christian love. In the fifth section, therefore, I will argue that love is to be understood as a form of revolutionary altruism. Its revolutionary effects originate from its power to transform social relations by reshaping them from the point of view of a new reality. Here, love can be described as a central dynamic in human life that introduces radically new perspectives and social practices. Beyond Kierkegaard's focus on the presence of God, the revolutionary nature of love can be seen in the interruption of the normality of social relation and interaction by introducing the relation to a third of universal nature into the ordinary relation of self and other. Finally, it will be shown that love is misunderstood by focussing solely on the relationality of human beings, because the understanding of love also requires an understanding of the interruption of social relations.

6.2 The Problems and Limitations of a Holistic Anthropological Model

The *Homo amans* project attempts to collect and synthesize an assortment of developments within the study of human nature and philosophical anthropology from the past few decades. It does so in a very inspiring manner and grounds these recent advances in a philosophical anthropology of relationality. However, relational anthropology, as presented here, is mainly concerned with the dynamics of *becoming* human rather than the state of *being* human. It has the conviction that humans *become what they are,* in and through the relations which form and inform their lives and self-understanding. Relational anthropology, therefore, moves away from understanding human nature as an essence or core of the human being. It conceives it anew, not as a given but as a dynamic structure. This means, the nature of humans is not assumed to be the same or self-identical all the time. Rather, it develops in a certain direction out of a varied network of relationships with oneself and others. Hence, in this approach, crucial questions concerning humankind shift from the nature of human beings to the nature of their relationship with themselves and others.

In my view, it is not quite clear whether this approach and its shift of perspective has been fully acknowledged and valued in the given outline of the *Homo amans* project. The crux of my concern here would be the starting point of the project, which is in strict opposition to the *Homo economicus* model prevalent in economics and the social sciences. The outline of the project expressly refers to John Stuart Mill's definition. *Homo economicus* is defined as a human being capable of judging the comparative efficacy of the means for obtaining an end, as the outline paper says. *Homo economicus* thus refers to the mainly self-concerned utility maximizer who manifests an egotistic type of rationality in his preferences, choices, and behavior. In the outline of the project, this model of *Homo economicus* is taken to be a mere idea or concept, which appeared at a certain point in the history of ideas. As a result, its reality content is devalued. Furthermore, it is criticized for being too narrow to account for the full spectrum of human behavior, although no mention is made of the possibility of there being at least some truth in it as far as human beings are concerned.

In contrast, the *Homo amans* project, as it is outlined here, aims to introduce love and the Christian virtues of faith and hope into the picture and form a wholly new understanding of human sociality. *Homo amans* thus provides a fuller picture of human life and its relationality, i.e. concern for the well-being of others, for the common good, and for the crucial role given to the prevalence and protection of social norms. As appropriate and rightful as this endeavor undoubtedly is – and I have the utmost respect for it – there is an inherent danger in the strict opposition between *Homo economicus* and *Homo amans* and also, very often, in the broader discourse about changes to this model in the social sciences. When the concept of virtues and human relationality, on the one hand, is contrasted with a mistaken understanding of the human being as merely a rational utility maximizer on the other, two problems can arise from this starting point: (a) the limited but nonetheless existing reality content of the *Homo economicus* model could be marginalized and overlooked; and (b) the model of *Homo amans* could be taken as a full and definitive representation of the reality of human beings. In sum, the *Homo amans* perspective could then be implemented in the same totalitarian fashion as the other model was before.

Both points can now be seen to endanger a correct understanding of the *Homo amans* project because they could – perhaps not initially but later on – produce negative consequences in the continuation and building of a *Homo amans* anthropology. Whereas the first point mentioned above could result in the *Homo amans* model itself becoming ideological as it neglects and denies the reality of egotistic and self-concerned attitudes and behaviors in the study of humankind, the second point could imply a naïve bias, as with the *Homo economics* model previously, when taken to be the sole and exclusive model of human behavior. The first problem leads to the question of how *Homo economicus* and *Homo amans* (or human beings with egotistic and prosocial preferences) can coexist and/or interact with one another or how the second one can prevail over the first one in social interaction. The second problem leads to the question of how the concept of love can be focused and differentiated enough to discriminate between the ambivalent and multi-layered phenomenology of real-world phenomena.

To put it more succinctly, my concern is that the holism indicated in the *Homo amans* model could entrap and suppress the intrusions and ambivalences of sociality phenomena in real life. Therefore, what is needed here is a dual perspective involving (a) antagonizing or conflicting *Homo amans* with the reality of *Homo economicus* and (b) differentiating the inner reality of *Homo amans* by exploring and probing inner tensions and misunderstandings associated with love among human beings. The following sections will address the second research lacuna of the *Homo amans* project and the final part of this article will elaborate further on the antagonism between *Homo amans* and *Homo economicus*.

6.3 The Focus on Virtues and the Ambivalence or Failure of Love

The outline of the *Homo amans* project does not only motivate study of *Homo amans* by presenting it as "a viable alternative" to *Homo economicus* but also by pointing to the prosocial qualities of humans living a life of love. Thus, *Homo amans* is pictured in the project as an other-regarding, cooperative, and even altruistic being by nature. These prosocial qualities are further elaborated to constitute a phenomenology of human flourishing. However, at this point in the outline paper there is a certain changing of perspective which takes place; from the level of typifying and modeling human behavior to the level of an ethically informed phenomenology of human life. This change of perspective can be addressed by distinguishing between the terms "prosociality" and "human flourishing."

In behavioral sciences as well as in social psychology and evolutionary studies, the term "prosociality" denotes a type of behavior which contributes to the welfare of society as a whole insofar as it increases, for example, the cooperation level of a certain group (Gintis 2003; Henrich and Henrich 2006). "Prosocial" behavior may include concrete actions of helping or benefitting others, but also punitive actions, for example, the sanctioning of social norms (Fehr and Gächter 2002). Hence, the term "prosociality" also refers to the fact that not all actions which benefit the welfare and flourishing of human societies have to be at the same time actions benefitting the welfare of concrete others. As demonstrated in the case of social sanctions, such as the "altruistic punishment" (Fehr and Gächter 2002)[1] of norm violators and free riders, a prosocial behavior is not required to be beneficial to the other in either case. Instead, it can also contribute to the common good, for example: the enforcement of social and cooperation norms by introducing severe costs at the personal level of social interactions.

In contrast, the term "flourishing" does not refer to a certain mechanism of behavior which can be measured and observed or to an outcome-oriented approach to human action at all but to a psychological attitude or lifestyle of individuals that is seen to be balanced, resilient, and orientated towards positive emotions and well-being, in order to allow humanity as a whole to flourish (Keyes and Haidt 2007). Taken as a psychological term, it describes the optimal functioning of human beings or their ability to live their lives well – even in the face of suffering and frailty (Fowers 2017). The term has recently become prominent in the context of positive psychology but it can be traced back to the antique Aristotelian concept of *eudaimonia* which means striving to live an intrinsically good life (Aristotle 2014).

As Miroslav Volf has shown in his book *Flourishing*, a good life has to be understood as a life worth living viz. a meaningful life in late modernity (Volf 2015, pp. 1–26). Volf emphasizes that the turn towards flourishing points toward the fact that life has to be more than just the satisfaction of needs and the initialization of pleasures, but also has to have meaning (Volf 2015, pp. 195–206). Furthermore, he suggests that the goodness of life we are striving for should not be understood too idealistically or transcendently, but rather that flourishing requires a unity of meaningfulness, as well as the experience of pleasure and joy, in order to avoid a decline into nihilism (Volf 2015, p. 201).

Hence, the shift from the observation of prosocial behaviors to the study of human flourishing and the phenomenology of a good and meaningful life, which is taken by the proponents of the *Homo amans* project, is a step into an ethically informed perspective on human life as well as a step into developing a holistic, instead of a fractional, perspective. In this shift of perspective, what is called the phenomenological constitution of *Homo amans* is made understandable by elaborating on the inner reality and differentiation of human beings' capabilities and virtues. The latter are focused on the triadic interrelation of three core virtues, which

[1] For a critical commentary on the experimental studies on altruistic punishment see Klein (2011) as well as the article published together with Christine Clavien: Clavien and Klein (2010).

are assumed to be inseparable. Thus, the initiators of this project express their conviction that the inner reality of *Homo amans* can be made understandable by discriminating between three basic capabilities of the human being: love, hope, and faith. These virtues can be traced back to the biblical tradition and to the epistles of Saint Paul, who wrote in 1 Corinthians 13 that these three are the basic virtues of a Christian community, but that love is the greatest among them. In his epistle, the apostle makes it quite clear that neither the gifts of charismatic speech nor wisdom nor knowledge can build up Christian community as this is done by acts of love.

In the reading of this tradition by the proponents of the *Homo amans* project, faith represents the quest for meaning in human life. Hope reflects the universal human desire for a future, and love (taken as being the primary virtue) grounds all human capabilities and virtues in relation to other human beings, making it quite clear that human beings are social or rather prosocial beings. With regard to the primacy of love, the initiators of the *Homo amans* project argue that love is a feminine virtue that might lead to a complementary rather than exclusive understanding of human nature. This then stands in contrast to the masculine virtues, which are characterized as being more or less anti-relational or egotistic.

From the outline paper, it follows that the virtue of love is somehow seen to prevail over faith and hope because (a) it is of a fundamental nature, pointing towards the basic relationality[2] of human beings and (b) it relates to secular anthropology more easily because the core relation inherent in love is taken to be primarily interpersonal and not divine, given that God is not the main object of love but is certainly the main object of faith and hope. I would like to challenge the last thesis in particular, as we will see later.

For now, I want to stress another point and to question whether the virtue of love, in a very common theological fashion, is presented in an overly positivistic manner by the *Homo amans* project outlined so far. To address my suspicion, I would like to pose some exploratory questions concerning the nature of love and its visibility and appearance in human life: Where do we find love in our lives and can it actually be equated to the prosocial behaviors and attitudes of cooperation and altruism? Is love grounded in a feeling, or is it grounded in a rational choice made by us? Is love a capability and among the properties of human life, or rather is it a phenomenon of contingent appearance? Is love the solution, or key, to human flourishing, or is it a challenge that we do not normally master but which always proves to be a milestone for failure in our lives?

These questions suggest that it is not so clear or obvious what love is and which role it plays in our life. Furthermore, it can be said that the longing for love as well as the desire for bonding, for reliable commitment and rootedness, is a kind of child of the spirit of our age, and I think this should also be taken into account when we address the problem of exploring the possibilities and limits of an orientation towards a loving human being. Human beings have become increasingly uprooted

[2] See this claim regarding St. Paul's preoccupation with love also in Schnelle (1999, p. 84).

and separated from their original bonds in late modern societies since the industrial revolution and late-capitalist globalization movements. Hence, an orientation towards relationality as well as a strengthening of other-regarding attitudes and behaviors seem to be the solution to the pressing problem of growing anonymity and atomization of the human being in a liquid modernity with fluid identities (as, for example, sociologist Zygmunt Bauman [2000] has argued). Not for nothing, then, recent studies in science – for example, the social neurosciences and economics of empathy and care – have been inaugurated and conducted on the grounds that we need to develop mental training in empathy and other caring attitudes, particularly in a globalized world where we are confronted with "the stranger" every day.[3] A better understanding of the neural mechanisms of empathy and care could thus help to better position us in the advancement of human flourishing.

These remarks are given to indicate that the quest for an examination of *Homo amans* is in no way a timeless or contextless project. Rather, the study of *Homo amans* can be seen as an indicator of a growing uncertainty about formerly self-evident phenomena in the era of globalization. Because traditional means of social bonding and human relationality have been broken so dramatically and with such intensity in late modern times, people long for a deeper understanding and maybe also for a restoration, or for a new configuration, of these basics of human flourishing. Seen in the context of the current agenda, a virtue approach to *Homo amans* which is mainly elaborated in Neo-Aristotelian terminology might overlook the opportunity to reflect on this current context agenda, and, therefore, could create a superficial impression of a romanticized fairy-tale like world instead. But I think that this is in no way intended in the *Homo amans* project.

The following thoughts should not, therefore, be understood so much as a critique but as a continuation of the differentiation process of the *Homo amans* project. The differentiation achieved by discriminating between love, faith, and hope must be opened out into a differentiation process of the inner reality of love. This inner difference of love will continue to be explored in the next section with reference to the work of Søren Kierkegaard.

6.4 Kierkegaard: A (Self-)Critique of Love as the Key to Love's Flourishing

In his later work, gathering together a collection of upbuilding discourses, Søren Kierkegaard wrote a book on the realness and actuality of Christian love, entitled *The Works of Love* ([1847] 1995). He did so because he was concerned that love

[3] See "Ein mentales Training, um toleranter Weltbürger zu werden," Interview with Prof. Tania Singer, Director at the Max-Planck-Institute for Human Cognitive and Brain Sciences, 7. Oct. 2017, https://www.mpg.de/11514867/interview-singer-neue-meditationstechnik-fuer-empathie (accessed 26 Aug. 2019).

should not be taken as an idea but as a reality, not as an ethical ideal but as concrete work that can actually be done. At the same time, in his book, Kierkegaard directly addresses the problem that love cannot easily be discriminated from other actions and that it has a certain "invisibility" among human affairs. He writes at the beginning of his book: "There is no work, not one single one, not even the best, about which we can unconditionally dare to say: The one who does this unconditionally demonstrates love by it" (Kierkegaard 1995, p. 13).

This means that love is not a phenomenon which can be recognized easily and that there is no proof or demonstration of love which safeguards its existence. Love is not a certain type of action or a stable character trait at all. Rather, Kierkegaard determines the relation of love and action as follows: "It depends on *how* the work is done" (Kierkegaard 1995, p. 13). Obviously, the view that love is a general trait of human persons or actions is not helpful but only obfuscates the study of its phenomenality. Kierkegaard emphasizes that the reality of love is, let us say, more complicated. Its study requires a special form of phenomenology which Kierkegaard then aims to develop throughout his book.

In recent years, there has been an extended discussion about whether Kierkegaard's book, *The Works of Love*, and the phenomenology of love that is developed in it, can be considered to be ethical in nature. In it, Kierkegaard himself polemicizes against certain strands of modern moral philosophy. Arguments, therefore, have been put forward to suggest that it seeks to engender ethical wisdom (Grøn 1998, pp. 358–68) and that it can even be interpreted as the pursuit of love as virtue.[4] On the other hand, there have also been suggestions that Kierkegaard's ethical considerations in this book are built on a theology of sin and that he is sceptical about seeing love as a meritorious action (Welz 2007). Hence, Kierkegaard's intention could not have been to build an ethical theory of human virtues. Against the view that he is not a virtue theorist, it has been argued that there is some evidence in his book that he also thinks about the constitution of the author of loving action (Lippitt 2013, p. 7). Or at least, that he sees love as "a divinely inspired potential that we humans are required to actualize" (Krishek 2017, pp. 3–15, esp. pp. 3–4). It has also been pointed out that he argues that "emotion-virtues," understood as ways of seeing the other, can be cultivated in Christian faith.[5]

A more moderate view regarding this debate is taken by Claudia Welz when she argues that "Works of Love can be termed as a 'virtue ethics' only in a restricted sense", because in Kierkegaard's view "it is not the human agent himself who naturally develops the virtue of love, nor does (s)he receive a supernatural virtue for personal use" (Welz 2007, p. 272). Rather, love could be actualized by the human being only "by acting in the spirit of God's love" (Welz 2007, p. 281). As Welz

[4] An ethical theorist who has put this thesis forward in many publications is Robert C. Roberts. See Roberts (1995, pp. 142–66; 2008, pp. 72–92, and many more).

[5] Compare the argument that virtuists like Kierkegaard are committed to upbuilding and ethical education, including a formation of proper concerns and dispositions of emotion, in Lippitt (2017). The approach to Kierkegaard as an emotion-virtuist is also elaborated in Welz (2007); Evans (2008).

argues, the relation of the human being to the other is built up by the reality of God's love alone.

Against the backdrop of this debate, one's attention should be turned to the phenomenology at stake in *Works of Love*. The term "phenomenology" here refers to a study of the way love comes into being and how it can be identified in its significance. In this regard, Kierkegaard emphasizes that love has a "hidden life" that we have to explore and carefully discover (Kierkegaard 1995, pp. 5–16). Very often we invariably think we already live a life of love and we err precisely because of our certainty. According to Kierkegaard, it is very important, then, to acknowledge that love is not just given to us as an inherent part of our nature that can be exercised on a whim. On the contrary, in an in-depth analysis of interpersonal relationships and social interaction, he demonstrates that we are more often confronted with the impossibilities of loving ourselves and others than with the experience of love in the true sense of the word.

Kierkegaard writes parts of his book, then, to reduce his readers to despair and release them from their certainty that love is already there in their lives. Nonetheless, on the other hand, he also aims to encourage the reader to see that love is a way to live one's life before God. According to him, it is something which can manifest in our lives although we experience all the misunderstandings, failures, and aporias that exist in human togetherness. To experience the failure of love, then, does not mean that we have to call off the realm of love and social bonding completely. For him, a self-critique of love is, in the end, the key to the flourishing of love's true nature.

By taking this position, Kierkegaard makes it possible to introduce a critical view of human sociality into the picture of love. Love is not automatically a representative of the good life prevailing under all circumstances. Love is not just a token of a certain type but is contingent in nature. The latter is made clear when Kierkegaard develops his phenomenology of love from a decidedly Christian point of view. To him, love is not only one of a kind but the only true way of living one's life in the spirit of Christian faith. In no way does this imply a glorification of the Christian way of life. Hence, Kierkegaard develops the latter stance into a self-critical attitude of modernity and Christian religion. A part of his phenomenology of love, therefore, is a critical discussion of the modern ideal of romantic love as well as the Christian denial and demonization of self-love (Lippitt 2013). Furthermore, he reviews critically the tradition of the denial of bodily love in Christianity and Western culture, and, in the light of true selflessness, questions the high esteem for seemingly altruistic and selfless behaviors celebrating a cult of the self in the other.

Kierkegaard, hereby, again resists the view that loving action is to be seen as a self-evident outcome of human nature (Kierkegaard 1995, Chapter III.A, IX 90–IX 129, pp. 91–134). His phenomenology of love is not built on the seemingly solid grounds of anthropology. Instead, it opens the door for social criticism and for a critical debate on widespread preconceptions of what love is in the Christian tradition. Through the narrowly designed contrast between human love and that of true Christian love, Kierkegaard accounts for the problem that in real life, loving attitudes and behaviors mostly remain ambivalent and difficult in their nature.[6] In his upbuilding discourses, he argues that what true love is (or is not) can be judged neither from the object of love or its meaning to the subject, nor from the selfless outcomes of its actions, nor the spiritual versus bodily nature of love. Rather, proper love, as Christians understand the word, can only be identified in this world by acknowledging that God has put love close to us, namely, in our neighbor (Kierkegaard 1995, Chapters II.B and II.C, IX 47– IX 89, pp. 44–90). The core of concrete love, as Kierkegaard puts it, is to see others just as they are and respond accordingly.[7] Hence, love is not a distant ideal that we reach out for, but is rather a daily concrete encounter with someone near to us (Kierkegaard 1995, Chapter IV, IX 147–IX 194, pp. 154–204). At the same time, however, it is exactly this concrete person whom we generally neither address nor see in the right way because we all too often account for their presence only in the horizon of selfish preferences or even narcissistic attitudes. Hence, love is needed to open our eyes, despite the fact that it is seldom found and exercised.

According to Kierkegaard, it is only the language and performativity of the Christian tradition and its way of life which gives witness to the eye-opening process and dynamic of love in our lives. It is the term, or better, the metaphor of the "neighbor" from the biblical tradition which can help to illuminate the dynamic of transformation taking place in love. The "neighbor" then serves as a middle term in all our social relationships as Kierkegaard continually seeks to emphasize (Kierkegaard 1995, Chapter II.B, IX 60, p. 58). The other being seen as the neighbor enters social relationships as a qualifying dimension, transforming the dyadic relation of self and other into a social and universal one in the full sense of the term. Concretely, the neighbor stands for a different mode of seeing the other, i.e., of seeing the other as a child of God who is neither worth more nor less than me and is an equal.[8] Thus, seeing others as neighbors means to acknowledge the primacy of this equality in all the inequalities and injustices of human relationships. Seeing the other as an equal child of God, therefore, helps the human being to acknowledge the nearness of love and also its practicability.

What love is and how it can be sought and found in our lives is, for Kierkegaard, clearly committed to a Christian perspective. Here, God appears not as the object of love but as a "middle term,"[9] as Kierkegaard calls it, which helps to redirect our relationships in order to make them more equal, more consistent, more solid, more responsive and concrete. Consequently, these relationships will be mediated and

[6] For an emphasis on the difficulty of love and the rigor of its demands, see Critchley (2012, pp. 247–52).

[7] This has been referred to as Kierkegaard's "paradoxical embrace of both the universal and the particular" which could form a model for the commitment in the context of multicultural societies and globalism in Veninga (2018, p. 122).

[8] Kierkegaard (1995, Chapter II.B, p. 60): "The neighbor is one who is equal. […] He is your neighbor on the basis of equality with you before God, but unconditionally every person has this equality and has it unconditionally."

[9] Kierkegaard (1995, Chapter II.B, IX 60, p. 58): "in love for the neighbor, God is the middle term".

transformed into relationships of a new kind: relationships of love. It is this new perspective and the actions resulting from it which mark the dynamic of love as a dynamic of freedom. From this perspective, Kierkegaard can address the pressing questions arising in the ethical study of human helping and other benevolent actions, such as: Are works of love driven by feelings and emotions or by rational interests? Are they self-concerned or other-concerned? Is sacrifice for the other always a form of love? Etc. To all these questions, Kierkegaard can give a clear answer, namely that the crucial criterion in this regard is whether the loving action is oriented towards the other by seeing and addressing him as a neighbor (as a fellow child of God).

In the concluding section, I will now return to the question of what the nature of love is and how it can be addressed best by a scientific approach. Following the fundamental distinctions of Kierkegaard's phenomenology, I will argue that love is not an attitude, an action, or a virtue but a central dynamic in human life which has the power to transform all social relations into prosocial ones with a tendency towards universality. The structural dynamic of love, thus, can be characterized as disruptive. Thus, I will argue, secondly, that the invoked dynamic of love is marked by a certain kind of revolutionary potential. The nature of love, then, can be found in its power of social transformation. It opens certain social practices, as well as dyadic and egotistic relationships, to change by introducing a third one which works as the initiator of a different order and establishes social bridging and prosociality.[10] In the end, it will be shown that the dynamic of love will not be subsumed by social techniques aiming at human flourishing or the ethical quest for a good life, because, rather, it is of a non-conformist nature and aims at unmasking the ideological character of social techniques of human flourishing too.

6.5 The Nature of Love and Revolutionary Altruism[11]

Besides Kierkegaard who has written at length of the inner struggles of love, there remains the question posed earlier in this paper whether there is any valid content in the repudiated *Homo economicus* model and consequently whether there is a struggle for love to be won against the non-cooperative and egotistic behaviour of utility maximizing. In this regard, it might be interesting to note some critiques of the *Homo economicus* model in the field of neuroeconomics, a research approach combining experimental economics and social neuroscience (Vromen and Marchionni 2019; Glimcher et al. 2009). This newly emerging field of transdisciplinary research aims to overcome neoclassical economics and to "provide an alternative theoretical approach for predicting behaviour" (Glimcher et al. 2009, p. 7). Its major paradigms for studying human social behavior are behavioral experiments designed after the

[10] For a study of the role and order of the third in social philosophy, see Bedorf (2003).

[11] Parts of this section have already been published in: Klein (2012).

paradigms of game theory, as for example the trust game, the dictator game, and the third-party punishment game etc. (Gintis 2000). Neuroeconomics does not simply take leave of the model of *Homo economicus*. Rather, it takes egoism to be a continuing challenge to the prosocial orientation of altruistic and cooperative human beings. Hence, the research question posed here is how altruism[12] and prosocial behaviors can prevail over *Homo economicus*? (Fehr and Gächter 2002; Fehr and Rosenbach 2003).[13] A special focus in the field of prosociality is placed on the study of norm enforcement.

Several experimental studies on cooperation and prosociality in economics have shown that altruistic punishment plays a key role in understanding the evolution of norm enforcement in human societies.[14] Altruistic punishment does not directly benefit the welfare of an individual person, but society as a whole. Therefore, it is referred to as a "prosocial" behaviour. As already noted, the term "prosociality" is used in experimental economics but also in other behavioral sciences to indicate a behavior that does not directly benefit others (as does cooperation), but the well-being of group interaction as a whole.[15] The behavioral pattern of altruistic punishment has been clearly shown to be of great significance for the study of prosociality in a series of behavioral experiments in economics and neuroeconomics (Fehr and Gächter 2002; Fehr and Fischbacher 2003; Fehr and Rosenbach 2003; de Quervain et al. 2004).[16] These have been conducted in different behavioral laboratories since the first study on altruistic punishment was published by Ernst Fehr and Simon Gächter (2002).

In this study, altruistic punishment is defined as a non-selfish act of punishment which "[provides] … a material benefit for the future interaction partners of the punished subject but not for the punisher" (Fehr and Gächter 2002, p. 139). In an experimental setup with 240 participants[17] at the University of Zurich, Fehr and Gächter tested their subject's individual willingness to punish altruistically in a "public goods" experiment. In this type of experiment, several people have the option of investing a certain amount of money in a group project.[18] Afterwards, the sum of all contributions is to be shared among the group members equally. The

[12]The term "altruism" is used here in a behavioral sense referring to the outcomes and not the motivation behind this behavior. Thus, the economic use of the term has to be distinguished from its use in moral philosophy and psychology. See further discussion in Peacock et al. (2005); Clavien and Chapuisat (2013).

[13]Compare also Clavien and Klein (2010).

[14]The claim that social reciprocity (prosocial norm enforcement) provides the best explanation for the evolution of punishing behaviors has been defended in Carpenter et al. (2004).

[15]A definition of the distinction between prosociality and cooperation can be found in Henrich and Henrich (2006). For a model explaining the cultural evolution of prosociality and cooperation see Gintis (2003).

[16]An assessment of the evolutionary origin of altruistic punishment can be found in Boyd et al. (2003).

[17]All of the participants in the experiment were undergraduate students from the University of Zurich.

[18]The money they earn is paid to them actually after the experiment.

experiment in Zurich was conducted in 12 sessions and the group composition was changed after each session. The latter guaranteed that none of the subjects could again meet the same subjects during the experiment. This ensured that the subjects' decisions and behaviors were not based on a preference for reputation-building among group members. The opportunity to punish group members who did not invest in the group project, but benefited from its gain, was offered at the end of each session. In order to test whether the subjects' willingness to punish did include the willingness to suffer personal cost, the punishment was not only costly for the free rider, but also for the punishing subject himself, because he had to pay for it from his own gain.

The results of the experiment were as follows: over 12 sessions, the opportunity to punish social free-riding behavior was taken by 84.3% of the subjects at least once, and 34.3% of the subjects punished more than five times (Fehr and Gächter 2002, p. 137). A minority of 9.3% of the subjects punished more than ten times. Thus, the experimental results provide strong evidence that altruistic punishment is a stable behavioral pattern among humans. Additionally, a significant effect of altruistic punishment was shown in the later sessions of the experiment. After having been punished, the punished subjects invested a higher amount of money in the group project and changed from non-cooperative to cooperative behaviors in the following sessions. Thus, altruistic punishment caused a substantial increase in terms of the average cooperation level of the group over time. This was highly correlated with the subject's investment strategies and can, therefore, be considered among the facilitating conditions of the evolution of human cooperation. Hence, the remarkable result of the study by Fehr and Gächter was that the opportunity to punish free riders altruistically has a significant impact on the maintenance of the norm of cooperation and equity, even in anonymous encounters.

With regard to the interpretation of this evidence, the researchers suggested that the evolution of social norms has to be explained further in terms of the level of the individual's preferences. Thus, they asked how the willingness to punish might be triggered on a psychological level. As a suggestion, it was hypothesized that the subjects' negative emotions concerning the free-riding behavior of others might be the source of their decision to punish. Emotions such as anger and outrage could provide a proximate mechanism of altruistic punishment.[19]

To elicit the correlation between punishment and the individual's emotions, the researchers prepared a questionnaire given to the subjects after the experiment that asked them to indicate their intensity of anger concerning the free-riding behavior on a seven-point scale. The results recorded that 47% of the subjects had indicated the highest intensity of anger. Hence, it was concluded that these emotions might be a psychological trigger for punishment. This led them to seek a research tool to further investigate this correlation, which in turn led them to engage in a new research field investigating the neurobiology of prosocial and cooperative behaviors in humans.

---

[19] A definition of proximate causes of evolution can be found in Mayr (1961, p. 1503).

In a follow-up study (de Quervain et al. 2004, pp. 1254–8) to the first experiment on altruistic punishment in 2004, Fehr and fellow economist, Urs Fischbacher, started to work together with neuropsychologists for the first time. They added a neuroimaging tool to the experimental setup of their study on social norm enforcement and observed the neurological foundations of people's choices. The idea of combining experiments on norm enforcement with the neurological investigation of the human mind had already come up in a study in 2003 when neuroscientists Alan Sanfey, James Rilling and other colleagues had adapted an experimental design from economics, and started to investigate the neural substrates of the cognitive and emotional processes involved in decision making about altruistic punishment (Sanfey et al. 2003). After they brain-scanned the subjects with functional magnetic resonance imaging (fMRI), they found an increased activity in the "anterior insula"–a brain area associated with negative emotional feelings. They concluded that emotions might be the psychological and neurological driving force behind this behavior, a view which was still consistent with the 2002 findings of Fehr and Gächter.

However, the follow-up study by Fehr, Fischbacher and de Quervain in 2004 led to a rather different neurological finding. The procedure of this experiment was as follows: the subjects were brain-scanned during their decision to punish free-riding behavior by using positron emission tomography (PET). They were placed in a scanner immediately after the interaction with another player was over. The scanning started when subjects learned about the free-riding behavior of the other participant and it finished when they had determined the punishment. In the observation of the neural circuits of the subjects' brains, it was shown that not the "interior insula" but a brain area linked to the anticipation of reward – the "caudate nucleus"–played a prominent role when people decided to punish. Subjects who exhibited stronger activation of the "caudate nucleus" were ready to incur more personal costs to punish a free rider in comparison with subjects who exhibited low caudate activation.

Hence, the researchers interpreted the finding as evidence that the anticipation of "hedonic rewards" (de Quervain et al. 2004, p. 1257) was considered a benefit that altruistic punishers weighed against the costs of punishing. The punishing subjects seemed to feel relief when the violated social norm was established again through an act of retributive justice. Thus, it was concluded that, according to the underlying neurological processes, the subjects' decision-making was driven by hedonic motivation. Hedonic motivation is one of the key features in an evolutionary explanation of behavior, because there is natural selection for avoiding pain and unpleasantness. The correlation between hedonic motivation and altruistic punishment, then, might function as a proximate mechanism with respect to the evolution of human cooperation.

From the presentation and analysis of these pioneering experimental works it can be seen that the findings, in a way, renew the initial question of modern political philosophy posed by Thomas Hobbes (1651): How can human society with stable cooperation and norm enforcement evolve out of the nastiness and brutish character of the state of nature? At the same time this question is transformed in the laboratory setting of the neuroeconomic experiments by introducing a dual anthropology into this so-called "state of nature". It is no longer the question of how a society with stable cooperation and norm following can be built out of a bunch of egotistic individuals, but rather how it can evolve out of a group of egotistic and altruistic individuals interacting with each other. The interesting thing about this recent experimental research in neuroeconomics is, therefore, that it stimulates the perspective of a fighting antagonism between *Homo economicus* and *Homo amans*. This means, it regards the cooperative and prosocial orientation not just as a viable alternative which fully replaces the view that human beings are egotistic utility maximizers. Rather, prosociality is seen as an orientation that must establish and sustain itself in a direct confrontation with radically egotistic preferences and behaviors and can – under certain circumstances – be seen to prevail.

Experimental economists have examined in their research the individual conditions (of the human mind) and institutional factors (of setting and context) which can help altruism to win against egoism (Fehr and Fischbacher 2003, 2004, 2005). A combination of both perspectives, behavioral and neuroscientific, helps them to determine in more detail the nature of altruism and cooperative behaviors. What they discovered after extensive experimental research is that there is a mechanism in human brains which helps altruists and co-operators do their job. The experiments have therefore given an empirical proof that there actually exist altruists and co-operators which are willing to sacrifice their individual self-interest to safeguard the existence of common goods (such as social norms of fairness), and that they are naturally oriented towards the welfare and flourishing of society as whole.

What we can learn now from this research concerning a deeper understanding of the nature of love is the following: The modern romantic view that love is fully developed in an interpersonal relation is misleading. Instead, it can be argued from a Christian point of view, but also from the insights of recent experimental studies, that love has a prosocial nature insofar as it is reliant on introducing a third into the interpersonal relation and transforming it in the light of a universal signifier. Likewise, the view is false that love is always aiming at a personal benefit or at the welfare of others. Rather, it can require personal sacrifice or even loss of self and other in order to safeguard the welfare of society and its ethical virtues such as fairness, justice, and norm compliance.[20]

Further, what has been shown by Kierkegaard to be true for the inner struggle of love is also shown to be true in the neuroeconomic experiments for the outer dynamics of prosocial behavior: the significance of *Homo amans*, a human being with a preference for loving and cooperative behavior, lies in its potential for social transformation which, in the behavioral experiments, is manifest in the establishment and protection of social norms as a main public good of every society. Other orientations do not disappear when *Homo amans*, i.e. human beings with prosocial

[20] This reference to the virtue of institutions or society can be traced back to John Rawls (1971).

preferences, appears on the scene. Hence, the *Homo economicus* has reality content as well, but – as the experiments have shown – the love for the third, the prosocial action, can definitely prevail due to its revolutionary nature. Thus, a convincing model of *Homo amans* and the nature of love should also provide a good analysis and explanation of the disruptive dynamic of love introducing a third that transgresses interpersonal relations.

6.6 Conclusions

Love is not a stable core of human nature nor a character trait that can be educated or trained. Rather, it should be seen as a dynamic structure at work in human attitudes and behaviors, arising out of a change of perspective concerning the world, oneself, and others. This change of perspective cannot be determined but happens for contingent reasons. This makes it uncomfortable to account for it in the realm of hard sciences with its focus on the measurability of love and cooperative behaviors. As has been shown, the characteristic of the dynamic structure of love is that it is creative in its nature because it brings into being a wholly new social reality, which transforms the *status quo* and the shape of human relationality completely by introducing a horizon of universality. Crucial for the prevalence of love in its true nature is the introduction of a notion of the third that opens the space for prosocial action and sets the focus on the welfare of all humankind or society as a whole.

Hence, it could be fruitful in future to explore in more detail the revolutionary potential of love – love's potential to induce social transformation and the role it plays in the implementation of radically new perspectives and social practices in human life. As has been further shown, the orientation of love is an orientation towards the third in the relationship with the other. Thus, it can be seen as structurally equal to what Kierkegaard already described in the language of Christian faith as the central dynamic of love of neighbor. The interpersonal relationship, which can be of a cooperative or non-cooperative nature, is transformed through love by introducing a third – in the experiments represented by a universal social norm of fairness and in the Christian faith represented by the universal perception of humans as children of God. Both orientations have in common that they describe the two terms "love of neighbor" and "prosociality" as revolutionary, i.e. disruptive dynamics which transgress the current social state and open it for a human sociality of a different kind. It inaugurates the existence of universal norms (in the horizon of a new and yet invisible social order) and overcomes the unstructured interaction of atomized individuals. Thus, love can be seen to set up the rules by setting out the rules first. It distances current social practice, for example, of free riding and exploiting the common good, and introduces a new one. Suspending the reigning unwritten rules is in itself an act of non-conformity. Building new structures of interaction by setting the rules for it in a kind of violently nonconformist act is, thus, a crucial capability of love.

References

Aristotle. 2014. *Nicomachean Ethics*. Transl. and ed. R. Crisp. New York: Cambridge University Press.

Bauman, Z. 2000. *Liquid Modernity*. Cambridge: Polity Press.

Bedorf, T. 2003. *Dimensionen des Dritten: Sozialphilosophische Modelle zwischen Ethischem und Politischem*. Munich: Fink.

Boyd, R., et al. 2003. The Evolution of Altruistic Punishment. *Proceedings of the National Academy of Sciences of the United States of America* 100 (6): 3531–3535.

Carpenter, J.P., et al. 2004. Why Punish? Social Reciprocity and the Enforcement of Prosocial Norms. *Journal of Evolutionary Economics* 14: 407–429.

Clavien, C., and R.A. Klein. 2010. Eager for Fairness or for Revenge? Psychological Altruism in Economics. *Economics & Philosophy* 26: 267–290.

Clavien, C., and M. Chapuisat. 2013. Altruism Across Disciplines: One Word, Multiple Meanings. *Biology and Philosophy* 28: 125–140.

Critchley, S. 2012. *Faith of the Faithless. Experiments in Political Theology*. London: Verso.

de Quervain, D.J.-F., et al. 2004. The Neural Basis of Altruistic Punishment. *Science* 305: 1254–1258.

"Ein mentales Training, um toleranter Weltbürger zu werden," Interview with Prof. Tania Singer, Director at the Max–Planck–Institute for Human Cognitive and Brain Sciences, 7. Oct. 2017. https://www.mpg.de/11514867/interview–singer–neue–meditationstechnik–fuer–empathie. Accessed 26 Aug 2019.

Evans, C.S. 2008. Can Love be Commanded? Kierkegaard's View of Neighbor Love. In *Visions of Agapé: Problems and Possibilities in Human and Divine Love*, ed. C.A. Boyd, 73–83. Aldershot: Ashgate.

Fehr, E., and U. Fischbacher. 2003. The Nature of Human Altruism. *Nature* 425: 785–791.

———. 2004. Social Norms and Human Cooperation. *Trends in Cognitive Sciences* 8: 185–190.

———. 2005. Human Altruism: Proximate Patterns and Evolutionary Origins. *Analyse & Kritik* 27: 6–47.

Fehr, E., and S. Gächter. 2002. Altruistic Punishment in Humans. *Nature* 415: 137–140.

Fehr, E., and B. Rosenbach. 2003. Detrimental Effects of Sanctions on Human Altruism. *Nature* 422: 137–140.

Fowers, B.J. 2017. *Frailty, Suffering, and Vice: Flourishing in the Face of Human Limitations*. Washington, DC: American Psychological Association.

Gintis, H. 2000. Beyond *Homo economicus*: Evidence from Experimental Economics. *Ecological Economics* 35: 311–322.

———. 2003. Solving the Puzzle of Prosociality. *Rationality and Society* 15: 155–187.

Glimcher, P.W., et al. 2009. *Neuroeconomics: Decision-Making and the Brain*. Amsterdam: Elsevier/Academic Press.

Grøn, A. 1998. Kierkegaards 'zweite' Ethik. Transl. H. Schmid. In *Kierkegaard Studies Yearbook 1998*, ed. N.J. Cappelørn and H. Deuser, 358–368. Berlin: De Gruyter.

Hirsch-Hadorn, G., et al. 2008. The Emergence of Transdisciplinarity as a Form of Research. In *Handbook of Transdisciplinarity Research*, ed. G. Hirsch-Hadorn, 19–39. Frankfurt a.M.: Springer.

Hobbes, T. 1651. *Leviathan, or, The Matter, Form and Power of A Common–Wealth Ecclesiastical and Civil*. London: Printed for Andre Crooke.

Henrich, J., and N. Henrich. 2006. Culture, Evolution and the Puzzle of Human Cooperation. *Cognitive Systems Research* 7: 220–245.

Keyes, C., and J. Haidt, eds. 2007. *Flourishing: Positive Psychology and the Life Well-Lived*. Washington, DC: American Psychological Association.

Kierkegaard, S. 1995. *Works of Love: Some Christian Reflections in the Form of Discourses*, Kierkegaard's Writings 16. Ed. and transl. H. V. Hong and E. H. Hong. Princeton: Princeton University Press.
Klein, R.A. 2011. *Sociality as the Human Condition: Anthropology in Economic, Philosophical and Theological Perspective*. Leiden: Brill.
———. 2012. The Neurobiology of Altruistic Punishment: A Moral Assessment of its Social Utility. In *Philosophy of Behavioral Biology*, ed. K. Plaisance and T. Reydon, 297–313. Dordrecht: Springer.
———. 2017. Theologie als transdisziplinäres Wissen: Wissenschaftliche Reformimpulse im Diskurs reformatorischen Denkens. *Evangelische Theologie* 77 (6): 437–450.
Krishek, S. 2017. Love as the End of Human Existence. In *Kierkegaard's God and the Good Life*, ed. S. Minister, J.A. Simmons, and M. Strawser, 3–15. Bloomington: Indiana University Press.
Lippitt, J. 2013. *Kierkegaard and the Problem of Self-Love*. Cambridge: Cambridge University Press.
———. 2017. Kierkegaard's Virtues? Humility and Gratitude as the Grounds of Contentment, Patience, and Hope in Kierkegaard's Moral Psychology. In *Kierkegaard's God and the Good Life*, ed. S. Minister, J.A. Simmons, and M. Strawser, 95–113. Bloomington: Indiana University Press.
Mayr, E. 1961. Cause and Effect in Biology. *Science* 134: 1501–1506.
Mittelstraß, J. 1982. *Wissenschaft als Lebensform. Reden über die philosophische Orientierung in Wissenschaft und Universität*. Frankfurt a.M.: Suhrkamp.
———. 2003. *Transdisziplinarität. Wissenschaftliche Zukunft und institutionelle Wirklichkeit*. Konstanz: Universitätsverlag Konstanz.
Nowotny, H. 1997. Transdisziplinäre Wissensproduktion: Eine Antwort auf die Wissensexplosion? In *Wissenschaft als Kultur: Österreichs Beitrag zur Moderne*, ed. F. Stadler, 177–195. Vienna: Springer.
———. 1999. The Place of People in Our Knowledge. *European Review* 7: 247–262.
Nowotny, H., P. Scott, and M. Gibbons. 2001. *Re-Thinking Science: Knowledge and the Public in an Age of Uncertainty*. Cambridge: Polity Press.
Peacock, M.S., et al. 2005. Altruism and the Indispensability of Motives. *Analyse & Kritik* 27: 188–196.
Peitz, D. 2019, June 3. Macht menschlich! *DIE ZEIT*. https://www.zeit.de/kultur/2019–06/spd–andrea–nahles–ruecktritt–machtkampf–parteivorstand. Accessed 9 Aug 2019.
Rawls, J. 1971. *A Theory of Justice*. Cambridge, MA: Belknap Press.
Roberts, R.C. 1995. Kierkegaard, Wittgenstein and the Method of 'Virtue Ethics'. In *Kierkegaard in Post/Modernity*, ed. M. Matustik and M. Westphal, 142–166. Bloomington: Indiana University Press.
———. 2008. Kierkegaard and Ethical Theory. In *Ethics, Love and Faith in Kierkegaard*, ed. M. Westphal, 72–92. Bloomington: Indiana University Press.
Sanfey, A.G., et al. 2003. The Neural Basis of Economic Decision-Making in the Ultimatum Game. *Science* 300: 1755–1758.
Schnelle, U. ^{3}1999. *Einleitung in das Neue Testament*. Göttingen: Vandenhoeck & Ruprecht.
Veninga, J.E. 2018. Loving the Ones We See: Kierkegaard's Neighbor–Love and the Politics of Pluralism. In *Kierkegaard and Political Theology*, ed. R. Sirvent and S. Morgan, 105–126. Eugene: Pickwick.
Volf, M. 2015. *Flourishing: Why We Need Religion in A Globalized World*. New Haven: Yale University Press.
Vromen, J., and C. Marchionni, eds. 2019. *Neuroeconomics, Vol. I–IV, Critical Concepts in the Social Sciences*. London: Routledge.
Welz, C. 2007. How to Comprehend the Incomprehensible Love? Kierkegaard Research and Philosophy of Emotion. *Kierkegaardiana* 24: 261–286.

Chapter 7
Searching for the Anthropological Foundations of Economic Practice: Controversies and Opportunities

Gerrit Glas

Abstract This chapter is a comment on the contribution of Rebecca Klein in this volume, preceded by a conceptual analysis of the argument that is developed in the *Homo Amans* discussion paper.

The main question that is raised is twofold and concerns the relation between science and worldview on the one hand, and between science and economic life on the other. With respect to the science – worldview relationship, it is doubted that science can play the role the authors of the *Homo amans* project expect it can have. What they have in mind is that science helps in validating and legitimizing a biblically informed concept of love. This author disagrees, to a large extent. Science can indeed orient itself on ideas and intuitions that are based on one's worldview. But it cannot prove the truth of these intuitions and ideas. To think so, is to commit a naturalistic fallacy.

With respect to the relationship between science and economic life, the author is also not convinced that science and philosophy as academic disciplines will by themselves be able (and should be expected to be able) to transform deeply ingrained, institutionally anchored economic practices. New theories, concepts, and paradigms are a precondition for change, but they do not bring about change by themselves. What is needed is a change in the practices themselves, a change that is both personal and comprehensive. What is needed is a clear, succinct, and encompassing view on the intrinsic normativity of economic interactions between relevant stakeholders in what we call 'the' economy. This is a huge undertaking, that requires painstaking 'phenomenological' analyses of a wide variety of economic practices. The chapter agrees with most of Klein's observations and concerns with respect to the discussion paper. These observations and concerns gain even more depth and relief given the conceptual distinctions that are made in the chapter.

G. Glas (✉)
Vrije Universiteit, Amsterdam, The Netherlands
e-mail: g.glas@vu.nl

J. van Nes et al. (eds.), *Relational Anthropology for Contemporary Economics*, Ethical Economy 61, https://doi.org/10.1007/978-3-030-84690-9_7

7.1 Introduction

In this response I will first focus on the argument in the discussion paper by Nullens and Van Nes (Chap. 2) in this volume. I will introduce a distinction to be made between four perspectives on economic practice and show its relevance for the conceptualization of the *Homo amans* project. I proceed by giving some comments on the paper by Rebekka Klein and conclude with a few more general, evaluative comments.

7.2 The Discussion Paper: Structure of the Argument

The discussion paper presents itself as "…a modest attempt to encourage a multidisciplinary dialogue on anthropology in contemporary economics by

1. rethinking human personhood
2. introducing the concept of *Homo amans* as a potential alternative to *Homo economicus*
3. exploring some dimensions of human relationality that deserve future study."

The paper builds on well-known oppositions such as that between mechanistic and teleological views of humanhood; and between materialistic and other, richer views on man. Sources of inspiration in the development of a new, relational view on man are critical realism, as developed by C. Smith (2015); personalism, as can be found in the work by Pope John Paul II (Wojtyla 1993); and the plea for non-reductionism and anti-scientism that, for instance, has been voiced by C. Taylor (1989). Nullens and Van Nes quote Smith (2010), when he describes the human person as "a conscious, reflexive, embodied, bodied, self-transcending center of subjective experience, durable identity, moral commitment, and social communication who – as the efficient cause of his or her own responsible actions and interactions – exercises complex capacities for agency and intersubjectivity in order to develop and sustain his or her own incommunicable self in loving relationships with other personal selves and with the nonpersonal world." This thick notion of personhood grounds a eudaimonistic ethics, i.e., the understanding that the human good can be conceived as a realization of human nature and a rediscovery of the wisdom of old moral systems that are often already in line with our own intuitions. In other words, the paper builds on the idea that universal traits such as love, justice, generosity, and the like, should be enacted and developed for the benefit of others and ourselves and that this is made possible by the fact that they are in some way already present in us because they are part of our nature.

This anthropological intuition is then undergirded by a wide variety of arguments derived from the Bible, positive psychology (Peterson and Seligman 2004), behavioral economics (McCloskey 2006), insights on religious behavior based on evolutionary theory (Wildman 2009), neuroscientific insights into the neuroendocrine 'basis' of prosocial behavior (Pfaff 2015), the psychology of hope (Scioli and Biller 2009), leadership studies focusing on servant/responsible/spiritual leadership, trust and cooperation; and on a phenomenology of multiple perspectives (economic, philosophical, theological) on love.

7.3 Four Perspectives

Although I sympathize with the general intentions of *Homo Amans* as a theological/empirical program and recognize the relevance of antireductionist findings in contemporary psychology, neuroscience, and (as I now understand) economy, I still have difficulties with (a) the structure of the argument and (b) the lack of clarity of the concept of *Homo amans* itself. To get a grasp on the project *Homo Amans* it is helpful to make a distinction between at least four perspectives: the perspective of one's life- and worldview, the perspective of philosophy (core concepts; conceptual frameworks; paradigms; argumentative structures), the perspective of theoretical knowledge (marked by abstraction and based on methodic reduction), and the perspective of practical (professional) knowledge and know-how. In other contexts, I have added a fifth perspective relating to the lay knowledge and everyday experiences (of a particular topic or situation). Since I will not deal here with lay perspectives, I will continue with the four perspectives mentioned earlier.

Each of these perspectives offers a way of looking at the phenomenon under study. One can, for instance, study empathy as a human capacity (or virtue) and give an account of it in terms of one's *life- and world view* (let us say, as one of the sources of self-surrendering love or as an evolutionary advantageous adaptation); one can study empathy from a *philosophical/conceptual* perspective (is empathy a feeling, a disposition, or a form of behavior?); one may formulate *scientific* hypotheses about empathy (mentalization is a prerequisite for the development of empathy; or: empathy is a capacity that builds on "earlier" abilities such as successful performance of perception-action cycles); and one may approach empathy from the point of view of the *professional* who, for instance, is interested in the empathic capacities of an offender or a person with personality disorder. One of the premises on which my account is based, is that these four perspectives are more than merely conceptual and epistemic and that they are part of, and intrinsically intertwined with, practices of knowing, interaction, and action, that diverge in scope, aim, function, content, and role (Glas 2019a, Chapters 6 and 7). Professional knowledge is not just a way of knowing. Professional knowing cannot be defined apart from the practices in which it is embedded. It is, for instance, characteristic of these practices that the relevance of a model, theory, or explanation (rational choice theory, for instance) for the understanding of a phenomenon (behavior of consumers) is weighed, and that different pieces of knowledge (rational choice theory versus, for instance, theories about prosocial behavior) compete for recognition of their relevance. In other words, scientific knowledge needs to be translated into relevant practices. This translation process requires awareness of contexts, the infrastructure, and the interactions between relevant parties. The translation process itself is not scientific, it is not based on methodic reduction and fixing and standardization of boundary conditions. Translation requires, instead, that the relevance of a certain theory for the understanding of a phenomenon is seen and weighed against intuitions about the relevance of other theoretical insights. Recognizing this relevance requires contextual knowledge, practical experience within the field, 'insight', holistic knowledge, and so on.

The context of scientific knowledge is scientific practice, i.e., the world of laboratories, technology, experiments, publishing, texts, libraries, peer competition, fund raising, and so on. The context of economic practice is the market as the platform for real life interactions and negotiations between consumers, producers, and other stakeholders. How relevant rational choice theory is for the behavior of a group of consumers in a segment of the market depends on the contribution of other possible factors that influence economic behavior. There is, in other words, no logical (deductive, straightforward 'applicative') relation between scientific knowledge and economic practice. There are also no such (logical, deductive) relationships between philosophical views on man and labor and economic theory; nor between the images of man based on life- and worldview and economic theory.

This does not imply, however, that there are no relationships at all between the different epistemic perspectives. There are, for instance, overarching intuitions, analogies, and metaphors that enable communication between the different perspectives. These intuitions and analogies need to be elucidated and tested in the relevant contexts: are they creative fictions or do they really hit the phenomenon under study. Moreover, people learn from their experiences, also in the application of scientific insights to the practices in which they are embedded. Professionals learn when these applications lead to something and when they lead them astray. They build up experiential expertise with the concepts, the techniques, the algorithms, and other implementations of scientific knowledge. This largely tacit expert-knowledge may in turn inform scientists when they reformulate their hypotheses and ideas.

7.4 The Four Perspectives in the Discussion Paper

Diagram 7.1 gives an impression of the argument in the discussion paper based on the distinctions I made in the previous section, i.e., the distinction between life- and worldview, philosophy, scientific theorizing, and professional practice. According to the *life- and worldview* of the authors, man is driven by faith, hope, and love. These and other virtuous are constitutive of human nature (perspective 1, life and worldview). The paper describes how this overarching idea might be supported by philosophical analysis and by insights found in theology, psychology, neuroscience, and sociobiology. This 'enriched' view leads to a relational view of human nature, as *philosophical* paradigm (perspective 2). This paradigm should then be operationalized in terms of new economic *theories* (perspective 3) and lead to better *economic practices* (perspective 4).

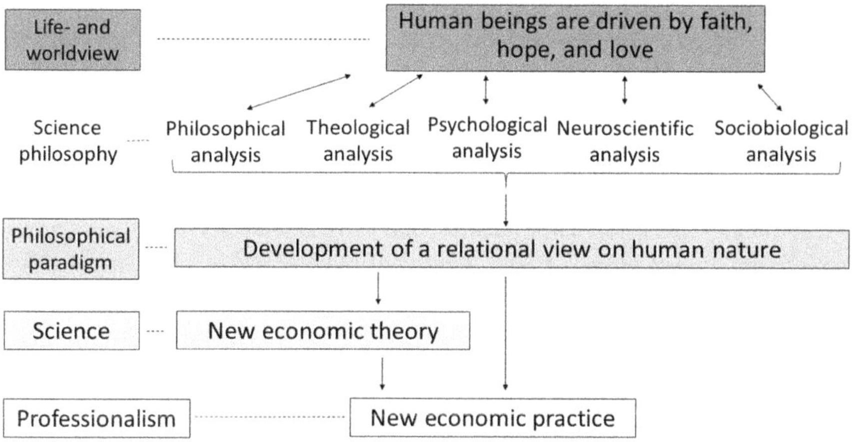

Diagram 7.1 Structure of the argument in the *Homo Amans* discussion paper

However, these expectations are based on mixed and somewhat shaky grounds. There are, as I said, no strictly logical, deductive, or purely empirical grounds to expect that the combined efforts of the empirical sciences will lead to a 'richer', or 'more biblical', philosophical image of man. That is to say, judging a view as richer and/or more biblical is a value judgment that cannot be based on the combination of empirical research and logical reasoning *per se*.

We are dealing with different transitions here, for instance with the transition from philosophy to the sciences (and back); and from the sciences to theology. By viewing these transitions as logical, deductive, or self-evident, the authors run the risk of committing a *naturalistic fallacy.* By this, I mean the error of considering scientific evidence as evidence for a normative position. Views based on, for instance, developmental psychology do not necessarily lead to a better (richer) philosophical theology or anthropology. Such theology or anthropology has obvious normative implications that the sciences will never deliver. Scientific evidence may be consistent or convergent with one's life- and worldview, but it cannot serve as the basis for it. Theories about the capacity to empathize with fellow human beings may be consistent with (aspects of) certain philosophical views on man, but they don't entail the full spectrum of meanings associated with the notion of man as a relational, virtuous being. Understanding how empathy develops does not necessarily lead to recognition of empathy as moral virtue. The first is an empirical hypothesis or theory, the latter is a normative valuation. There may be moral and religious reasons for thinking empathy is an important phenomenon to understand. But empirical understanding of a phenomenon that we value on the basis of our moral and other convictions, does not add to the normative force of these convictions. Consistency is something other than validity and legitimacy.

One other problem of this view on the relationship between philosophy/theology and the sciences is the risk of circularity, lack of precision, and pseudotheorizing. The idea of the project is that a richer, relational view on man will lead to better economic theories. However, philosophical accounts of man are typically caught in general and abstract terms. Definitions of these terms are based on theoretical reflection and discussions that are primarily philosophical and that relate to a philosophical/conceptual context. The aim of these definitions is to shed light on and articulate the content of a term or theory in the context of a wide range of competing philosophical theories and ideas. These abstract and general terms are usually not precise enough to serve as a basis for solid empirical hypothesizing and experimenting. They are difficult to operationalize and refer to contexts that are distant from the experimental practice. Using them to support empirical hypothesizing easily leads to circular reasoning, vagueness, and pseudo-theorizing. The philosophical term is defined in terms of the phenomena it is supposed to explain; the *explanans* entails the *explanandum*, then, which is a logical error.

With respect to the transition from *philosophy to professional activities,* the idea of the paper seems to be that a richer, relational view on man will lead to better education, better economic practice, and better working ethics. Surely, overarching ideals and views do guide all kinds of practices. They may serve as legitimation for one's approach, they highlight the general perspective. But there are again a number of risks: risk of ambiguous interpretation of the overarching ideas and concepts; risk of ignorance of differences in the application of these ideas and concepts on varying practices. The umbrella term itself may mean different things in different contexts; but the term may also lead to different practical applications. A more urgent risk is the suggestion of moral superiority that comes along when one's own view serves as touchstone for other conceptions. In short, to say this in a somewhat different formulation, it is crucial to recognize that the implementation, application, and translation of scientific discoveries are not by themselves scientific activities. They presuppose in-depth knowledge and contextual sensitivity. But the search for meaningful application and the weighing of the relevance of scientific evidence within a particular context build on something other than scientific scrutiny.

7.5 Different Routes to 'Integration'

All this, I need to say, does not imply that I am negative about the possibility of connecting philosophical discussions with issues in the sciences and professional practices. Earlier, I mentioned that the implementation of scientific insights in applied contexts requires insight and creativity to discern the potential relevance of scientific evidence for a certain practice. This innovative mindset does not primarily consist of deductive reasoning and logic. It does not work with the idea of a linear process from basic research via the applied sciences to professional practices. It does not derive distal changes from proximal causes. The innovative mindset supports the view that successful implementation is based on (circular) learning processes and on socialization into ways of interacting and collaborating that further and enhance insight and creativity.

Let me zoom out and briefly indicate four ways to conceptualize this process of learning, translating, and collaborating. An essential component is building a culture of interaction and collaboration that is sharply aware of the different mindsets of scientists, philosophers, professionals, and designers. Given these differences, there are nevertheless ways to cooperate fruitfully and to gain deeper understanding.

Iain Barbour, for instance, who has written extensively about the interaction between science and religion, discerns four forms of interaction: conflict; parallelism; dialogue; integration (Barbour 1997). Scientists and practitioners may perceive each other as being in conflict; as operating in different domains without any interaction (parallelism); as being in dialogue with one another; and as operating conjointly and moving toward integration of perspectives.

Jochemsen, Hoogland and this author have developed a so-called normative practice approach (NPA) to medicine and healthcare. This NPA has been elaborated for other fields too: media and communication, public administration, military ethics, and philosophy of organizations. The cornerstone of this approach is the idea that practices should be seen as responsive to clusters of intrinsic norms, rules, and/or values. Within these groups of norms (rules, values), one needs to make a distinction between norms that form the basis for a practice; norms that undergird the (economic, jural, institutional, and political) conditions for a practice; and norms that qualify that practice. Qualifying norms indicate the kind of normativity that guides a certain practice. Economic practices could be evaluated along similar lines as being founded on a variety of norms that are foundational, conditional, or qualifying with respect to these practices. Economic theories function as cognitive artefacts in these practices, in the sense that they highlight certain aspects of the practice. Religious and philosophical anthropological ideas inform one's view on the *Homo economicus*; they may be seen as constructs that help to articulate the ethos or spirit that dominates economic life (Dooyeweerd 1953–1958; Glas 2019a, b, c; Jochemsen 2006; Jochemsen and Glas 1997; Hoogland and Jochemsen 2000; Verkerk et al. 2015; de Vries and Jochemsen 2019).

One other approach that is worth mentioning is the so-called actor-network approach as developed by Latour (1987); and applied by scholars such as Callon et al. (1986). The actor-network theory is often seen as belonging to social constructivism. It suggests that a practice (technological, medical, social, economic) is not solely determined by the acts and intentions of economic subjects, but also equally by all kinds of contextual factors (from the physical to the political).

In terms of Barbour's four models of interaction between science and religion, what can be achieved with this approach is dialogue between contributions from different fields. The next step could be convergence between the results based on the sciences, philosophy and worldview. This would be no small result: the interaction between the fields would lead to "richer" conceptualizations in each of the interacting practices.

In terms of the normative practices approach, one could start with an attempt to analyze the "intrinsic" normative core of economically qualified practices. From that point on, one could proceed with an analysis of how economic functioning might be opened up by (analogical) references to higher order (jural, social, moral, esthetic) norms and ideals. Another approach could consist in the analysis of qualifying, foundational, and conditioning norms for the interactions between economic subjects and their micro-, meso-, and macro-environments.

In terms of the actor network approach one could analyze how economic practices develop under the influence of technology (ICT), globalization, migration, ecological crises, political leadership, and the like.

7.6 Response to Rebekka Klein

After these lengthy introductory remarks, it is time to focus on Rebekka Klein's 'What is the Nature of Christian Love? *Homo Amans* and Revolutionary Altruism' (Chap. 6, this volume). Let me start by saying that I agree with most of what she says. It will come as no surprise that I agree with Kleins's warning that the *Homo amans* should not be taken as a comprehensive and definitive representation of the reality of human being. That would lead to similar totalitarian implementations, she says, as with the older *Homo economicus* model. Philosophical models should play a role that is different from dictating scientific hypothesizing. The project seems to require too much from scientists in this respect. They are expected "… to prove the anthropological, psychological, societal and political usefulness and the pragmatic and ethical impact of its insights instead of merely safeguarding the correct methodological fabrication of scientific facts." I agree, that this is simply too much. The idea that science can prove the truth of a prescientific (philosophical, religiously inspired) view on man comes dangerously close to the idea that science can prove metaphysical claims, whatever their content. This view could also easily drive us into the arms of scientism.

There are, therefore, "limits and problems inherent in the argument." I will briefly discuss another five of these limits, problems and issues that are mentioned in Klein's contribution. One of them is that the holism and integrationism implied in notions like well-being and love disregards the fracturedness and ambivalences of the phenomena under study. Man is not the rational calculating being that traditional economic theory has supposed him to be. He is driven by ambiguous, skewed, and sometimes downright contradictory motives and impulses. The things people value and are willing to invest in, emotionally, financially, or in terms of efforts, depend on their individual and collective histories. Identification of the fracture lines, and the active search for issues that evoke tensions and feelings of unease, is a condition for understanding what people avoid or strive for. I am convinced that searching for such fracture lines and areas of unease and tension is crucial for the detection of underlying values in economic life, values that do matter and have proven to matter in the lives of concrete groups and individuals, also and especially in the economic sphere.

Klein's second concern originates from the question of how the proposal takes notice of the independence, objectivity, and cool mood of science? What is left from these? What is the validity and legitimacy of the concept of *Homo amans*? My response is, briefly, that this is a matter of concern for me too. As I have argued above, the transdisciplinary perspective, as such, does not guarantee the wholeness and integration the discussion paper is aiming at. In the act of abstraction, scientists lose by definition the connection with this wholeness. They may retain, of course, prescientific intuitions about this wholeness and they may try to do justice to these intuitions in their hypothesizing and model-building. But they are not able to reconstruct this wholeness and its inner coherence by scientific means (Dooyeweerd 1953, Vol. I, p. 1). Attempts to do so, for instance in systems theory or (other) computational approaches to a given field of science, will by definition be colored by the language and the perspective of the supposedly overarching and connecting science (mathematics, for instance).

Third, Klein raises a question about the concept of love. What is love? Can it be equated with prosocial behaviors and attitudes of cooperation and altruism? Like Klein, I am inclined to suggest that this is not, or at best only partly, the case. There exists a huge amount of research on empathy and altruism, suggesting that there is continuity between animal and human behavior. However, the issue here is love in the biblical sense, i.e., self-giving, self-surrendering, altruistic love that doesn't expect to get anything in return for one's "investment"; love of one's enemies; love that is ready to sacrifice oneself and one's own interests. This self-giving love is not instrumental, it is the expression of one's deepest self, of one's giving, caring, and life-preserving motives.

How about love as grounded in a feeling or in a rational choice? Is it a capability? Is love essential or contingent in the definition of who we are as human beings? Is love a remote ideal, or should we conceive it as a fulfilment of a latent capacity, a fulfilment that leads to human flourishing? These are again big questions, that cannot adequately be addressed in a couple of paragraphs. But let me briefly indicate in which direction I am thinking. With Klein, I am inclined to reject all these options, except the latter, the virtue-ethical approach to love. I feel sympathy for this latter approach, which conceives love as an excellence of human nature and as an important aspect of human flourishing. But there are also important differences between the virtue-based approach to love and the biblical emphasis on love as a form of self-surrender and as a counter-intuitive movement in the presence of often overwhelming suffering and tragedy. Biblical love emerges against a background of broken relations, anger, suspicion, negativity, shame, ambivalence, and deception. Love is indeed central to our existence as human beings, but it is not what we are inclined to do, especially not in situations in which we ourselves feel threatened, devalued, put to shame, and so on. Love is indeed a central dynamic within our existence, a driving force that helps us focus on doing well by our fellow human beings; whoever this fellow human being is and whatever the difference is between their and our situation. But this will to love is always, in a way, in opposition to other inclinations we also have; inclinations that manifest themselves as egotism, lack of trust, misanthropy, lack of self-disclosure, narcissism, and tendencies to grandiosity.

Fourth, Klein expresses as a special worry that the concept of love should be defined by acknowledging the societal context. What love is, can only be identified given the alienation and atomization of individuals and given the liquid society in which we live with its increasingly fluid identities of individuals and groups. By not systematically adopting this perspective of alienation, individualization, and loss of identity, the *Homo amans* project runs the risk of "dreaming away." I agree, again, and I am inclined to include systematic and institutional injustice as important other contexts against the background of which acts of love gain meaning and prove to be transformative.

Fifth, with Kierkegaard, Klein is inclined to suggest that love is not a virtue nor an expression of human nature, but something in the concrete world, that God has put next to us, in our neighbor. Love is a "middle-term" instead of an end-term (or object), she says. It is that through which we reshape our relationships.

I agree that love is not a goal in itself, but a mediating power with transformative potential. As I said, I see love as a central, transformative dynamic. Love gets shape in the struggle with egotistic and disconnecting forces. It is accompanied by a hidden creativity in finding out what is good for others and for society in spite of all sorts of resistance and animosity.

So, in sum, I agree with most of Klein's observations and concerns with respect to the discussion paper. These observations and concerns gain even more depth and relief given the conceptual distinctions that were made earlier in the chapter.

7.7 Final Comments and Conclusion

Let me finish by summing up my most important hesitations with respect to the *Homo Amans* initiative and the role it is supposed to fulfill in the context of economic theory and economic life.

My main question is twofold and concerns the relationship between science and worldview on the one hand and between science and economic life on the other. With respect to the science – worldview relationship, I doubt that science can play the role the authors of the *Homo amans* project expect, in validating and legitimizing the biblically informed concept of love they have in mind. Science can orient itself on ideas and intuitions that are based on one's worldview. But it cannot prove the truth of these intuitions and ideas.

My strictness on this point is not based on the idea that biblical love and love in the mundane economic sphere are completely distinct realities. It is based on the conviction that the epistemic attitude of scientists fundamentally differs from the epistemic attitude of believers (citizens, entrepreneurs, employees, consumers, or experts in a certain profession). Each scientific discipline highlights a different and distinct aspect of a phenomenon; and the combined sum of all these partial insights does not reproduce the original coherence and holism of the phenomenon under study. This also holds for the concept of love. The combined efforts of all the sciences will not deliver us the coherence and holism of the idea of love the authors of the *Homo amans* project have in mind.

With respect to the relationship between science and economic life, I am also not convinced that science and philosophy as academic disciplines will by themselves be able (nor should be expected to be able) to transform deeply ingrained, institutionally anchored economic practices. New theories, concepts, and paradigms are a precondition for change, but they do not bring about change by themselves. Economy will not be changed by a new model or paradigm about human nature *per se*. Nor can the economy be rescued by implementing legal, institutional, political, or moral innovations alone. What is needed is a transdisciplinary approach guided by an overarching and inspiring view, which is informed by a worldview or worldviews, with contributions from all relevant stakeholders and a set of useful conceptual distinctions. What is needed most of all is a clear, succinct, but also encompassing view of the intrinsic normativity of economic interactions between relevant stakeholders in what we call "the" economy. This is a huge undertaking, that requires painstaking "phenomenological" analyses of a wide variety of economic practices. But this new view and these analyses are worthy of being strived for, given the needs of our time.

The idea that there exists someone like a *Homo amans* or a *Homo economicus* is also vulnerable in a more practical and empirical sense. Does the *Homo economicus* actually exist? Is it not a strawman? Are we not tilting at windmills? Does the term refer to essences, attitudes, relational characteristics, or something else? And, has economic theory not already recognized for quite some time the importance of collaboration, a certain measure of non-selfishness, and sustainable interactions? All these questions need to be addressed. The answers will determine which conclusions can be drawn from the *Homo amans* project.

References

Barbour, I.G. [2]1997. *Religion and Science: Historical and Conceptual Issues*. New York: Harper Collins.

Callon, M., A. Rip, and J. Law, eds. 1986. *Mapping the Dynamics of Science and Technology*. London: Palgrave Macmillan.

de Vries, M.J., and H. Jochemsen, eds. 2019. *The Normative Nature of Social Practices and Ethics in Professional Environments*. Hershey: IGI Global.

Dooyeweerd, H. 1953–1958. *A New Critique of Theoretical Thought*. Vol. I–IV. Amsterdam/Paris/Philadelphia: P&R Publishing.

Glas, G. 2019a. *Person-centered Care in Psychiatry: Self-relational, Contextual, and Normative Perspectives*. New York: Routledge.

———. 2019b. Roots of the Normative Practice Approach: The Philosophy of Herman Dooyeweerd. In *The Normative Nature of Social Practices and Ethics in Professional Environment*, ed. M.J. de Vries and H. Jochemsen, 15–30. Hershey: IGI Global.

———. 2019c. A Normative Practice Approach to Healthcare. In *The Normative Nature of Social Practices and Ethics in Professional Environment*, ed. M.J. de Vries and H. Jochemsen, 164–184. Hershey: IGI Global.
Hoogland, J., and H. Jochemsen. 2000. Professional Autonomy and the Normative Structure of Medical Practice. *Theoretical Medicine and Bioethics* 21 (5): 457–475.
Jochemsen, H. 2006. Normative Practices as an Intermediate between Theoretical Ethics and Morality. *Philosophia Reformata* 71: 96–112.
Jochemsen, H., and G. Glas. 1997. *Verantwoord medisch handelen: Proeve van een christelijke medische ethiek*. Amsterdam: Buijten & Schipperheijn.
Latour, B. 1987. *Science in Action*. Cambridge, MA: Harvard University Press.
McCloskey, D.N. 2006. *The Bourgeois Virtues: Ethics for an Age of Commerce*. Chicago: The University of Chicago Press.
Peterson, C., and M.E.P. Seligman. 2004. *Character Strengths and Virtues: A Handbook and Classification*. Oxford: Oxford University Press.
Pfaff, D.W. 2015. *The Altruistic Brain: How We Are Naturally Good*. New York: Oxford University Press.
Scioli, A., and H.B. Biller. 2009. *Hope in the Age of Anxiety: A Guide to Understanding and Strengthening Our Most Important Virtue*. Oxford: Oxford University Press.
Smith, C. 2010. *What is a Person? Rethinking Humanity, Social Life, and the Moral Good from the Person Up*. Chicago: The University of Chicago Press.
———. 2015. *To Flourish or Destruct: A Personalist Theory of Human Goods, Motivations, Failure, and Evil*. Chicago: The University of Chicago Press.
Taylor, C. 1989. *Sources of the Self: The Making of the Modern Identity*. Cambridge, MA: Harvard University Press.
Verkerk, M., J. Hoogland, J. Van der Stoep, and J. De Vries. 2015. *Philosophy of Technology: An Introduction for Technology and Business Students*. London: Routledge.
Wildman, W.J. 2009. *Science and Religious Anthropology: A Spiritually Evocative Naturalist Interpretation of Human Life*. Surrey: Ashgate.
Wojtyla, K. 1993. *Person and Community*. Transl. T. Sandok. New York: Lang.

Chapter 8
Altruistic Concern for the Other and the Development of the Virtue of Humility

James A. Van Slyke

Abstract Humility is often defined by what it is not; as the antithesis to various vices such as pride, arrogance, conceit, or vanity. This negative definition leaves open the possibility of some underlying characteristic or trait that influences the formation of this virtue. *Homo amans* lays out the classic theological triad of faith, hope, and love as a natural inclination in humanity. This chapter explores one aspect of this triad, love, as a possible underlying characteristic or trait that uniquely informs the formation of the virtue of humility: specifically, love as altruistic concern for the other that puts them ahead or before the self. Contemporary psychological studies of humility demonstrate a connection between this virtue and altruistic concern for the other. Altruistic concern becomes a part of moral schemas that greatly influence moral behavior and are the basis for the development of moral identity. Holocaust rescuers demonstrate that moral schemas, which contain altruistic concern as a primary component of their view of the world, cultivate a moral identity that makes rescuing a consequence of their self-identity and naturally leads to humility about their actions.

8.1 Introduction

Humility is commonly defined according to what it is acting against; most often some form of pride.

> Humility is most easily defined as the virtue that opposes pride, that is, the virtue which opposes ascribing to oneself an excellence one does not possess, or wrongly thinking of oneself as the cause of one's own excellence, or wishing to be the exclusive possessor of the excellence (Pinsent 2012, p. 261).

Aquinas defines humility as a restriction against thinking too highly of oneself and a type of restraint against forming an identity based on the over-estimation of

---

J. A. Van Slyke (✉)
Fresno Pacific University, Fresno, CA, USA
e-mail: james.vanslyke@fresno.edu

J. van Nes et al. (eds.), *Relational Anthropology for Contemporary Economics*, Ethical Economy 61, https://doi.org/10.1007/978-3-030-84690-9_8

oneself (1912/1981). Humility is foundational to the formation of virtue, generally through the actions and resistance it takes against pride.

Wherefore, the first step in the acquisition of virtue may be understood in two ways. First by way of removing obstacles: and thus humility holds the first place, in as much as it expels pride, which "God resists," and make man submissive and ever open to receive the influx of Divine grace (Aquinas 1912/1981, ST II-II.161.5.ad 2).

Both of these definitions focus on a type of negative claim, the presence of humility is the absence of some other sort of vice. Humility is present when something else is regulated or restricted.

Roberts and Wood (2010) argue that humility is best described by paying attention to its vice counterparts because it has a negative character. They list a number of its opposite vices including "arrogance, vanity, conceit, egotism, hyper-autonomy, grandiosity, pretentiousness, ..." among many others (p. 236). Humility is ultimately defined by being opposed to vanity and arrogance. Vanity is excessive concern or anxiety with how one appears to others, which can be focused on a number of personal qualities such as intelligence, attractiveness, or social status. Thus, a humble person is one who is unconcerned or inattentive to their appearance to others, based on these qualities (Roberts and Wood 2010). Arrogance is defined as a type of entitlement that is afforded to oneself based on some quality (real or imagined) where a person sees himself or herself as superior to others and thus deserving of special treatment. The humble person may accurately perceive a special quality in themselves (a skill, a strength, or some other asset), but the difference is that they do not use that information to see themselves as superior or requiring special treatment.

Descriptions of some property using contrasts are certainly helpful, and aspects of the virtue of humility contain elements that are antithetical to its corresponding vices. Roberts' (2003, 2013) overall method of focusing on detailed descriptions of virtues, using a Wittgensteinian family resemblance approach, is very helpful to understanding virtue formation. However, definitions focused on absence or restriction seem to indicate the possibility that there might be a separate property or character trait that lies underneath, which actually plays an essential role in the overcoming of vice. My suggestion is that altruistic concern, which views the other as intrinsically valuable, is the ultimate foundation or bedrock of the virtue of humility.

The idea of *Homo amans* uses St. Paul's tripartite view of the theological virtues of faith, hope, and love as a new paradigm for understanding certain predispositions in humanity and argues against the typical idea of *Homo economicus* as a foundation for human anthropology (See Chap 1, this volume). One aspect of this view, love, understood as altruistic concern for the other, is foundational for the development of the virtue of humility. Part of the development of this virtue is dependent upon a certain view of other people, a view that sees intrinsic worth and value in the other. When this altruistic view of the other is present, humility becomes a natural consequence because the temptations to various vices related to selfishness no longer take hold in the virtuous person.

In this way, a certain sense of relational connection and identification with the other provokes the various cognitive states and behaviors associated with the virtuous state of being humble. Humble people have moral schemas that include a distinctive valuation for the other and places a high value on those relationships. Their moral identities are partially constituted based on this altruistic view of other people, which influences their actions and view of the world. Other people have an inherent value simply based on their status as fellow humans and this perspective promotes many of the factors commonly associated with the virtue of humility. This view of *Homo amans* is a helpful starting point for reconsidering human nature and the possibility of developing humility as a virtue.

8.2 Human Nature and Altruistic Concern

Selfishness is often perceived as a core aspect of human nature. Theologically, original sin and the doctrine of total depravity describe human nature as fully corrupted by sin (Augustine 1961/1996; Calvin 1559/1999). Philosophically, Hobbes viewed the essence of human nature as egoistical, eventually leading to a brutal competition among people, absent a proper monarch to rule over them (1651). More recently, Dawkins' idea of a selfish gene has been interpreted as evidence that human nature itself is also inherently selfish (1976). De Waal (2006) has argued that a popular view among many biologists is that human morality and culture are just a façade that covers the selfish core of human nature. The view of *Homo amans* is a helpful corrective to the assumptions of human selfishness presumed to be foundational to human nature. By emphasizing the aspects of human nature that are searching for meaning, projecting the self into the future, and focusing on the inherent worth of human relationships, it is possible to re-imagine the basic characteristics of human nature and highlight the most positive attributes rather than relegating them to a secondary or cursory status.

Elsewhere, I have argued that this focus on the inherent worth of others or, as I have defined it here as altruistic concern, is not antithetical to the evolution of human nature. Rather, the evolutionary or natural processes that produced human nature as we know it today actually allows for the *possibility* of altruistic concern and behavior (Van Slyke 2010). The altruistic concern that is such a noteworthy part of many forms of moral exemplarity is actually based on the everyday evolved characteristics of human nature (Van Slyke 2012). Sociality is a basic aspect of many mammalian species and is most prominent in the primate lineage (de Waal 2005). Attachment processes establish a trajectory of care and concern for offspring that can later influence altruistic concern in other relationships (Shaver et al. 2016). Neuroeconomics has shown in a variety of experiments that people often prefer various types of transactions that emphasize cooperation and fairness rather than self-interest (Camerer and Fehr 2006; Fehr and Camerer 2007). When one person experiences empathy for another, similar areas of the brain are activated in the two people, thus each feels a facsimile of what that other person is feeling, based on shared neural circuitry (Singer and Lamm 2009). Neural systems underlying empathy in concert with human mirror systems involved in imitation and specialized circuitry for theory of mind encompass a natural human propensity towards understanding another (Van Slyke 2014).

These human characteristics (along with a host of others) make the development of altruistic concern a very natural part of human nature. It is not so much working *against* a selfish core or intrinsic self-interest, rather it is an emphasis and development of the parts of human nature related to cooperation, trust, attachment (among others), toward the end of viewing the other as intrinsically valuable. The development of altruistic concern is foundational to the development of humility, in that showing humility seems to be dependent upon viewing the other as having an intrinsic worth simply by being a fellow human being. Thus, part of the development of this virtue will be dependent upon developing the relational or love facet of the *Homo amans* triad.

8.3 Recent Definitions of Humility

Recently, there has been a revival in the study of humility, both as a virtue and as a positive character trait associated with optimal human flourishing. Although humility has historically been defined in terms of low self-esteem, unworthiness, and self-deprecation, more recent definitions focus on the positive contributions it makes to human relationships and individual psychological functioning. Three components stand out as important characteristics of humility that have taken center focus in recent definitions of this virtue. Those components are (1) accurate self-assessment, (2) openness, and (3) low self-regard. Each of these components is related to how a person views the other and their relationship to other people in their lives.

Emmons initially identified accurate assessment as one of the primary components of a humble person.

> To be humble is not to have a low opinion of oneself, it is to have an accurate opinion of oneself. It is the ability to keep one's talents and accomplishments in perspective … to have a sense of self-acceptance, and understanding of one's imperfections, and to be free from arrogance and low self-esteem (Emmons 2000, p. 7)

Humble people are able to understand the limitations to their own knowledge; an understanding of their intellectual accomplishments without the belief that they are somehow all-knowing (Templeton 1997). Humble people are able to perceive themselves accurately, both their strengths and weaknesses, without defensiveness (Exline and Hill 2012).

Part of their accurate assessment is related to their understanding of dependence on others. Humble people realize that their accomplishments and relationships are not produced in a vacuum, but are dependent upon others. Humble people recognize that the formation of any virtue occurs in particular groups with unique characteristics that help to foster the relational conditions necessary for virtue formation. It is through social formation that we begin to acknowledge our dependency on others for moral formation and virtue, even though dependency is not often acknowledged especially in academic circles.

> Dependence on others is of course often recognized in a general way, usually not as something that we need in order to achieve our positive goals. But an acknowledgement of anything like the full extent of that dependence and of the ways in which it stems from our vulnerability and our afflictions is generally absent (MacIntyre 1999, p. 3).

This view of virtue demonstrates that dependency on others is an essential element of overall flourishing; each of us is indebted to our parents, teachers, siblings, etc. for the type of formation they bore in us (Boyd 2014).

The second primary component in humility is a sense of openness, both towards others as well as in regard to taking advice from others, hearing new ideas, and graciously receiving criticism. Humble people are often open-minded and willing to admit their mistakes in different areas while also interested in learning from and seeking advice from others (Tangney 2000; Templeton 1997). They are able to see and acknowledge their own imperfections and refuse to use their own influence or power to control others (Sandage 1999). Humble people recognize the importance and need for others based on an accurate appraisal of their own limitations and gaps in their knowledge, often in regard to some form of a higher power or spiritual truth (Tangney 2000). This openness to others is foundational to their development of altruistic concern because so much of their life is built upon and sustained by relationships. When relationships are valued at that level and the openness to the other includes emotional availability, the development of altruistic concern is a natural outcome.

The third primary component of humility is related to the stereotypical definition of humility in terms of low self-regard; humble people lack a strong focus on the self. However, this focus on others does not include the types of self-effacement often associated with the stereotypical definition. Humble people show empathy, respect, and kindness toward others; they value others in such a way as to promote equality and compassion (Sandage 1999). Humble people are not preoccupied with themselves and are willing to share the spotlight with others. They do not have an exaggerated sense of self-importance, but are able to forget themselves while recognizing that they are one part of a much larger universe (Exline and Geyer 2004; Tangney 2000). They are much less likely to distort information about themselves, because of, in part, the type of security experienced by them both in terms of their estimation of themselves and their self-esteem deriving from more stable sources (such as unconditional love in relationships; devotion to meaningful causes) rather than transient sources such as physical attractiveness, climbing the social ladder, or projects focused on self-enhancement (Exline and Geyer 2004; Peterson and Seligman 2004).

Nadelhoffer and Wright (2016) condensed these three components along two primary dimensions, low self-focus and high other focus. Their definition assumes a "particular psychological positioning of oneself … one that is both epistemically and ethically aligned" (Wright et al. 2017, p. 4). Epistemically aligned refers to the proper knowledge of oneself as but one person that is a part of a much larger universe and all the limitations and imperfections this imparts on one's singular perspective. Ethically aligned refers to the recognition of the moral value of the other who is worthy of dignity, respect, concern, and compassion. As other definitions have emphasized, low self-focus does not necessitate an overly negative or diminished view of the self, rather the attention is directed to a low level of "self-prioritization or self-importance" while high other-focus refers to an "increase in one's orientation outwards – towards other morally relevant beings" (Wright et al. 2017, pp. 5–6). This suggests a type of re-orientation in which a person does not necessarily need to diminish or downplay the self in order to focus on the other but adjusting the balance between emphasis on self and other towards more of an integration between the two.

8.4 Humility and Concern for the Other

Recent research on the psychological functions of humility demonstrates a relationship between humility and concern for the other. Humility is related to a host of pro-social relational variables including generosity, helping behavior, repair of social bonds, forgiveness, and gratitude. These types of pro-social variables would seem to include a component of concern for the other in that they naturally involve showing affection (at some level) for another whether through giving generously, showing gratitude or extending forgiveness to another. I would argue that altruistic concern and humility actually build on each other such that displays of humility engender more closeness and connection between people and the feeling of relational connection induces more humility towards others. People are more likely to show humility and contribute to a common purpose when they know and experience a sense of affinity with particular individuals. Thus, altruistic concern creates the context in which humility is more clearly experienced and displayed among persons of similar character and conviction.

Exline and Hill (2012) found that humility was often associated with generosity. Humility predicted higher levels of charitable donations as well as mailing back an extra survey to the researcher. Humble people most often passed on anonymous donations to future participants, and this form of generosity was positively correlated with a lack of self-focus. Humility was also associated with greater levels of self-reported motives to be kind to others, such as close friends, strangers, and enemies. Humility played a larger role in the generous acts in contrast to other individual variables such as self-esteem, entitlement, religiosity, gratitude, or social desirability.

LaBouff et al. (2012) found that humility was associated with different instances of helping behavior. Both explicit and implicit measures of humility were used to analyze the presence of humility as a character trait in participants. Humility was most strongly correlated with a self-reported measure of helpfulness and was also correlated with agreeableness, conscientiousness, extraversion, and impression management (IM), however the effect of humility on helpfulness remained even when IM was statistically controlled. In a second study, participants who scored high on an implicit measure of humility (IAT) were more likely to offer help to a fellow student in need. The same effect was found when agreeableness was added as a covariate, and there were no gender differences in the amount of help offered. In a third study, two different conditions were introduced one with high social pressure to help (five out of seven confederates had already agreed to help) and a second with low social pressure to help (two out of the seven confederates had already agreed to help). Although humble people did not help out more than others in the social pressure condition, they did offer more help in the low social pressure condition (76.9%) in comparison to the non-humble group (47.8%).

Gratitude is the recognition that something of value was received from another person, which was given and received openly and freely. Grateful people are less likely to engage in hierarchical comparisons with others, which often leads to envy or resentment (Emmons and Mishra 2011). Being in a state of gratitude toward another is incompatible with feeling envy and resentment toward them, thus this type of state in a sense blocks out negative comparator judgments and emphasizes the good qualities of another person (Smith et al. 1996). Psychological measurement scales of gratitude have been shown to be negatively correlated with envy (Ger and Belk 1996; McCullough et al. 2002). Gratitude also has a reciprocal relationship with humility. Participants who wrote a gratitude letter demonstrated a higher level of state humility in comparison to those who wrote a neutral one. Persons identified as being humble felt higher levels of gratitude after writing a gratitude letter and in a 14-day diary study, humility and gratitude mutually predicted each other (Kruse et al. 2014). Thus, gratitude is another form of relational connection that may be related to concern for the other and may help to develop altruistic concern over time for a wider network of social relationships.

8.5 Humility in Relationships and Organizations

Not only is humility associated with a host of prosocial variables, it is also associated with the maintenance and repair of social relationships. It is a preference in potential romantic partners, business leaders, and coworkers. I would argue that part of the reason for this is that humility is related to the perception of care and concern in others. A humble relationship partner demonstrates that they value the perspective of the other and a humble business leader demonstrates that they value the contributions of those in their charge. Although this may not be full-blown altruistic concern, it sets people on a trajectory toward valuing the other beyond a mere instrumental relationship. It allows for the development of a concern that goes beyond self-interest toward a type of humility that tips the scales away from the self toward the other.

A longitudinal study of couples that had experienced some sort of hurt or offense in their relationship rated their feelings of unforgiveness as significantly less over time when they saw their partner as more humble rather than viewing their partner as superior (Davis et al. 2013). Thus, perceiving a romantic partner as more humble is associated with greater levels of forgiveness on the part of the romantic partner who was hurt in some way. In a second study, groups of participants who were told they were part of a leadership workshop were also measured based on relational dynamics and humility. Based on ratings of individual members by the group, the trait of humility was positively associated with group acceptance and status. A second analysis also demonstrated that the same effect occurred over time, in that as people demonstrated more aspects of the humility trait during the group activities, they were rated higher in terms of acceptance. There was also some evidence that the group was able to discriminate between genuine and feigned humility, in that there was a negative relationship between people who scored *themselves* as higher in humility in comparison to observer scores who scored them lower.

In the initiation and maintenance of romantic relationships, Van Tongeren et al. (2014) found in an initial study that potential romantic partners who were considered very humble were rated more favorably and people were more likely to initiate a romantic relationship with them in comparison with less humble people. In a replication of the first study, participants found humble potential dating partners as more attractive in comparison to arrogant dating partners. Humility also had a demonstrated effect on the maintenance of long-distance relationships, by helping to facilitate greater levels of forgiveness and relationship satisfaction, especially in connection to higher levels of commitment in romantic relationships (Farrell et al. 2015).

Humility has also recently been identified as a helpful factor for various business organizations and a character trait sought after in corporate leaders. Among students who participated in ten-week-long project teams, those identified as expressing different cognitive and behavioral traits of humility were significantly related to identifiable positive traits including overall contributions to the team and individual performance (Owens et al. 2013). Humility was also shown to help compensate for lower mental ability on tasks, presumably by helping to better facilitate different social factors involved in group dynamics. Honesty-humility, as a unique personality trait, was strongly predictive of positive ratings of job performance by supervisors especially in jobs that involve some form of care taking (Johnson et al. 2011). Vera and Rodriquez-Lopez (2004) argue that humility actually offers a competitive advantage for organizations because humility helps to foster more realistic perspectives on a number of different factors related to organizational effectiveness.

Humility has been identified as a primary contributor to leadership effectiveness, too. Humility expressed in leaders, which was identified by group members, was positively correlated with job engagement (individual investment in work-related activities) and job satisfaction, while being negatively correlated with voluntary job turnover (Owens et al. 2013). Through an analysis of 55 in-depth interviews of leaders who implement humility in their organizations, these types of leaders were identified as effective by acting as role models for growth over time and creating space for team members to express their own areas of growth and uncertainty, leading to more positive organizational outcomes (Owens and Hekman 2012). Additionally, humility is able to counteract certain negative effects of narcissism. Among a large health insurance organization, survey data revealed that interactions between the traits of narcissism and humility were actually associated with more positive perceptions of leader effectiveness, increased job engagement by followers, and both subjective and objective measures of job performance in members of the organization (Owens et al. 2015).

Psychological research on humility demonstrates its association with a number of different types of relationships at various levels of intimacy from co-workers and friends to both potential and current romantic partners. This indicates that humility is part of a general suite of relational pro-social capacities at the heart of which, I would argue, is the general foundation of relational connection to, and value of, another human being. In the formation of humility in individuals, it would be impossible to separate out the valuation of the other from humility itself, both would be highly intertwined and interdependent in their workings toward the development of this virtue. It would seem that a part of us prefers or seeks out individuals who demonstrate these qualities because we believe they will be better relationship partners, leaders, and coworkers. This intuition is connected to our own need or desire for relationships that value others and the opportunity to show love, care, and concern for another person. The next section explores different cognitive and psychological mechanisms involved in the development of altruistic concern and humility – specifically moral schemas and morality identity. Finally, these two mechanisms will be fleshed out in Holocaust rescuers, exposing how they demonstrated humility and altruistic concern for Jews during the Holocaust.

8.6 Moral Schemas

Schemas have been used in a variety of different domains such as social psychology, perception, and cognition to demonstrate how expectations and learned information can affect current interpretations of a context or visual scene. Schemas are based on "general knowledge or expectations, which is distilled from your past experiences with someone or something" (Matlin 2013, p. 152). Schemas decrease cognitive load by creating expectations for familiar contexts and people by encoding in memory the regularities of various situations so that each time the situation is re-experienced the entire scene does not need to be re-encoded. Piaget (1970) originally suggested that schemas play an important role in learning through assimilation (encoding bias based on current schemas) and accommodation (adjusting schemas to fit new information). Brewer and Treyens (1981) demonstrated that when remembering a scene (in the case of this experiment the contents of an office), people will use an office schema to help remember different items. Items often associated with this schema (i.e. desk, chair, pencils) are easier to remember than items not consistent with the schema (a skull placed on the desk). People will also *mistakenly* remember items consistent with the schema that were not actually present in the setting. Schemas are not limited to perceptions of a visual scene; the actions associated with different contexts are also present in memory through the use of a particular schema often referred to as a script. For example, going to a restaurant has specific actions to be performed in a particular order, which is widely shared in particular cultures without the need for detailed conscious recollection (Bower et al. 1979).

Based on their general usage in human cognition, several authors have suggested the importance of *moral* schemas for understanding the factors associated with moral action in children and adults (Narvaez and Lapsley 2009). Moral schemas primarily involve social information, especially regarding the self in relation to others.

> Schemas are structured parcels of knowledge from memory situating the self in relation to others. Schemas can give rise to scripts or conceptual representations of action sequences associated with particular social situations (Reimer et al. 2011a, p. 72).

Moral schemas are the ethical lenses people use to perceive the world and their place in it. Moral schemas contain perceptional content in terms of how different situations are interpreted as well as potential action sequences to be enacted.

Several lines of research indicate that moral formation is significantly dependent on relational ties and variables in the formation of a self-concept. This self-concept would be at least partially substantiated and demonstrated in a particular moral schema that viewed the self in connection to other important social relationships. Adolescents from an urban neighborhood were selected based on their identification as care exemplars who embodied several moral traits including community involvement, responsibility toward family, helpfulness toward others, emotional maturity, leadership, and others (Reimer 2003; Reimer and Wade-Stein 2004). Using computational analysis, it was identified that a significant proportion of their understanding of the self was based on the integration of peer and parental representations into their own internalized representation of the self in comparison to matched controls who did not demonstrate this tendency. These representations would be a part of the moral schemas that these adolescents used in their development as care exemplars. Among L'Arche caregivers (people who willingly volunteer to live with and serve the mentally and physically disabled) who have served for more than three years, aspects of their moral schemas were related significantly with expectations regarding close intimate partners who may act as models for moral action (Reimer et al. 2011b). Among spiritual exemplars, adolescents who are actively involved in a specific religious group report more resources in terms of social capital (including positive peer and family relationships), which led to higher levels of positive views on various moral perspectives (empathetic concern, perspective taking, and altruism) (Ebstyne, King and Furrow 2008).

Several perspectives in psychology demonstrate the importance of relational ties to moral development and character formation (Narvaez and Lapsley 2014). Parental socialization plays an important role in the development of self-regulatory functions and the development of moral emotions and, ultimately, conscience (Kochanska and

Aksan 2006). From birth, parental interaction plays a vital role in the development of the physical, emotional, and cognitive systems of the infant, while many forms of dysfunction in these systems is at least partially attributable to deficits in parental interaction and regulation (Narvaez and Gleason 2013; Schore 2001, 2002). Insecure attachment styles (anxious and avoidant) negatively affect pro-social emotions, motives, and behaviors while secure attachment styles are positively related to increases in empathetic concern, compassion for others, and different forms of altruistic behavior including gratitude and forgiveness (Shaver and Mikulincer 2012). Although some perspectives have argued that young infants and children have little to no interaction with moral concerns, new perspectives seem to indicate a wealth of different social and moral information that is being processed and used by children throughout their early development (Narvaez and Lapsley 2009; Thompson 2012).

This evidence suggests that moral behavior generally is related to representations of relationships that are a part of the self-concept and, ultimately, facets of a moral schema. How other people are perceived within their moral schema is at least partially constituted by past relationships, which form the expectations that are so critical to moral perception in the present. Thus, our relational connections, both from our past and our current relational ties, inform the way that we view the world and others as well as modifying the ability for someone to develop certain aspects of humility. As altruistic concern and valuation of the other increases, the ability to exercise and sustain humility increases because these two aspects of both cognition and behavior are so highly intertwined. Our ability to show altruistic concern is based on the relationships from our past but can also be modified based on new relationships and new experiences. Thus, moral schemas can be adaptive and transformed over time and lead to greater levels of humility. Related to moral schemas is the concept of moral identity, which also plays a key role in moral development generally and humility specifically. This will be discussed in the next section.

8.7 Moral Identity

Generally, moral identity refers to the importance of morality to the self-conception of the individual (Hardy and Carlo 2011). Thus, moral identity increases as a particular moral perspective becomes more central to the way in which a person understands themselves and identifies with the moral perspective. Morality and self-identity become more closely linked such that a person with a high moral identity, a moral exemplar for example, tends to prefer or purse personal goals that are morally right (Colby and Damon 1992). Moral schemas are foundational to the development of moral identity; having a moral schema that is readily accessible to process current social situations in terms of their morality would be key to proper accounts of moral action (Narvaez and Lapsley 2009). Thus, moral identity forms as the moral schemas used to instantiate moral actions become solidified and consistent over time such that certain forms of moral action become part of one's identity (Van Slyke 2015).

Several areas of research indicate that moral identity has an important effect on moral actions in a variety of different domains. Aquino and Reed (2002) found that the importance of moral identity for self-identity had a marked effect on moral behaviors. Participants with a strong internalized sense of moral identity donated more food and had an increased commitment to various forms of volunteerism. For each step upwards on a measure of internalization of moral identity there was a corresponding increase in the probability of some form of volunteer work such as working in a homeless shelter, mentoring troubled youth, or visiting patients in a nursing home. In a second study, among high school students, higher scores on the same moral identity internalization measure (which was second only to gender differences) was associated with more donations of food to an end-of-the-year food drive that was conducted three months after the instrument was originally given to the students (Aquino and Reed 2002).

Moral identity was found to play a mediating role between adolescent religiosity, empathy, and aggression (Hardy et al. 2012). Using structural equation models to analyze an online survey of 502 participants, religious commitment was indirectly related to aggression (through decreased scores on the measure) and empathy (through increased scores on the measure) through the variable of moral identity. Religious commitment and involvement also predicted scores on the moral identity measure, which suggests that the pro-social behaviors often associated with religiosity may be closely associated with moral identity. Similarly, religious identity has been shown to be associated with a variety of prosocial personality factors including empathy, perspective taking, helpfulness, and personal responsibility (Furrow et al. 2004). Adolescents who were highly committed to their religion were involved in twice the national average of acts of service to homeless and needy people in comparison with non-religious people (Smith and Denton 2005).

In terms of humility, moral identities become formed in such a way that the value of the other person becomes a dominant theme of the way a person interacts with and views the world, and engenders the types of humility demonstrated in moral exemplars and others. Several areas of research show a close association with moral identity and concern for out-group members. This would suggest that an important aspect of moral identity is developing a proper concern for other people, especially people who are different or represent different groups and ethnicities.

From a national online database, it was demonstrated that activating moral emotions associated with in-group solidarity increased negative associations with out-groups (Smith et al. 2014). Moral foundations theory, which suggests intuitive moral categories that function as the foundational building blocks of different cultural moral systems, has identified three categories primarily involved in binding groups together: loyalty/betrayal, authority/subversion, and purity/degradation (Graham et al. 2011). Reliance on the three binding categories strongly predicted low support for helping out-groups through the sharing of water, and negatively predicted condemnation for torture of out-groups. However, moral identity actually mitigated this effect in that for those who relied heavily on the binding foundations, if they also had a strong sense of moral identity, they were more supportive of offering water to out-groups and showed more condemnation for torture of out-groups (Smith et al. 2014).

An earlier study also demonstrated similar results in that a strong sense of moral identity was associated with a more positive view of out-groups (Reed and Aquino 2003). Those who scored high on a measure of the self-importance of moral identity (meaning those individuals whose moral identity was central to their self-conception) also scored higher on a measure of moral obligation toward out-groups (while also controlling for gender and ethnicity variables). The same measure of moral identity also showed a positive relationship with perceived worthiness of relief efforts for an out-group (Afghanistan, which at the time was identified as one of the countries related to the 9/11 attacks). This was studied further by directly comparing support to in-groups (New York police, fire widows, and children's benefit fund) vs. out-groups (UNICEF for Afghan children and families). The self-importance of moral identity also predicted higher levels of donation to the out-group in this situation as well. In a final study, higher levels on the self-importance of moral identity scale were significantly related with lower levels of acceptable collateral damage to civilian Afghanis, negatively correlated with the morality of killing the perpetrators of 9/11 attacks, and positively correlated with the morality of forgiving the perpetrators of the 9/11 attacks (Reed and Aquino 2003).

Moral schemas are foundational for the development of moral identity, which ultimately effects developing prosocial behaviors such as volunteerism, donating food, and donating time to various agencies working for the needy. Additionally, moral identities are related to more positive views of various types of out-groups in a variety of contexts. Both of these areas of research suggest that how a person views the other affects the types of positive moral actions they will initiate on their behalf. Thus, the development of altruistic concern is an essential component of moral schemas that view the world in such a way that others are perceived as having intrinsic value. This value becomes important to a sense of self-identity, which links this value to how one sees the self and one's natural inclinations toward treating others. Once this viewpoint is a part of the self-identity, moral actions on the behalf of others are not perceived to be extraordinary, but simply a natural outgrowth of altruistic concern for others. Thus, people can more easily be humble about their moral actions because they don't see themselves doing anything beyond what each person deserves based on their intrinsic worth. This becomes apparent when looking at the moral exemplarity of Holocaust rescuers who demonstrate altruistic concern, heroic acts of compassion, and humility.

8.8 Moral Exemplars

Moral exemplars provide a unique window into the virtue of humility through the minds of people who have performed incredible acts of moral courage. Biographical investigations of moral exemplars often cite humility as one of their primary qualities (Colby and Damon 1992; Oliner and Oliner 1988). One particular group,

Holocaust rescuers, is an example of people performing astonishing acts of bravery and compassion on behalf of Jews being persecuted, tortured, and exterminated at the hands of the German Nazis. Monroe (2004) has conducted extensive interviews with these people in order to begin to understand the rationale behind their extraordinary behavior. For example, Otto was an ethnic German who lived in Prague and saved 100 Jews before ending up in a concentration camp. John was a Dutchman who was placed on the Gestapo's most wanted list, yet was able to organize an escape route to Switzerland and Spain. He was ultimately captured and tortured by the Gestapo, but never revealed any information about his collaborators or their escape route. Irene was a Polish nurse who was forced into slave labor under the Nazis, but was able to rescue 18 Jews by hiding them in the basement of the Nazi general whom she was forced to work for. Knud took part in the rescue of 85% of the Jews who were living in Denmark, but was captured by the Gestapo. He was eventually able to escape from his captors and re-joined the underground rescue effort (Monroe 2004).

Despite the fact that these people put themselves and their families at enormous risk of retaliation from the Nazis (and in fact, many of them experienced retaliation in the form of violence and torture), most of them didn't feel like they had done anything that extraordinary. One of the rescuers remarked during a long interview about different factors involved in his actions that he didn't do anything that extraordinary, he simply did what anybody would do (Monroe 2004). Thus, despite incredible acts of bravery, courage, and compassion, these people showed astonishing amounts of humility in comparison to the type of moral actions they took on behalf of the Jews during The Holocaust. Yad Vashem, one of the primary organizations involved in remembering and documenting the atrocities of the Holocaust, has done considerable work to identify and reward Holocaust rescuers for their actions. However, many of the rescuers often refuse the monetary rewards and medals or give the money to charity. These types of moral exemplars demonstrate several different forms of virtue, including courage and compassion, while displaying an inordinate amount of humility in comparison to the moral acts they performed. Their form of humility is uniquely intertwined with their altruistic concern for other (which is a part of their moral schemas) and ultimately their morality identity, which made their actions during The Holocaust a natural outcome of their self-identity.

8.9 Moral Schemas of Rescuers

Monroe conducted several long-form interviews with Holocaust rescuers to investigate different components of the moral schemas used by rescuers to understand the reasons behind their actions (Monroe 2004, 2008, 2011b). Interestingly, many of the features of the moral schemas of Holocaust rescuers match some of the primary characteristics of humility discussed earlier (accurate self-assessment, openness, and lack of self-focus). They demonstrated accurate self-assessment in that they did not unduly elevate themselves because of their heroic actions; they recognized the importance of the contributions of others to their rescue efforts. They often worked in groups and underground organizations to accomplish their goals and viewed themselves as part of a network of rescuers, rather than as solitary heroic individuals. In fact, rescuers did not see themselves as doing anything spectacular, they simply did what they felt was right. Rescuers thought it was simply natural to help others, not necessarily deserving of merit or praise, because each person was assigned a sense of common dignity and worth, simply by being a human being (Monroe 2011a).

Rescuers demonstrated an openness to others and considered themselves to be a part of a common humanity that did not discriminate against others, even the Nazis. One rescuer, Tony, remarked,

> I was to understand that you're part of a whole; just like cells in your own body altogether make up your body, in our society and community, we all are like cells of a community that is very important. Not America. I mean the human race. You should always be aware that every other person is basically you. Always treat people as though it is you. That goes for the evil Nazis as well as for Jewish friends in trouble. Always see yourself in those people, for good, or for evil both (Monroe 2008, pp. 711–2).

Tony even extended humanity to the Nazis, despite their terrible violent actions. Rescuers placed a high value on the sanctity of life and their definition of what it meant to be human was wide and expansive and included many different types of people and points of view. Rescuers did not make strong in-group vs. out-group distinctions (which is consistent with research discussed previously on moral identity and views of out-groups), but rather saw themselves as part of a common universal humanity with each person being granted dignity and worth based on the sanctity of life (Monroe 2008).

This leads naturally into the final component of their moral schemas that matches one of the components of humility, lack of self-focus. This is clearly demonstrated in their moral actions of courage and compassion on behalf of the Jews. They perceived Jews as having a common humanity and worth that required action, and they sacrificed themselves, their families, their fortunes, their health, and risked the potential for capture, torture, and even death, which some of the rescuers, unfortunately, actually had to experience. This kind of forgetting of the self in the face of danger indicates that they lacked many of the features of selfishness and conceit common in the vices of pride. In contrast, bystanders during the Holocaust perceived the potential costs to be too great and the threat of loss of possessions, dignity, or life too severe to be pursued.

Thus, rescuers demonstrate many of the common features of contemporary definitions of humility. My contention is that their humility regarding their actions during the Holocaust was a natural consequence of the moral schemas of these types of exemplars, moral schemas which placed such a high value on the inherent worth of other people. It would seem strange to them to display the various vices of pride by bragging, showing arrogance, or being conceited about performing actions necessary to save something as precious to them as a fellow human being. It did not occur to them that their actions deserved abundant praise because their behavior and cognition were simply consistent with their moral schemas and the way they saw other people, the world, and their role in it. Thus, displaying the vice of pride was simply not within their current repertoire of potential actions. Their humility was a natural extension of their altruistic concern for other people and the value they placed on a common humanity represented in their moral schemas and moral identity.

8.10 Importance of Moral Identity

The primary thesis of this paper is that altruistic concern or love is a primary underlying factor in the trait of humility. Humility is not simply *the contrary to* several different vices, but is an outgrowth of altruistic concern for other persons. Humility as a virtue is not detachable from an underlying altruistic ethic that consistently values others. In Monroe's study of Holocaust rescuers, she found that moral identity was the primary causal factor in the moral actions of Holocaust rescuers during World War II (2011a). This moral identity was uniquely intertwined with an ethical perspective that saw unique value in other people, expectations about how they should be treated, and an emotional connection that created a sense of responsibility toward Jewish people.

> It is this ethical perspective that helps us make sense of the ethical situations presented to us. The way we categorize and classify others, our perceived relationship to the person in need, our idealized cognitive models, and our canonical expectations about what constitutes appropriate behavior all work through the ethical perspective to produce both a cognitive menu of choice options we find available and a sense of moral salience, the feeling that the suffering of others is relevant for us and therefore demands action to help, not just a generalized sense of concern or sympathy (Monroe 2011a, p. 5).

Monroe's theory of moral choice highlights the importance of a bundle of character traits that facilitate the kind of moral actions exhibited by rescuers, primarily their view of the other.

The care, concern, courage, and compassion of rescuers toward the Jews was tied up in their moral schemas, identity, and views of others, which ultimately informed their humility in terms of the courageousness of their actions. Because they viewed the moral situation in Nazi Germany from a particular ethical perspective, it constrained the action possibilities that came to mind when faced with the situation. This was part of the reason for their humility because they viewed their actions as the norm, not something heroic or extraordinary. As one rescuer commented, "But what else could I do? They were human beings like you and me" (Monroe 2011a, p. 3). Thus, their humility cannot be separated from their underlying view of other people; in fact, it is a consequence of that view.

8.11 Conclusion

Homo amans provides a new foundation for understanding human nature that argues against the assumption that humans are inherently selfish. In this chapter, I have argued that one aspect of *Homo amans*, love, understood as altruistic concern for the other is foundational for the development of the virtue of humility. Research demonstrates that humility is related to a variety of pro-social variables, which at their core seem to revolve around some sense of concern for the other. Similarly, humble people seem to be preferred in both romantic and business relationships, based in part on the concern they show for others. This association reveals the importance of a relational connection for developing humility in people. Humility develops best, not in opposition to the vice of pride, but through the development of relational values and connection that provide the bedrock for forming this virtue. This type of concern for the other is the foundation for a more developed sense of altruistic concern that is demonstrated in moral exemplars such as Holocaust rescuers.

Humility is not merely the absence of the various vices associated with pride. Instead, altruistic concern is the bedrock or foundation for the development and sustainability of humility. Those who value the intrinsic worth of other people are less likely to express the various vices of pride and will more readily demonstrate humility towards others. Moral exemplars, especially Holocaust rescuers, embody moral schemas that contain particular views of others, specifically their value and worth simply by being a member of the human race. Holocaust rescuers demonstrate many of the characteristics associated with humility and it is my contention that their humility is a consequence of those characteristics associated with their moral identities and schemas, especially the altruistic concern they show for others.

References

Aquinas, T. 1981. *Summa Theologiae*. Transl. E. Dominicans. New York: Christian Classics.

Aquino, K., and A.I. Reed. 2002. The Self-importance of Moral Identity. *Journal of Personality and Social Psychology* 83 (6): 1423–1440.

Augustine. [1961] 1996. *The Enchiridion on Faith, Hope, and Love*. Transl. J.B. Shaw. Washington, DC: Regnery.

Bower, G.H., J.B. Black, and T.J. Turner. 1979. Scripts in Memory for Text. *Cognitive Psychology* 11: 177–220.

Boyd, C.A. 2014. Pride and Humility: Tempering the Desire for Excellence. In *Virtues and Their Vices*, ed. K. Timpe and C.A. Boyd, 245–268. New York: Oxford University Press.

Brewer, W.F., and J.C. Treyens. 1981. Role of Schemata in Memory for Places. *Cognitive Psychology* 13: 207–230.

Camerer, C., and E. Fehr. 2006. When Does "Economic Man" Dominate Social Behavior? *Science* 311: 47–52.

Calvin, J. 1559/1999. Institutes of the Christian Religion. Oxford: Oxford University Pres.

Colby, A., and W. Damon. 1992. *Some do Care: Contemporary Lives of Moral Commitment*. New York: The Free Press.

Davis, D.E., et al. 2013. Humility and the Development and Repair of Social Bonds: Two Longitudinal Studies. *Self and Identity* 12 (1): 58–77.

Dawkins, R. 1976. *The Selfish Gene*. Oxford: Oxford University Press.
de Waal, F.B.M. 2005. *Our Inner Ape: A Leading Primatologist Explains Why We Are Who We Are*. New York: Riverhead.
———. 2006. Morally Evolved: Primate Social Instincts, Human Morality, and the Rise and Fall of "Veneer Theory.". In *Primates and Philosophers: How Morality Evolved*, ed. S. Macedo and J. Ober, 1–58. Princeton: Princeton University Press.
Ebstyne King, P., and J.L. Furrow. 2008. Religion as a Resource for Positive Youth Development: Religion, Social Capital, and Moral Outcomes. *Psychology of Religion and Spirituality* S (1): 34–49.
Emmons, R.A. 2000. Is Spirituality an Intelligence? Motivation, Cognition, and the Psychology of Ultimate Concern. *The International Journal for the Psychology of Religion* 10 (1): 3–26.
Emmons, R.A., and A. Mishra. 2011. Why Gratitude Enhances Well-being: What We Know, What We Need to Know. In *Designing Positive Psychology: Taking Stock and Moving Forward*, ed. K.M. Sheldon, T.B. Kashdan, and M.F. Steger, 248–262. New York: Oxford University Press.
Exline, J.J., and A.L. Geyer. 2004. Perceptions of Humility: A Preliminary Study. *Self and Identity* 3 (2): 95–114.
Exline, J.J., and P.C. Hill. 2012. Humility: A Consistent and Robust Predictor of Generosity. *The Journal of Positive Psychology* 7 (3): 208–218.
Farrell, J.E., et al. 2015. Humility and Relationship Outcomes in Couples: The Mediating Role of Commitment. *Couple and Family Psychology: Research and Practice* 4 (1): 14–26.
Fehr, E., and C. Camerer. 2007. Social Neuroeconomics: The Neural Circuitry of Social Preferences. *Trends in Cognitive Sciences* 11 (10): 419–427.
Furrow, J.L., P. Ebstyne King, and K. White. 2004. Religion and Positive Youth Development: Identity, Meaning, and Prosocial Concerns. *Applied Developmental Science* 8: 17–26.
Ger, G., and R.W. Belk. 1996. Cross-cultural Differences in Materialism. *Journal of Economic Psychology* 17: 55–77.
Graham, J., et al. 2011. Mapping the Moral Domain. *Journal of Personality and Social Psychology* 101 (2): 366–385.
Hardy, S.A., and G. Carlo. 2011. Moral Identity: What is It, How Does It Develop, and is It Linked to Moral Action? *Child Development Perspectives* 5 (3): 212–218.
Hardy, S.A., L.J. Walker, D.D. Rackham, and J.A. Olsen. 2012. Religiosity and Adolescent Empathy and Aggression: The Mediating Role of Moral Identity. *Psychology of Religion and Spirituality* 4 (3): 237–248.
Hobbes, T. 1651. *Leviathan*. New York: Pearson Longman.
Johnson, M.K., W.C. Rowatt, and L. Petrini. 2011. A New Trait on the Market: Honesty-humility as a Unique Predictor of Job Performance Ratings. *Personality and Individual Differences* 50 (6): 857–862.
Kochanska, G., and N. Aksan. 2006. Children's Conscience and Self-regulation. *Journal of Personality* 74 (6): 1587–1618.
Kruse, E., J. Chancellor, P.M. Ruberton, and S. Lyubomirsky. 2014. An Upward Spiral between Gratitude and Humility. *Social Psychological and Personality Science* 5 (7): 805–814.
LaBouff, J.P., et al. 2012. Humble Persons are More Helpful than Less Humble Persons: Evidence from Three Studies. *The Journal of Positive Psychology* 7 (1): 16–29.
MacIntyre, A. 1999. *Dependent Rational Animals: Why Human Beings Need the Virtues*. Chicago: Open Court.
Matlin, M.W. [8]2013. *Cognition*. Hoboken: Wiley.
McCullough, M.E., R.A. Emmons, and J.-A. Tsang. 2002. The Grateful Disposition: A Conceptual and Empirical Topography. *Journal of Personality and Social Psychology* 82: 112–127.
Monroe, K.R. 2004. *The Hand of Compassion: Portraits of Moral Choice during the Holocaust*. Princeton: Princeton University Press.
———. 2008. Cracking the Code of Genocide: The Moral Psychology of Rescuers, Bystanders, and Nazis during the Holocaust. *Political Psychology* 29: 699–736.
———. 2011a. *Ethics in an Age of Terror and Genocide: Identity and Moral Choice*. Princeton: Princeton University Press.

———., ed. 2011b. *Science, Ethics, and Politics: Conversations and Investigations*. Boulder: Paradigm Publishers.
Nadelhoffer, T., and J.C. Wright. 2016. The Twin Dimensions of the Virtue of Humility: Low Self-focus and High Other-focus. In *Moral Psychology, Vol. 5: Virtues and Vices*, ed. W. Sinnott-Armstrong and C. Miller, 1–88. Cambridge, MA: MIT Press.
Narvaez, D., and T. Gleason. 2013. Developmental Optimization. In *Evolution, Early Experience and Human Development: From Research to Practice to Policy*, ed. D. Narvaez, J. Panksepp, A. Schore, and T. Gleason, 307–325. New York: Oxford University Press.
Narvaez, D., and D.K. Lapsley. 2009. Moral Identity, Moral Functioning, and the Development of Moral Character. In *The Psychology of Learning and Motivation*, ed. D.M. Bartels et al., vol. 50, 237–274. Burlington: Academic.
———. 2014. Becoming Moral: Development of Moral Agents through Social Interaction. In *Empirically Informed Ethics: Morality between Facts and Norms*, ed. M. Chisten et al., 227–238. Heidelberg: Springer.
Oliner, M.P., and S.P. Oliner. 1988. *The Altruistic Personality: Rescuers of Jews in Nazi Europe*. New York: The Free Press.
Owens, B.P., and D.R. Hekman. 2012. Modeling How to Grow: An Inductive Examination of Humble Leader Behaviors, Contingencies, and Outcomes. *Academy of Management Journal* 55 (4): 787–818.
Owens, B.P., M.D. Johnson, and T.R. Mitchell. 2013. Expressed Humility in Organizations: Implications for Performance, Teams, and Leadership. *Organization Science* 24 (5): 1517–1538.
Owens, B.P., A.S. Walker, and D.A. Waldman. 2015. Leader Narcissism and Follower Outcomes: The Counterbalancing Effect of Leader Humility. *Journal of Applied Psychology* 100 (4): 1203–1213.
Peterson, C., and M. Seligman. 2004. *Character Strengths and Virtues: A Handbook and Classification*. New York: Oxford University Press.
Piaget, J. 1970. *Genetic Epistemology*. Transl. E. Duckworth. New York: Columbia University Press.
Pinsent, A. 2012. Humility. In *Being Good: Christian Virtues for Everyday Life*, ed. M.W. Austin and R.D. Geivett, 242–264. Grand Rapids: Eerdmans.
Reed, A.I., and K.F. Aquino. 2003. Moral Identity and the Expanding Circle of Moral Regard toward Out-groups. *Journal of Personality and Social Psychology* 84 (6): 1270–1286.
Reimer, K.S. 2003. Committed to Caring: Transformation in Adolescent Moral Identity. *Applied Developmental Science* 7: 129–137.
Reimer, K.S., and D. Wade-Stein. 2004. Moral Identity in Adolescence: Self and Other in Semantic Space. *Identity* 4 (3): 229–249.
Reimer, K.S., Spezio, M.L., Brown, W.S., Van Slyke, J. Peterson, G.R. 2011a. Virtuous courage: New methods for the interdisciplinary study of virtue. In K. R. Monroe (Ed.). *Science, Ethics, and Politics: Conversations and Investigations*. Boulder, CO: Paradigm Press.
Reimer, K.S., Young, C., Birath, B., Spezio, M.L., Peterson, G. Van Slyke, J., Brown, W.S. 2011b. Maturity is explicit: Self-importance of traits in humanitarian moral identity. *The Journal of Positive Psychology* 7(1) 36–44. https://doi.org/10.1080/17439760.2011.626789
Roberts, R.C. 2003. *Emotions: An Essay in Aid of Moral Psychology*. Cambridge: Cambridge University Press.
Roberts, R.C. 2013. *Emotions in the Moral Life*. Cambridge: Cambridge University Press.
Roberts, R.C., and W.J. Wood. 2010. *Intellectual Virtues: An Essay in Regulative Epistemology*. New York: Oxford University Press.
Sandage, S.J. 1999. An Ego-humility Model of Forgiveness. *Marriage and Family: A Christian Journal* 2: 259–276.
Schore, A. 2001. Effects of a Secure Attachment Relationship on Right Brain Development, Affect Regulation, and Infant Mental Health. *Infant Mental Health Journal* 22 (1–2): 7–66.
———. 2002. Dysregulation of the Right Brain: A Fundamental Mechanism of Traumatic Attachment and the Psychopathogenesis of Posttraumatic Stress Disorder. *Australian and New Zealand Journal of Psychiatry* 36: 9–30.

Shaver, P.R., and M. Mikulincer. 2012. An Attachment Perspective on Morality: Strengthening Authentic Forms of Moral Decision-making. In *The Social Psychology of Morality: Exploring the Causes of Good and Evil*, ed. P.R. Shaver and M. Mikulincer, 257–274. Washington, DC: American Psychological Association.

Shaver, P.R., et al. [3]2016. A Lifespan Perspective on Attachment and Care for Others: Empathy, Altruism, and Prosocial Behavior. In *Handbook of Attachment: Theory, Research, and Clinical Applications*, ed. J. Cassidy and P.R. Shaver, 878–916. New York: Guilford Press.

Singer, T., and C. Lamm. 2009. The Social Neuroscience of Empathy. *Annals of the New York Academy of Sciences* 1156 (1): 81–96.

Smith, C., and M. Denton. 2005. *Soul Searching: The Religious and Spiritual Lives of American Teenagers*. New York: Oxford University Press.

Smith, R.H., et al. 1996. Envy and Schadenfreude. *Personality and Social Psychology Bulletin* 22: 158–168.

Smith, I.H., K. Aquino, S. Koleva, and J. Graham. 2014. The Moral Ties that Bind . . . Even to Out-groups: The Interactive Effect of Moral Identity and the Binding Moral Foundations. *Psychological Science* 25 (8): 1554–1562.

Tangney, J.P. 2000. Humility: Theoretical Perspectives, Empirical Findings and Directions for Future Research. *Journal of Social and Clinical Psychology* 19 (1): 70–82.

Templeton, J.M. 1997. *Worldwide Laws of Life*. Philadelphia: Templeton Foundation Press.

Thompson, R.A. 2012. Whither the Preconventional Child? Toward a Life-span Moral Development Theory. *Child Development Perspectives* 6 (4): 423–429.

Van Slyke, J.A. 2010. Evolutionary and Cognitive Factors in the Emergence of Human Altruism. *Zygon* 45 (4): 841–860.

———. 2012. Naturalizing Moral Exemplarity: Contemporary Science and Human Nature. In *Theology and the Science of Morality: Virtue Ethics Exemplarity, and Cognitive Neuroscience*, ed. J.A. Van Slyke et al., 101–116. New York: Routledge.

———. 2014. Moral Psychology, Neuroscience, and Virtue: From Moral Judgment to Oral Character. In *Virtues and Their Vices*, ed. K. Timpe and C. Boyd, 459–480. Oxford: Oxford University Press.

———. 2015. Understanding the Moral Dimension of Spirituality: Insights from Virtue Ethics and Moral Exemplars. *Journal of Psychology & Christianity* 34 (3): 205–215.

Van Tongeren, D.R., D.E. Davis, and J.N. Hook. 2014. Social Benefits of Humility: Initiating and Maintaining Romantic Relationships. *The Journal of Positive Psychology* 9 (4): 313–321.

Vera, D., and A. Rodriquez-Lopez. 2004. Strategic Virtues: Humility as a Source of Competitive Advantage. *Organizational Dynamics* 33 (4): 393–408.

Wright, J.C., et al. 2017. The Psychological Significance of Humility. *The Journal of Positive Psychology* 12 (1): 3–12.

Chapter 9
Trust, Faith, and Social Imaginary: Prolegomena to an Anthropology of Personhood

Emilio Di Somma

Abstract Amidst the many problem that our societies are facing today, there is acknowledgment of the fact that the current economic system is unable to create and foster a just and stable society. This becomes increasingly true the more we continue to rely on the paradigm of the *Homo economicus*, which reveals itself as a fragile basis for a just and functioning society.

The paradigm of the *Homo economicus* does not allow us to build a workable society; but then, the first question remains, what is the fundamental feature of the *Homo*, what does it mean to be human? And how can we build a just and functioning society?

The theme of this work focuses on finding an answer through the paradigm of the *Homo amans,* that is, a paradigm in which we take into account not only human self-interest but also of those other features that are strongly linked with human life: the need for a meaning in our life, our relationship with our future and our relationship with other human beings. However, to change an anthropological paradigm, there is a necessary step that has to be addressed. To say that the paradigm of *Homo economicus* has been the dominant one so far, means that we have had a society that was imbued within a specific framework of customs, values, and traditions. Our society has been developed on a set of assumptions about human behavior, and on these assumptions have been developed institutions and procedures in which we *trust*.

The attitude of trust is the main topic of this essay. To develop a society on the paradigm of *Homo amans* and to further develop the debate, one should ask what kind of expectation we should encourage in people, and what should the foundations for such expectations be. What, then, is the foundation of this sensible assurance? Why do we trust people and institutions? This chapter aims to analyze this fundamental requirement for the development of any kind of society: the need for trust between persons and communities.

E. Di Somma (✉)
Evangelische Theologische Faculteit, Leuven, Belgium
e-mail: Emilio.disomma@etf.edu

J. van Nes et al. (eds.), *Relational Anthropology for Contemporary Economics*, Ethical Economy 61, https://doi.org/10.1007/978-3-030-84690-9_9

9.1 From *Homo Economicus* to *Homo Amans*

Amidst the many social and financial problems that our societies are facing today, there is growing acknowledgment of the fact that the current economic system is increasingly unable to create and foster a just and stable society. This becomes increasingly true the more we continue to rely on the paradigm of the *Homo economicus*, which reveals itself as a fragile basis for a just and functioning society and more of a theoretical instrument to justify the existing balance of power, with unpleasant consequences for the life of the majority of citizens. As Fleming (2017) has argued, the current social and economic landscape can be likened to the destruction left after a tsunami, where people make the catastrophic error of believing that, after the crisis, things will return to normal. All the while a new, much more catastrophic wave, is making its way toward us.

The more our societies have displayed disfunction and contradictions during crises, especially in recent years, the more the paradigm of the *Homo* economicus reveals itself not as an analytical tool, but as an a-rational assumption to justify the contingent, historical, structure of society. Robert H. Nelson (2001, pp. 2–8) offers us a good preliminary description of the problem we are facing. Nelson affirms that a suitable value-foundation for the market should approve the pursuit of self-interest only in those instances that it is expressed *legitimately*. The problem, that is a moral as well as a theological one, lies precisely in this definition of *legitimization*. Much like any theological/political/moral system, economics requires a normative foundation for the market that involves a dual attitude with respect to self-interest. We are presented with strong cultural inhibitions against the expression of self-interest in many areas of society, but, at the same time, strong encouragement for another powerful form of self-interest in the individual pursuit of profit that is specific to the confines of the market. According to Nelson, to avoid this conundrum, modern society developed a surprising solution: *It may be that economists have themselves been acting in the requisite religious capacity.* In fact, in the moment of policy making, economists try to advocate for the ethical assumptions and consequences of the system they are supporting, they do not just propose a set of technical assumptions for the scientific evaluation of reality. In this way, the role of the economist in government already assumes an ethical normative dimension. Another interpretation of a theological function in economic assumptions has been provided by D. S. Grewal (2016). He argues that the idea of self-love, channeled through commerce, producing a collectively optimal result, first appeared in seventeenth-century French debates about grace and redemption in interpretations of Augustine. Eighteenth-century socio-economic thought made this assumption its own, transforming a theological problem into a secular model of commercial sociability. The idea that an invisible mechanism – the market functioning according to providential design – makes private vices conducive to public benefit suggests an account of social order generated through essentially non-political processes.

Critiquing the paradigm of the *Homo economicus*, then, should be treated similarly to a theological debate, not just an economic, *scientific* one. While we can accept Mill's (1844) definition of the economic human being as *a being who desires wealth, and who is capable of judging the comparative efficacy of means for obtaining that end*, we should ask ourselves whether that is what it means to be *Homo,* to be human, and, furthermore, whether such a foundation would allow us to build a stable and just society. Seeing the economic and social upheaval of recent years, we could assume that the answer to the latter question is negative. The paradigm of the *Homo economicus* does not allow us to build a workable society; but then, the first question remains, what is the fundamental feature of the *Homo*, what does it mean to be human? And how can we build a just and functioning society?

The theme of this work focuses on finding an answer through the paradigm of the *Homo amans,* that is, a paradigm in which we take into account not only human self-interest (the desire for wealth and material benefits), but also those other features that are strongly linked with human life: the need for a meaning in our life, our relationship with our future and our relationship with other human beings. In this sense, then, the paradigm of the *Homo amans* wishes to re-discuss the fundamental concepts through which we establish a sense of personhood. While *Homo economicus* limits human personhood to its capacity to have and satisfy desires, the paradigm of *Homo amans* takes into account those elements of human life that cannot be described trough a paradigm of desires, costs, and benefits. The need for a meaning, the love toward our families, neighbors and communities, the need for hope and a clear vision of the future to foster and inspire human action, all these elements, that do exist in the life of a person, cannot be subsumed within the boundaries of the *Homo economicus.*

However, to change an anthropological paradigm, there is a necessary step that has to be addressed. To say that the paradigm of *Homo economicus* has been the dominating one so far, means that we have had a society that was imbued with a specific framework of customs, values, and traditions. Our society has been developed on a set of assumptions on human behavior and on these assumptions have been developed institutions and procedures in which we *trust.* The attitude of trust is the main topic of this essay. In fact, to become the foundation of a social structure, the paradigms of both *Homo economicus* and *Homo amans* need to stress the importance of actions, traditions, customs, and institutions that are supported and nurtured by the trust of the people participating in them. A social convention, or an institution, that does not have the *trust* of the people involved in it, is in fact unable to sustain itself to the point of becoming a historical factor. Trust, however, should not be mistaken for a feeling or sentiment. One does not need to love, or be affectionate toward the person or institution in which one trusts, one only needs the sensible expectation and assurance of a determined outcome from them.[1] At the same time, however, to develop a society on the paradigm of *Homo amans,* and to further develop the debate, one should ask what kind of expectation we should encourage in people, and what the foundations for such expectations should be.

[1] The fact that the paradigm of *Homo economicus* could impose itself as the explanatory paradigm of modern society, thus reinforcing the model of society to which it was connected, is proof that trust does not necessarily need love.

What, then, is the foundation of this sensible assurance? Why do we trust people and institutions? This chapter aims to analyze this fundamental requirement to develop any kind of society: the need for trust between persons and communities.

9.2 The Need for Trust, a Short History of the Concept

To be clarified and encouraged, the paradigm of *Homo amans* requires clarification of what trust is, and of what it means to trust someone. As Nullens and Van Nes have indicated, *Homo amans* needs to be founded on the three virtues of faith, hope, and love. A first tendency would be to subsume trust within the category of faith. In this sense, trust would be faith of a different order. After all, the technical definition of trust is the assured reliance of one character, ability, strength, or truth of someone or something. However, the act of trust, to be meaningful, has to rely on a sense of consistency possessed by the person (or institution/situation) in which we place our trust. We do not trust someone or something because of a future expectation, but because of the actions/events that have already happened. These allow us to build the sense of consistency and coherence we need to enter into a relation of trust. On a social level, the act of trust is possible because we all adhere to what Taylor has called a *social imaginary*.

As he explains in his work (Taylor 2004), we can understand a social imaginary as an epistemic structure through which human beings interpret their relations with, and within, their society. It is not only a simple scheme of relation, a collection of beliefs about the common life. It incorporates some sense of how we all fit together, both on a social and a normative plane. Through our social imaginary, we have a sense of how social things go and how should they go. This generates in us the perception of what steps are acceptable, and which ones, instead, go against social practice, both in a factual and normative way (Taylor 2004, pp. 25–6). The framework is something we are born into, it is a system in which we trust because it is imbued with a sense of coherence and consistency provided by its past. It is because things have been done in a certain way in the past that we feel compelled to keep the system going on as it has always been. It is because we engage, from the moment we are born, with related sets of values and institutions that we can perceive their history and draw on that past, which is part of our story, to build our sense of trust in them. Faith and trust, then, are certainly related, although it would be incorrect to subsume them within the same sphere of consciousness. If we espouse Taylor's theory of the *social imaginary,* it would be much more precise to say that trust is embedded within all the three virtues required to develop a paradigm of *Homo amans.*

Trust, then, is not only a necessary component of faith, but also of hope and love. We can say that all our relations require an underlying component of trust, to make sense both socially, ethically, and existentially. The necessity of a foundation of trust is something that, if we explore the history of the concept, has been evident since ancient times. Much more interesting, however, is to note how, in the classic tradition, the vocabulary for expressing *faith* was the same as the one used to express *trust*. In the Greco-Roman tradition, we lack a meaningful distinction between faith and trust at a conceptual/linguistic level, to the point that the same term (*pistis* in Greek and *fides* in Rome) were used in a multiplicity of instances to express different relations of trust or faith.

For examples, in the *Iliad* and *Odyssey* we see the appearance of the adjective *pistos* (Seidl 1952, pp. 21–32), especially in the form *pistos etairos* that indicates the trustworthy companion, usually the closest companions of the hero. Moreover, *pistos* also appears together with *xenia* in the context of ritualized friendships and hospitality, thus marking its centrality in the aristocratic ethos of ancient Greece. (Faraguna 2012) Another example can be found in Theognis. Being trustworthy was the quality that allowed the *aristos* to establish reciprocal relations of hospitality and friendship, thus marking their radical difference from the common people. *Pistis* was one of the fundamental qualities that made them *agatos*, better than the people of lower classes, *apistos*, who were unworthy of trust and were deceitful.

With the change of political order in the Greek *polis* and the establishment of democratic regimes, the concept of *pistis* also undergoes some etymological changes. As Faraguna tries to show us, the concept of *pistis* is made democratic. Its meaning transformed to indicate the fundamental prerequisite for the good functioning of society and its prosperity (Faraguna 2012, p. 363).

It becomes the fundamental attitude that makes every social activity possible. *Pistis*, in the Greek democratic stage, becomes the mutual trust and confidence that allows the citizens to undertake agreements in good faith and preserves the social stability of the community. Another useful source of information on this topic can be found in Angelica Taglia's (1998) work. In the context of Greek democracies, *Pistis* was related to *peitho*, the persuasion, as the fundamental pre-political quality that allowed any kind of agreement within the social body. If *pistis*, born from *peitho*, is the benevolent and rational consensus obtained through an act of persuasion, *peitho*, as the act in itself, is only possible and meaningful precisely because the good Greek citizen has a natural tendency to adopt *pistis*. Without *pistis*, any kind of agreement or act of persuasion becomes impossible and we regress to a state of *bia*, a state of violence. *Pistis,* therefore, not only indicated the process through which the democratic system of the polis could work properly, it also preserved its aristocratic, pre-political value. Precisely because the citizens of the polis were capable of *pistis*, could the *polis* keep itself united and function properly. In an ideal *polis*, *pistis* was the fundamental human feature that allowed any collective action (Taglia 1998, pp. 14–27).

In the Greek context, *pistis* was more similar to a form of knowledge – a form of awareness – than an act of abandonment. In Plato's *Laws*, *pistis* is described as the sensible acknowledgment, by the wise man, of the presence of a higher order in the *cosmos*, an order of which the *polis* is just a fraction. This rational acknowledgment would allow the wise man to guide his fellow citizens into the creation of a harmonious political order that would complement and emulate the higher order of the universe. It is the acknowledgment of, and submission to, a fundamental hypostasis that provides the existential background for everything that happens within the *cosmos,* and by consequence, would allow for the submission to the laws of the community (Taglia 1998, pp. 39–44).

It is a fundamental acknowledgment of the Greek worldview that allows the Greek citizen to make sense and find meaning in the web of social relations and institutions in which they were involved. The Greek citizen could submit to the laws of their city because they were aware that they represented, locally, a state of being affirmed throughout existence as whole. It was because things *were* in a certain way, that social actions *should have gone* in a certain way and hence, that things *made sense*.[2]

If we move our examination from the Greek context to the Roman concept of *fides*, we will see that the historical analysis of the idea becomes even more complex. The Roman concept of *fides* presented an enormous variety of fields of application spanning the categories of politics, morality, the divine sphere, and legal principles. Lombardi (1961), in his study on the Roman word-group of the term *fides,* described how it is impossible to determine one predominant meaning to ascribe to the constellation of contents referred by the concept.

However, a fundamental meaning of *fides* traced by Lombardi indicated the fundamental, practical virtue that allowed stable social relations within Roman society. Friendships, associations (*socii*), families, and the range of different Roman groups were sustained and sustainable because of the fundamental value of *fides* that allowed the single Roman citizen to navigate through the world with stable points of civil and social reference. In this sense, then, we see a similar scenario to the Greek *pistis* (Lombardi 1961, pp. 26–7). We see that faith is a social virtue inherent in human sociality and always connected to it. It is only because the single individual had the capacity to have faith that it was possible to establish meaningful social relations.

A similar interpretation is given by Freyburger (2009), in his work *Fides,* where he affirms that a fundamental meaning of *confiance* (trust) can be found in all the successive applications of the term, and it should, then, be considered equivalent, if not related, to the Greek *pistis*. Even more, says, Freyburger, we should consider the concept of trust in the Roman vocabulary as the fundamental basis that sustains all the other meanings of *fides* (Freyburger 2009, pp. 30–2). Building on this theory, we can affirm, then, that without this fundamental trust, we could not have all the successive acts of *fides* in the Roman sense. Pre-political trust was considered a necessity for any social act in Roman society.

The concept of faith/trust, independent of specific given contexts, seems to imply a relational value in the strong sense. It may be between two different people, between an institution and its members, or about the individual and the world/divine

[2]An example of how the law of the community must align, in a more general way, to universal laws, can be found in Sophocles' *Antigone.* In the play, Antigone wishes to bury his brother because of the unwritten laws of the world. While king Creon forbids it by virtue of his legal role as a king. It is true that king Creon had the legal right to order that the body of Polynices be left without burial; however, Antigone tries to remind him that there is a higher order of things to which the legal order of the polis should always conform.

sphere, but faith preserved the meaning of a relationship based on a form of awareness and legitimate expectation (the degree and mix of these two aspects changing according to the context). *Pistis* and *fides* denoted *trust* and *loyalty/promise*. The basis for this sense of *trust*, however, had to be something solid enough to give legitimization and sustenance to the acts of relationality in such societies. To borrow Taylor's vocabulary: what was the social imaginary that gave sustenance to the ancient forms of sociality?

At this stage, Jacob Taubes comes to our aid. In his work on Pauline theology, Taubes (1993) presents the argument that the different components of society in the Roman Empire all shared a common hypostasis, a sort of hidden conspiracy.[3] For Taubes, this common hypostasis was carried through in adherence to the *Law*, the *nomos*, the *ius*, as a foundational structure of all the different societies under the rule of Roman authority. It could be constituted specifically to suit the needs and language of a specific group (thus, for Taubes, we had a Hellenistic, Roman, and Jewish version) but all shared a foundational character through which the different groups could find a common ground of agreement. For Taubes, this is one of the most important reasons that Judaism, despite refusing to recognize the divine figure of the emperor, was still considered as *religio licita* and allowed to exist. It shared with Roman society the foundational acknowledgment of the *nomos* as hypostasis. Thus, it was still possible to integrate it within the social structure of the empire (Taubes 1993, pp. 23–5).

In Taubes' presentation of the *nomos* as the fundamental hypostasis of the Roman Empire, we are seeing the *socio-ontological character* of the relation of trust and the strong socio-existential character of the *social imaginary* described by Taylor.

According to Taubes, in fact, we should not interpret the *law* just as a legal instrument, but as a cultural/ontological awareness. It was because existence was organized in a certain way, that the authority of the city, or of the empire, made sense. It was, then, not just a legal agreement, but also an ontological understanding of the world that Romans and Greeks shared, and that Judaism, was at least not willing to call into question. We are not talking about a specific source of value, but of a more implicit acknowledgment of a whole structure of existence. In this sense, the relationship of trust always refers to a metaphysical hypostasis, a sense of implicit order in which the things that have value find their own position and structure.

With the advent of Christianity, the concept of faith began to be distinguished from the concept of trust and was used to describe only *religious* faith. On this topic, in her short work on the medieval concept of *fides*, Weijers (1977) has demonstrated how the Christian concept of faith was the result of two different processes that affected the related word-group. First, there was the expansion of the use of *fides* as it was developed within the *Christian faith*. Alongside this first process, Weijers assumes a second development. The same universal extension of the authorized use of *fides* as *Christian faith* caused the gradual decline of other meanings of the word.

[3] I am not using the term *conspiracy* in a negative sense, but in the sense of hidden or silent agreement between the parties involved.

At a time when *fides* was primarily associated with Christian faith, the word probably grew less apt for designating quite different concepts.

Yet, the features presented above were not relinquished. The Christian individual retained a sense of trust in the institutions around him (the church, the king, etc…) because of his social/cultural framework. Of course, such frameworks were connected to the eschatological promise of the final salvation in a universal sense and, on a particular level, the Christian was enveloped in various relationships of *fidelitas* and *confidentia* that guaranteed respect of the promises made in his social context. All these relations made sense because they were connected and structured through the divine order of the universe that was emulated, on an immanent level, by the divine authority of kings, popes, and the nobility. In this sense, then, while the concept of *faith* became more and more connected to the religious sphere of human life, the need remained for a more fundamental concept of *trust* connected to a *sense of the world*, an ontology, if we want, that worked as the foundational binding of sociality and relationality.

9.3 Trust, Social Imaginaries and the Origin of Personhood

To be *Homo amans* we have to develop a model of society in which we evaluate human beings, not in their capacity to take rational economic decisions that aim to maximize their profit, but in their capacity to develop relationships and social bonds, together with their capacity to find meaning and seek meaning in their own life. The *amans* adjective can only have a positive[4] meaning in the extent to which this love is directed toward other human beings, not just towards the activities and interests of an individual. As Nullens and Van Nes have argued in their essay, the *Homo amans* is found at the crossroads between hope, faith, and love. Only when we are able to develop a concept of society and of human being that envelops these three virtues, can we meaningfully propose a functioning moral framework and ask its implementation in society.

However, to be able to do so we should discard the concept of *individual*, assumed within the concept of *Homo economicus* and, instead take into account the concept of *person*. The difference, in adopting this conceptual stance, is radical. When we define a human being as an *individual*, we are assuming such a human being in its own *separateness* from the other: as a lonely monad within a cosmos that is only mechanically and instrumentally related to it. The paradigm of the *Homo economicus* can work with such an assumption only because it assumes that all of human relations have a utilitarian and instrumentalist nature, that a human being undertakes activities and relationships with other human beings only to gain some measure of benefit, be it pleasure or material wealth. Instead, when we take into account the being *person* of a human being, we assume the fact that this person is

[4] In the sense of being descriptive, but also in the sense of being morally right.

always immersed in a web of relations that cannot be reduced just to instrumental economic calculations. A *person* is always socially, culturally, and historically situated; what we are as persons is the fruit of our own experiences and relationships with the human beings around us. It is always the result not only of our own actions, but also the result of the actions of other people (and of the cultural influence of society) on us. It is certainly not an easy, or comfortable process. A person may, through their own free will and capacity of self-analysis, be at odds with the society or the people around him, but this would still not deny the influences that are exercised by these cultural factors, instead, it is a re-affirmation of such influence.

In this sense, in his work on Hegel (Taylor 1975, 1979), Charles Taylor has already affirmed that, when we are talking about a *person,* we are talking about a culturally and historically situated phenomenon. Taylor describes how, for Hegel, the fulfilment of morality is reached when society reaches a superior state of *Sittlichkeit.* Taylor focuses on the fact that, when we discuss human identity, we always discuss a culturally situated phenomenon. We can think about a single individual in abstraction from his community only as an organism, but when we develop thoughts about a human being, we also think about related sets of ways to experience the world, which are culturally produced and that form his identity. *What we are as human beings*, Taylor says, *we are only in a cultural community* (Taylor 1979, pp. 85–7).

In Hegel, the concept of *Sittlichkeit* indicates the moral obligations we possess toward an ongoing community of which we are members. The *Sittlichkeit* refers to a common life that already exists. It also contributes to the constitution of the *sittlich*[5] of an individual. It is by virtue of this ethical order being an ongoing affair that the individual possesses these obligations. The fulfilment of these obligations is what sustains the ethical order and maintains its existence. Therefore, this ethical order is different from *Moralität*, in which the individual has an obligation to realize something which does not exist, that may even be in contrast with the existing moral order. The obligations provided by *moralität* bind the individual not by virtue of being part of a larger community, but as an individual and rational will (Hegel 1991, p. 193). For Hegel, *Sittlichkeit*, the world of common customs or shared life, is extremely important for the development of an ethic of duty, a philosophical trait

[5] With the term *Sittlich,* we mean the ethicality of the single individual. For a discussion of the Hegelian *Sittlichkeit* see: Ferrarin (2001, pp. 325–72). Also, Singer (1983, pp. 24–44). Particularly interesting is Singer's use of Hegelian categories in his criticism of the principles of the neo-liberal economy.

that Taylor has inherited. The *Ethos* of the individual has its source in custom.[6] For this reason, custom is described by Hegel as a *zweite Natur*, a second nature that permeates the purely natural will and creates the substance of the ethical mind. This train of thought is vital for the development of a paradigm of *Homo amans* as it re-affirms the fact that values, and the good, can be objectively identified outside of the subjectivity of a single individual. In the development of liberalism, which led to the development of the *Homo economicus* paradigm, something has value only insofar as it belongs to someone – it has no universal meaning or significance. Its own meter of judgment is exclusively what is or could be of benefit to its owner. In the *Homo economicus* paradigm, economic theory does not need a theory of ethics and value outside of itself; it is, in itself, a value-theory, although an extremely dysfunctional one. To affirm the paradigm of *Homo amans* means to go against this cultural trend. In this sense, if we affirm that the human-that-loves is found at the crossroads between hope, faith, and love, then this human being is not a lonely component, abstracted from their own community; it is immersed within it and has to recognize a good outside of themself, something that can describe as *objectively good*, to be in a meaningful relation with their fellow citizens and neighbors. In this sense, then, Taylor's connection of the sense of the self with the moral framework is well placed.

In his philosophical work, Taylor has discussed how this relationship influences the formation of our own identity, and he focuses especially on the historical process that allowed the development of the *modern* western identity (Taylor 2001). In his work, Taylor focuses on how the modern concept of identity has reached its present form and what its social function is in western civilization. He affirms that the concept of self is strictly intertwined with the concept of morality (Taylor 2001, p. 3).[7] Our identity is strictly connected with the social background that surrounds us, our framework. It involves the problems of our *strong evaluations*, namely, the

---

[6] This because the *ethos*, the ethical consciousness, can be realized only in the social life and find its highest objective, in Hegel's philosophy, in the state system. Hegel aims to criticize the Kantian concept of individual morality, as it considers only the *moral intention*, not the actual reality of moral facts, creating a conflict between *being* and *have-to-be*, making morality like a duel in front of a mirror, in which the existence of the person is always in conflict with a tyrannical duty imposed by abstract rationality. Against this interpretation, Hegel re-affirms the importance of an ethics developed in the here and now, through the interaction of the person with the ethicality of its own community. Ethics, therefore, *can* be conflictual, but can also a much more pacific process of negotiating personal ethics through the ethos of the community. For this reason, Hegel denies that there is a natural law, a law that is pre-existing in respect to the laws set forth by the state. According to Hegel, morality is not a personal matter; it is not a relationship with an absolute law nor a relationship with a Destiny. Humans can achieve an ethical consciousness only through the dialectical process that starts in the category of the *family*, find its antithesis in *civil society* and is fully realized in the *state*, as *synthesis*. According to Hegel, we reach ethical achievements only through social phenomena.

[7] Taylor tries to understand how western modern civilization achieved its peculiar concept of the *self* and its (allegedly) unique features. He analyzes three great fundamental sources as the foundation of modern self-conscience: the first is the modern inwardness (sense of ourselves as beings with inner depths), the second is the affirmation of ordinary life and the third is the expressivist notion of nature as an inner moral source.

fact that we engage in moral dilemmas in order to define our own identities. For Taylor, morality has two facets. An instinctive one, which is tied to our spontaneous feelings of right and wrong, and a second facet tied to a given *ontology of the human*. An important strand of modern consciousness has tried to diminish the ties that morality has with this second facet: mainly because of the risks involved in discussing the characteristics of this ontology of the human that history has presented to us. Taylor aims to criticize the naturalistic and secular assumption that it is possible to create a set of moral values based only on universal assumptions, abstracted from a community of reference. For Taylor, instead, it is impossible to create morality without a social framework. In addition, our strong evaluations are deeply connected with a moral source, or constitutive good, that is, a center of value which receives the greatest importance in our framework and is considered as the ultimate source of our moral reasoning (Taylor 2001, pp. 28–32).

As Abbey (2004) has argued, Charles Taylor is attempting to open up a non-anthropocentric perspective on the good, to allow us to see the *sovereignty of good* over the moral agent. In moving the philosophical argument in this direction, Taylor's philosophy aims to be explicitly a retrieval of this non-anthropocentric perspective that philosophy, since the Enlightenment, has been motivated to occlude. To achieve this outcome, Taylor has to postulate, in my opinion correctly, a strong connection between the source of moral good and the individual identity connected to it.

At this stage, we can return to Taylor's concept of social imaginary as a foundation for building the necessary trust to create a coherent and functioning society. I have referred to this concept of social imaginary several times in the previous pages. With this concept, to which Taylor will dedicate a whole work (Taylor 2004), he indicates something much more broad and deeper than just an intellectual or mental scheme. A social imaginary is more like a common framework or reference for explaining and justifying social existence. It is different from a social theory, according to Taylor, because of three fundamental features:

1. it is not used to explain social realities; it is used, instead, to *imagine* social surroundings. It does not necessarily work through theoretical categories, instead it relies also on images stories and legends that are relevant to the community. It relies then, equally on feelings and sentiments as much as on intellectual faculties.
2. A theory is, usually, the field of a restricted circle of experts. A social imaginary, instead, is available to all members of the community. It is shared by all the persons belonging to the same society.
3. A social imaginary is tied to common sense more than to complex knowledge. It instils, within the community, a wider sense of legitimacy for social practices and institutions; it allows for customs, traditions, and institutions to *make sense* within a community (Taylor 2004, pp. 23–7).

A social imaginary, however, is never a simple thing. Instead, it reveals various levels of complexity. It involves a sense of normal and legitimate expectation around our own social actions and the actions of the people that participate in society along with us. It provides a sense of normalcy and meaning on how we all fit together in our common practices, both at a factual and at a normative level. Not only, then, does it make sense of our immediate particular practices, it also offers a wider metaphysical or moral background through which we make sense of how we stand in relation to each other, how we relate to each other and with other groups.

The relationship between this background and our practices is not one-sided. A social imaginary is not a cultural, untouchable, authority that prescribes all of our actions. Instead, it is a framework of reference that help us to make sense of our relations and actions towards other human beings. However, such understanding, while influencing our actions, is also is also influenced and reinforced (or questioned) by the actions themselves.

It can be likened, as Descombes (1994) implies, although not referring directly to the concept of social imaginary, to Hegel's *objective spirit*. According to Descombes, Taylor retains a sort of positivist Hegelianism, a baggage of Hegelian concepts freed from their theological/ontological value and now used as sociological instruments. The fundamental assumption behind Taylor's Hegelian interpretation of social events is that social life is not reducible to the necessities of common life, but that it has a meaning. The individuals that partake in any social life derive a fundamental something, a meaningfulness, from it. The problem, then, would be to understand properly the effective social reality of this meaningfulness, defined by Descombes as the objective spirit of a society, in a Hegelian sense. He affirms that to understand Taylor's philosophical proposal correctly, we must interpret this concept of objective spirit as *a sharable state of mind or a rule to follow*. That is, a condition for the social exercise of intelligent activity, a condition to which individuals would be subject in a manner that does not require their expressed consent. According to Descombes, Taylor's strategy is twofold, he shows how any social practice presupposes common (as opposed to merely shared) meaning. In addition, he argues that institutions express the ideas and meanings mentioned that resemble the Hegelian objective spirit. The functions of institutions, therefore, can be compared, to those of a language (Descombes 1994, pp. 97–106). We could interpret the concept of social imaginary as the full, conceptual, inheritance of the Hegelian concept of *objective spirit* and its complete assimilation in Taylor's social theory, although devoid of any ontological cosmic reference to the absolute spirit. The social imaginary, then, would an *immanent* objective spirit, a framework of reference that does not need, necessarily, a connection with an absolute being; although many social imaginaries in western history did rely on this connection.[8]

The social imaginary can be described as one of the cultural-ontological foundations of trust. We can develop a sense of trust in the institutions and traditions in our surroundings because, as I argued in the previous pages, we can base our trust on a

[8] The topic of debate, at this point, would be to evaluate the eventual *success* or lack of it of such social imaginaries. Did social imaginaries connected to a spiritual source achieve a stable and just society more successfully than those social imaginaries that did not? This chapter, obviously, does not aim to answer this question, or even debate it, but the question is left here to stimulate the reader's thoughts.

sense of consistency. The social imaginary is the foundation on which this sense of consistency is built. Therefore, if the *Homo amans* can be so only socially, that is, within a society and a set of shared values with his community of reference, then we need to investigate how we can structure a new social imaginary on which the relation of trust between persons and between persons and institutions, within a community, can be born and developed. It is only because we trust other human beings that we can entertain them in social relations. It is only because we start with a fundamental attitude of trust towards our neighbors, that we do not fear to relate with them and have relationships with other human beings. It is vital, then, to provide a strong sense of consistency and meaning on which we can build such trust and foster it in our own communities.

9.4 Trust, Faith and *Homo Amans*, the Need for a New Social Imaginary

In the Reith Lectures of 2002, philosopher Onora O'Neill admitted that our society is facing a crisis of trust. I believe it is not hard to find evidence that confirms this in our current social landscape. The crisis of trust does not involve just the loss of legitimacy and the increase of suspicion with which citizens look upon their governing institutions. It involves the whole of a society that is becoming increasingly fractured by more and more restricting boundaries, tied by subjective identities and the wishes of restricted groups. Today, in western societies, we witness the increasing impossibility of the citizenry as a whole standing together behind a common position, political or moral.

It becomes immediately clear that, clear though the concept may be, the concrete reality of the act of trust cannot be so easily identified. So far, I have described trust as the necessary foundation for building any successive relational act. In this sense, love, hope, and faith would be possible only when trust has been built into a relationship.

However, when we want to examine the concrete relationship between these concepts (and in so doing, how they reveal themselves in human action and in social/cultural reality), the phenomenon appears much less clear. It may well be a chicken or egg dilemma: does sociality starts with trust (that then allows successive relational acts that foster the virtues of hope, faith, and love) or are those virtues practiced on a gradual scale that can then give birth to social customs and wider relational forms?

The only thing we can be sure of is that we are born when the social game has already started and is ongoing. Our personal social interactions may well start with our birth, but society (and sociality) is already in progress when we make our appearance in the play. In this sense, it may be in our more immediate interest to understand the ongoing rules of meaningful social interaction, rather than focus on the origin of said interaction.

The ongoing rule of this game, as we have assumed at the beginning of this essay and building on Taylor's work, is that a social paradigm is built on a social imaginary. I believe the best definition of social imaginary, as suggested by Taylor, would be that of *epistemic structure*. In *A Secular Age,* Taylor further expands the concept by also describing its role in developing the modern, scientific and liberal social imaginaries. It was the transformation of the social imaginary that allowed the birth of modernity. According to Taylor, the processes involved in the transformation of social imaginary are not necessarily linear and do not need, at least at the moment of their origin, institutional support. A social imaginary can start as a set of claims belonging to a restricted niche group and then expand to embrace the whole community. This is what happened in the modern age, for example, with the theories of Locke and Grotius. Thanks to Locke's philosophy of nature and Grotius' view of normative order, modern society acquired, slowly but steadily, the sensibility that society exists for the mutual benefit of the individuals and to protect their rights. A new picture of society was, thus, developed, one in which individuals come together to form a political entity against certain pre-existing moral backgrounds and with particular ends in view. In modernity, the moral background was one of natural rights, where people already have certain moral obligations toward each other, while the ends sought were certain common benefits, of which security was the most important. In the specific case of modernity, the new social structure – with its underlying concept of moral order – influenced the development of modern society along three axes. First, in extension – starting from a restricted niche of thinkers and philosophers, it influenced the social discourse in other niches until it encompassed the whole of western society. Second, in intensity – the demands people made on society became more complex and ramified. And lastly, in the demands society itself made on the people – while making our demands, it is incumbent on us to take some kind of action or attitude as a counterpart, as a duty. These three axes of modification also involved a separation of the modern moral order from any kind of connection to a transcendent source of good. The pre-modern understandings of moral order (egalitarian, such as the law of the people, or hierarchical, inspired from the platonic/Aristotelian philosophy) were connected to a transcendent order of the cosmos, such that a breach of the law was equivalent to a breach of the order of the cosmos itself. According to Taylor, the modern moral order had no such ontic or cosmic reference, it was an order made for the here and now (Taylor 2007, pp. 4–15).[9]

It is within this enormous transformation of social imaginary that Taylor identifies three, very specific, forms of social self-understanding as social imaginaries born from Locke's and Grotius' theories of moral order. The first one has been *Economy*, which came to be considered as an objectified reality. Taylor finds the greatest example of this new development in Adam Smith's theory of the *invisible*

[9] The difference is a great one, while the previous concept of moral order stated that the individual is complementary to the whole, so that the first task of the individual is to work to preserve the community, with the modern concept of people and moral order, the relationship is reversed. It is now the individual that should be preserved, and the purpose of the society is to guarantee his safety.

hand. Where economy becomes the fundamental model of society,[10] not only as a metaphor, but also as the dominant end of human activity.

The second social imaginary was the public sphere. This concept indicates not only the official sphere of government, but communication in society as a whole. The public sphere is a common space in which members of society meet through a variety of media. In addition, communication is not only present between members of society, but also between media themselves. The public sphere is so important that, even in conditions where it is controlled or abolished, its existence is still faked to retain control over the population. We have come to consider this space as distinct from the political space, and, at the same time, a benchmark of legitimacy for the political authority (Taylor 2007, pp. 86–99).[11]

The final social imaginary has been popular sovereignty. The two great revolutions of the eighteenth century (French and American) created the conditions for the interplay of social imaginaries, new and traditional, that helped determine their respective courses and culminated with the affirmation of popular sovereignty. According to Taylor, revolutionary brutality made it possible for ideologies that found support only in minor circles (such as the republican theory of Rousseau), to spread among the people. This generated the development of the new social imaginary in which the legitimization of the power resides in the population (Taylor 2007, pp. 109–41). In this way, we shifted from a vertical society to a horizontal society.[12]

To build a society on the paradigm of *Homo amans,* then, we should, with plausibility, assume that western society has to go through the same, painful, process of transformation. The plight of our contemporary society, and the social crises it is currently facing, can no longer be addressed through the modern liberal presuppositions of an absolute individual, completely independent and separate from other human beings and from its societies of reference. It is born out of a cultural assumption that spatial and temporal separations are an absolute that has to be taken for granted. That our physical separateness from our neighbors translates into an

[10] Economy was obviously linked with the self-understanding of polite civilizations as grounded in a commercial society. However, the eighteenth century adds an appreciation of the way human life is designed to produce mutual benefit. Emphasis is put on the *invisible hand* factor. With this, Taylor means the theory in which we are supposed to be *programmed* to commit to specific actions and attitudes that systematically have beneficial results for the general happiness. Adam Smith, in the *Wealth of Nations*, provide us with the better example of this mechanism. This new understanding of providence is already evident in Locke's formulation of natural law theory in the *Second Treatise*; we can see how much importance the economic dimension is taking on in this new notion of order. The two main goals of an organized society become, therefore, security and economic prosperity. This leads to a study of economics as an objectified reality with its laws and mechanisms, as an object of *science*; but this also determines the complete independence of economy from the political plane.

[11] Taylor describe the public sphere as a *meta-topical common space*; a topical common space is a space where people come together in a common act of focus for whatever purpose (a ritual, a conversation, the celebration of a major event, etc…). A meta-topical common space transcends such topical spaces; it knits together a plurality of such spaces into one larger space of non-assembly.

[12] Taylor examines the shift that led to a society in which the order was guaranteed by a transcendental order, to a society in which the order is achieved by common action, as in the secular age.

impossibility of developing a relationship with them, that it is impossible to build a bridge over such division; or that, maybe, this bridge has always existed, we have just conveniently ignored it to avoid the responsibility it brings with it. Every cultural framework always develops a metaphysical image of the world, a social imaginary, which helps society to structure its own political and social institutions. The ontology of the world goes hand in hand with what a society consider acceptable as political/ethical organization. In this sense, then, if we wish to build a society on the paradigm of *Homo amans* and re-build a sense of trust within our own communities, we cannot simply acknowledge that faith, hope, and love can be good virtues. We have to find the courage to affirm their objective goodness, that they can be good virtues to be cultivated by all who have a stake in our society. We need to reclaim, then, a social imaginary that can be a stable foundation for the *Homo amans.*

References

Abbey, R. 2004. *Charles Taylor*. Cambridge: Cambridge University Press.

Descombes, V. 1994. Is There an Objective Spirit? In *Philosophy in an Age of Pluralism: The Philosophy of Charles Taylor in Question*, ed. J. Tully, 96–118. Cambridge: Cambridge University Press.

Faraguna, M. 2012. *Pistis* and *Apistia*: Aspects of the Development of Social and Economic Relations in Classical Greece. *Mediterraneo Antico*, *15*(1–2), 355–374.

Ferrarin, A. 2001. *Hegel and Aristotle*. Cambridge: Cambridge University Press.

Fleming, P. 2017. *The Death of Homo Economicus: Work, Debt and the Myth of Endless Accumulation*. London: Pluto Press.

Freyburger, G. 2009. *Fides: Étude sémantique et religieuse depuis les origins jusqu'à l'époque augustéenne*. Paris: Les Belles Lettres.

Grewal, D.S. 2016. The Political Theology of Laissez-Faire: From *Philia* to Self-Love. *Political Theology* 17 (5): 417–433.

Hegel, G.W.F. 1991. *Elements of the Philosophy of Right*. Transl. H.B. Nisbet. Cambridge: Cambridge University Press.

Lombardi, L. 1961. *Dalla Fides alla Bona Fides*. Milan: Giuffré.

Mill, J.S. 1844. *Essays on Some Unsettled Questions of Political Economy*. London: Parker.

Nelson, R.H. 2001. *Economics as Religion: From Samuelson to Chicago and Beyond*. State College: Pennsylvania State University Press.

Seidl, E. 1952. *Pistis in der griechischen Literatur bis zur Zeit der Peripatos*. PhD diss. University of Innsbruck.

Singer, P. 1983. *Hegel*. Oxford: Oxford University Press.

Taglia, A. 1998. *Il Concetto di Pistis in Platone*. Florence: Le Lettere.

Taubes, J. 1993. *The Political Theology of Paul*. Transl. D. Hollander. Stanford: Stanford University Press.

Taylor, C. 1975. *Hegel*. Cambridge: Cambridge University Press.

———. 1979. *Hegel and Modern Society*. London: Cambridge University Press.

———. 2001. *Sources of The Self: The Making of Modern Identity*. Cambridge, MA: Harvard University Press.

———. 2004. *Modern Social Imaginaries*. London: Duke University Press.

———. 2007. *A Secular Age*. London: Belknap Press.

Weijers, Olga. 1977. Some Notes on *Fides* and Related Words. *Medieval Latin, Archivum Latinitatis medii aevi* 40: 77–102.

Chapter 10
Homo Amans in the Economy: A Utopia?

Hendrik Opdebeeck

Abstract A *Homo amans* oriented transition economy is not a utopia. In essence, the transitional economy we so urgently need today concretely involves assigning an inter-cultural and inter-religious interpretation to responsibility within the economy. This means providing a response (transition) to social-economic questions based on a form of trust (transcendence). Effectively, this means responding to a form of trust or admiration that has been received. It involves concrete attitudes emerging from reasonable rationality within the economy. An economy in which the *Homo amans* takes the *Homo economicus* by the hand, becomes, step by step, a responsible economy. In its turn, a responsible economy corresponds to the ethics of virtue, which connects the rational to the reasonable. As a virtue, responsibility is that positive characteristic of trust that focuses on providing the proper response to the social-economic questions that we encounter. In this chapter we therefore call for concrete, *here-and-now* economic changes throughout the world. Instead of a *u-topia* or a *dys-topia* we can witness today the emergence of what we refer to as a '*u-globia*'. It therefore does not involve a polarization between *Homo economicus* and *Homo amans*, or between the economy and ethics.

10.1 Meaningfulness and Reasonableness Behind the Quest to Define and Understand the Need for Love Within an Economic Context

Dictionaries generally formulate meaningfulness in terms that involve us "assigning meaning to something." At the heart of the economy is the quest to satisfy our needs using the scarce resources available. If we consider this in the light of meaningfulness, the economy essentially boils down to *assigning meaning* to the fulfilment of needs. Compare this with Mill's definition of *Homo economicus* in the discussion paper (Nullens and Van Nes, Chap. 2, p. 10, this volume): "a being who desires

H. Opdebeeck (✉)
Universiteit Antwerpen, Antwerp, Belgium
e-mail: hendrik.opdebeeck@uantwerpen.be

J. van Nes et al. (eds.), *Relational Anthropology for Contemporary Economics*, Ethical Economy 61, https://doi.org/10.1007/978-3-030-84690-9_10

wealth, and who is capable of judging of the comparative efficacy of means for obtaining that end".

For the average citizen or business manager, however, to speak of meaningfulness in relation to the economy readily calls to mind the involvement of ethics. On many occasions during recent decades we have seen entrepreneurs make cheap use (or abuse) of ethical values. For example, consider the "Dieselgate" scandal at *Volkswagen,* and *Starbucks* that sells its "fair trade" coffee while evading taxes. The marriage of convenience between the economy and ethics is not evident. Both the economy and ethics proceed from rationality, as well as from reasonableness – a concept that is all too frequently confused with rationality. Both the economy and ethics can be elaborated from an exclusively intellectual judgment (known as rationality), as well as from an inclusive human judgment (known as reasonableness). Rationality approaches labor, technology, and nature from an exclusively intellectual perspective. The economy thus entails a risk of extremes, as with the elaboration of a free market economy or a communist economy which could theoretically be rationally justified purely in terms of freedom and equality, respectively. In ethics, pure rationality can lead to an exclusively materialistic ethic or to an ethics of utility: acting in order to acquire the greatest possible material comfort or utility, respectively. The perspective of reasonableness, however, offers a different standpoint from which to consider labor, technology, and nature. This perspective of a more human judgment, which also allows for feelings like fear, hope, empathy, and love, is a standpoint that goes beyond an exclusive rationality. For example, it could bring us to a social or ecological economy, or to an ethics of care or happiness. In the discussion paper by Nullens and Van Nes in this volume, it is interesting to read how behavioral economists, together with neuroscientists, today insist more and more on the importance of this reasonableness.

Both the economy and ethics can thus proceed along paths that either are or are not laudable from a humane perspective. The solution thus cannot simply be to adopt an ethical approach to problems arising in the economy. Moreover, it means that both the economy and ethics can evolve into either dystopia (in which everything will backfire) or utopia (which is allegedly not feasible). Today all over the world we hear people warning of the risks of a so called neo-liberal economic dystopia, with negative outcomes such as the climate crisis, burnout phenomena, financial disruptions, and excessively unequal income distributions. Another common interpretation equates an ethics of happiness with utopia (for example, as translated into Gross National Happiness in Bhutan).

However, as noted by, for instance, Stephen Toulmin (2001), both the economy and ethics originally emerged from within a broad sense of reasonableness such as that of Aristotle. With regard to progress, scholars up until the Enlightenment also called for moral recovery. The reasonable ethics underlying the economy would nevertheless degrade into the ever more dominant ethics of rational utility proposed by Jeremy Bentham. This occurred along with the breakthrough of the economic sciences in the transition from the eighteenth to the nineteenth century. As proposed today by Martha Nussbaum, however, one path that could bridge this tension between rationality and reasonableness might indeed involve the acknowledgement of human feelings. From the perspective of reasonableness, the identification of emotions, which transcend exclusive rationality by definition, can also generate knowledge concerning what is important to our actions – and, more specific to our topic, economic action. Think of current altruistic leadership theories such as servant leadership, as mentioned in the discussion paper by Nullens and Van Nes.

It is important to rediscover that emotions like fear and suffering, but also hope and desire, have been shown to have played at least some role in the foundation of the gradually emerging economy, as well as within the realm of ethics. On the one hand, consider the emergence of welfare economics, arising from the fear of not or never having enough, and the ethics of care, with its view to transcending feelings of suffering. On the other hand, consider the economics of well-being and the ethics of happiness, which express such feelings as hope and desire. One could even imagine that economic scarcity (the lack of resources with which to satisfy our needs) – the very heart of economics – arises from emotions. More specifically, scarcity emerges from both our fear of never having enough and our desire and hope of satisfying our ever-increasing desires. Our economic scarcity, or our lack, thus emerges from our fears concerning our desire for food and clothing, as well as from our desire for money (as argued by Locke) and for private property (as referred to by Rousseau 1755) and last but not least, from our fear of not being seen, or our endless desire to be loved (as discussed by René Girard 1978). The origin of the economy, you could say, is our endless need to be loved. This is expressed by feelings like fear and hope. The *Homo amans* within an economic context, started thus as a *Homo economicus* looking forward for recognition, for love.

10.2 Justice and the Natural Predisposition to Love

What could be a feasible principle for spanning the described tension between dystopia and utopia, or between rationality and reasonableness? Since the beginning of philosophy, the concept of justice has offered a solution in this regard. Justice is a virtue. It essentially consists of granting to others that to which they are entitled in order to survive. Also, Nullens and Van Nes in their discussion paper insist, with Christian Smith, that virtues are important. In the description of the virtue of justice, we can recognize the rational judgement that, if we rationally want to avoid dystopia in society, one arrives at the notion that each person has the *right* to survive. Just as plausibly, however, in justice we can recognize the reasonable judgment – which is connected to our feelings – according to which we must thus *grant* this to the other, if the human right to survive is not to become a utopia. Here *Homo amans* comes to the fore.

Like Joseph Torchia in the discussion paper by Nullens and Van Nes, the twentieth-century French personalist Ricoeur (1990) arrives at this point. Proceeding from his assumption of free human individuals, Ricoeur states that individuals are able to achieve full success in their freedom and attempts to be happy, only through a natural predisposition to love. It is through encounters with other people that an individual becomes a person. Each time, we do indeed feel called to respond to the invitations or challenges of the other – whether the other is our partner, an employee, a refugee, or that other who is regarded as strange, like nature around us. The desire to articulate freedom is also recognized in the other. Freedom should thus emerge from intersubjectivity, from the relational. However, according to Ricoeur, this should clearly be understood as an "option" with respect for the other (whether person or nature) an act of granting to the other. We know that we cannot live decently unless we promote that which is unique in ourselves and in others. This option does mean (compare with the view of Dennis Krebs expressed in the discussion paper by Nullens and Van Nes) that I must choose to restrict myself to some extent, in the sense of restricting my natural urge to see everything as an object of my endeavors. One aspect that is of fundamental importance in this regard is that Ricoeur opens this intersubjectivity to the entire world. Ricoeur thus rejects an individualistic ethics, as a human being is not merely an individual, but is rather constituted as a person, and this in the various layers of the "we," anchored within the whole of such entities as economic structures and institutions.

Since time immemorial, people have adopted two possible criteria for the concrete realization of this justice or granting to others that to which they are entitled in order to survive. We elaborate this justice either by emphasizing "to each according to his or her merits" or by focussing on "to each according to his or her needs." If we attempt to realize justice through the principle of "to each according to merit," the market takes center stage. If we attempt to realise justice through the principle of "to each according to need," however, the government takes center stage. With the market, we risk more individualism and inequality. With the government, we tend more towards collectivism and an equality that might be too strict. An excessive impact of the market within society is currently confronting us with the utopia of the free market, which ultimately risks transforming into a dystopia. We need only consider the climate crisis, burnout phenomena, and excessively unequal income distributions. When excessive place is reserved for the government in utopian and unaffordable plans, this also ultimately results in dystopia. It is therefore no coincidence that Joseph Amato (2002) describes a personalistic economist as a person who, out of respect for the human person, seeks to safeguard human beings from the consequences of such extreme individualism as well as from those of extreme collectivism.

Given the risk and the reality of all these excessively utopian and dystopian effects, along with the failure of the alliance between the market and the government, it looks like it is now up to the citizen to take the lead within our society. Consider the ideas of young people throughout the world who are taking to the streets to protest about climate change, or what we call the "yellow vests" who are challenging economic injustice in France and elsewhere. Not to forget the rise in the percentage of voters during the last European elections. It might refer to citizens attempting (in a personalistic way) to develop their own (economic) freedom but however in solidarity with others and the planet in search for adapted economic institutes: what we call *an economy in transition*. This means acting no longer rather as egocentric individuals (as in the pure *Homo economicus*) but at least as human persons (as in *Homo amans*). Only in such a circumstance can we speak of citizens who consider that – economically – everyone is of equal *value* with regard to our common lack of food, warmth, and recognition. It appears that the floor belongs to *Homo amans:* the human as an involved person expressed in compassion, love, and hope, rather than only as an egocentric individual or *Homo economicus*.

10.3 Factors that Encourage the Promotion of *Homo Amans* in the Economy

Which points of departure do we need to develop if we want to promote *Homo amans* in the economy?

10.3.1 Responsible, as in Responsible Economics

First of all, we can no longer consider data such as nature, labor, technology and, last but not least, our so-called infinite needs as neutral data that we can just use in our economic models. We discover that this cluster of data happens to contain the most important factors that cause the economy to degenerate into dystopia. Starting with compassion we can transform this cluster of data into a *cluster of responsibility*.

There is thus increasing talk of what one calls *Responsible Economics*, or a responsible economy. With regard to the ecosystem, labor, technology, as well as our infinite needs, one no longer escapes one's responsibility. The worldwide CSR (Corporate Social Responsibility) approach in the economy also illustrates this abundantly.

10.3.2 Inter-relational, as in the Social Economy

A result of this cluster of responsibility, which is receiving attention from the perspective of *Homo amans*, is that there is a greater emphasis on the inter-personal, the *inter-human*, than on individualism. The satisfaction of fundamental human needs – for respect and self-development – depends primarily on the quality of the inter-human relationships concerned. Only by way of a qualitatively rich personal relationship with the other do you encounter human needs at a deeper level. Whereas in the present economy, competition is steadily increased, the satisfaction of essential human needs demands co-operation and solidarity with the other. The other can be a colleague or client, a patient, the poor, a foreigner, the disabled, and so on. The *Social Economy* attempts to convert this into practice.

10.3.3 Enough, as in the Circular Economy

Subsequently, the choice for a *Homo amans* attitude in the economy calls the infinitude of human needs and desires into question. It is important to recommend a limit, a *finitude*, to human needs, if only for the sake of yet another element of the aforementioned cluster of responsibility, to wit, the environment. Thus, we will talk about *an economy of enough*, rather than our dystopian economy of dissatisfaction.

This is reflected in what we call a *Circular Economy*. Central to a circular economy is the prevention of the exhaustion of scarce resources, the recycling of waste, and the use of energy sources such as the wind and the sun. Actual applications include, among others, *Cradle-to-Cradle* projects, in which one produces on the basis of components that can be reused after their cycle of life has run out. A more radical form of a circular economy is what one calls an *Economy of Frugality* (Bouckaert et al. 2008). Here, far more than in a circular economy, moderation, temperance, is paramount.

10.3.4 Balanced, as in the Happiness Economy

Furthermore, the distinction in the economy between the means (such as labor or technology) and the ends that must be achieved (profit, for example) has to be criticized because this distinction detracts from our respect for the other. To receive the other as they are cannot be reconciled with using them as a means towards an end. On the contrary, in a sensible way, *means and ends* have to be balanced *relative to each other* in view of man's happiness.

In the *Happiness Economy*, we see that certain aspects of this view have been developed with, among others, Richard Layard (2005) as a pioneering thinker and *Gross National Happiness* as an application. Money is then a means and not an end. Through adapted forms of technology that do not undermine human happiness, we are given the opportunity not to regard machines as merely a means of achieving maximum efficiency. When labor as a means is too drastically reduced in favor of capital, we will feel the need to re-emphasize the neglected value of *qualitatively* rich and rewarding labor as an end in itself.

10.3.5 Authentic, as in the Purpose Economy

A fifth offshoot of the transition in the economy is the fact that the principle of rationality, according to which the economic subject takes those decisions that maximize utility, is put in perspective (Wilkinson 2008). In light of the cluster of responsibility and, among others, Maslow's hierarchy of needs, the emphasis has shifted towards the *more authentic needs* of man. Think of the need for respect and self-development that we discussed earlier.

It is this emphasis on authenticity that is also central to the *Purpose Economy* in which one embarks upon the search for meaningfulness. Not just through personal achievements, but at least as much through meaningful contacts with others and contributions to the *bonum commune*, the common good. Thus, economic growth is focused not so much on the further increase of the consumption of material goods, but much more on services that are useful for the ethical and cultural enhancement of living standards or happiness.

10.3.6 Meaningful, as in the Economy of Communion

Finally, from the perspective of *Homo amans*, an economy in transition will adopt a different attitude towards the price presupposition of the prevailing economy. This assumption makes it all too easy for individual utility seekers to co-ordinate their respective preferences. However, it is not because something or someone doesn't yield an immediate utility that it is therefore without value, or needs to be priced through some method of assessment.

By proposing that things can only be *partially expressed in money*, we can avoid reducing values that cannot be expressed in money to a common denominator of "price." We don't just reduce elderly people to a cost. The same goes for the daily labor of a spouse at home, for nature, and for human life in general. We do not merely propose so-called solutions such as an affordable retirement home, potential wages for homemakers, or cost–benefit analyses.

In all of this, we stop reasoning in terms of pure prices in the service of our self-interest. On the contrary: as in the worldwide *Economy of Communion*, the focus is on sharing. The profits of an enterprise of the Economy of Communion flow not only to sustainable investments, but also to meaningful work and concrete support for those who are on the edge of society, on whom it is hard to simply put a price.

10.4 The Interconnection with Trust

We have described justice as granting to others that to which they are entitled in order to survive. It is a fact that the transitional economy just described – that we need but that also is already appearing all over the world – attempts to substantiate this *being entitled to survive*. Think of the Circular Economy, the Social Economy, the Happiness Economy, The Economy of Communion, CSR, the Purpose Economy, and so on. If we wish to prevent this transitional economy from being labeled a utopia, however, we must also consider the question of how the *granting to others* that to which they are entitled in order to survive can be realised effectively. We therefore should actually question – as in the discussion paper by Nullens and Van Nes – whether we are not in need of the lung of transcendence, in addition to the lung of the contemporary social-economic transition. What do we mean by this? At the start of this chapter, I described the current economy in the light of meaningfulness as assigning meaning to the satisfaction of our needs (which for an entrepreneur often amounts to turning €1 into €2 as quickly as possible). In the economy, therefore, meaningfulness has traditionally meant using the market and the government to address our lack of food, money, and possessions, along with our desire for recognition. If the current generation behind the developing transition economy is also open to transcendence, the most prominent role is no longer played only by the act of *making* meaningfulness yourself (turning €1 into €2), but at least equally by the act of *discovering* meaningfulness outside of yourself. In the economy, discovering meaningfulness outside yourself thus refers to the situation in which citizens – however much in cooperation with the market and the government – truly acknowledge the common lack of and hope for food, money, possessions, and recognition all over the world and the planet. Moreover, this situation proceeds from compassion – from sharing in the suffering and hope of everybody, inclusive nature.

However, such an emerging evolution from a *making* of meaningfulness (turning €1 into €2) towards a *discovering* of meaningfulness within our current transitional economy is more than simply a pious return to a sort of religious transcendence that calls you to compassion. The origins of the transitional movement – the all too expansive dystopian effects of our economy – invite us to a re-interpretation of the mimetic desire that helped to bring about the economic dystopia. What does this mean? The eighteenth-century French philosopher Rousseau (1755) speaks of the important distinction between *amour propre* and *amour-soi. Amour propre* refers to the self-love of the individual, which imitates or mimetically desires that which is desired by another human (for example, consider the world of advertising). Rousseau distinguishes this *amour propre* or self-love from what he refers to as the *amour-soi* of the human person. The individual discovers – Ricoeur explains in *Soi-même comme un autre* (1990) – that only in a respectful relational context with the other in adapted institutions, can he truly develop his love for freedom. This *amour-soi* renders humans open to external models to be imitated. Humans today indeed seem again attracted by external models to be imitated. Not the internal models that we "like" or not via Facebook or Twitter, but external models as an expression of a transcendent desire that today's society needs so much. An external model to be imitated that has gained fascination today is the *Dalai Lama* with his compassion and the empathetic appeal of the Buddha; or *Pope Francis*, with his call with Christ for a new humanism, applied within what he refers to as a prophetic economy. Not to forget, of course, in this era of fake news, the external model of the philosophical admiration of *truth.* As it comes to the fore, we want to know the truth and we want and try to act in consensus with it.

The described receptiveness in the finding of meaningfulness ultimately amounts to trust. Trust indeed involves being open to the possibility that something (like truth) or someone (like the Buddha, Christ, or the o(O)ther) is ultimately to be trusted. With this trust, we surround ourselves with a relationship of love or equal value, which – and this is crucial – also calls us to see the concrete other as actually being of equal value. This trust replaces the fear or desire that leads us to treat the other – including nature – unequally or to enter into competition, to exploit the other, whether it's my employee or nature. In the discussion paper Christian Smith speaks about "loving relationships with other personal selves and with the nonpersonal world" (Nullens and Van Nes, Chap. 2, p. 15, this volume). The reception of this trust is tangible in the uniqueness of nature, in the admiration of truth, in the loving gaze that we feel from the Buddha, in the mystical consolation that we experience through Christ, and, last but not least, in an authentic meeting with the o(O)ther. In this context, the tension between the economy and ethics is surpassed by the transcendental dimension – in other words, by trust. As argued by another twentieth-century personalist Emmanuel Mounier in his *Manifeste au service du personnalisme* (1936), such openness to transcendence does not depend upon an exclusively Christian inspiration. But according to Mounier, a personalistic culture and economy are possible only when we are open to the transcendent. If we are not, we will not be able to move beyond modernity, with all of its technocratic awareness, he explains (Abicht and Opdebeeck 2015, p. 89).

10.5 Conclusion

In this reflection with reference to the discussion paper, I have tried to outline that a *Homo amans* oriented transition economy is not a utopia. In essence, the transitional economy we so urgently need today concretely involves assigning an inter-cultural and inter-religious interpretation to responsibility within the economy. This means providing a response (transition) to social-economic questions based on a form of trust (transcendence). This amounts to providing an ultimate response to a form of trust or admiration that has been received. In an article, Dries Deweer describes this art of receiving as follows: "the deep-seated awareness that life is given to us – that we receive it – which makes us willing to bear responsibility" (Deweer 2016, p. 716). In all cases, it involves concrete attitudes emerging from what we have previously elaborated as reasonable rationality within the economy. The core of the current economic dystopia – inequality – is called into question because, proceeding from trust, each person is indeed perceived as being of equal value, thereby giving rise to empathy, compassion, or mercy. Our era thus corresponds to what was emerging throughout the world even during what Karl Jaspers (1949) called the axial period (*Achsenzeit*) between 800 and 200 BC, and was expressed by such figures as Socrates, Confucius, Buddha, or Jeremiah: empathy, compassion, or mercy are a *conditio sine qua non* when a context is dystopian.

We can conclude that an economy in which *Homo amans* takes the *Homo economicus* by the hand, becomes, step by step, a responsible economy. In its turn, a responsible economy corresponds to the ethics of virtue that connects the rational to the reasonable. The justice, hope, compassion, and love of which we speak are all virtues. As a virtue, responsibility is that positive characteristic of trust that focuses on providing the proper response to the social-economic questions that we encounter. I therefore call for concrete, *here-and-now* economic changes throughout the whole world that can bring a sense of peace, as it were – on the part of humans in relation to their fellow humans and nature. It thus does not involve a polarization between the Homo *economicus* and the *Homo amans*, or between the economy and ethics, or between rationality and reasonableness – or between dystopia and utopia. Instead of a *u-topia* or a *dys-topia* we can witness today the emergence of what I refer to as a '*u-globia*': a concrete, worldwide development of transition and transcendence.

References

Abicht, L., and H. Opdebeeck. 2015. *The Point of Philosophy*. Oxford: Lang.

Amato, J. 2002. *Mounier and Maritain: A French Catholic Understanding of the Modern World*. Ypsilanti: Sapientia.

Deweer, D. 2016. Krijgkunst: Tegen het neergangsdenken. *Streven: Cultureel maatschappelijk maandblad* 83 (8): 711–716.

Girard, R. 1978. *Des choses cachées depuis la fondation du monde*. Paris: Grasset.

Jaspers, K. 1949. *Vom Ursprung und Ziel der Geschichte*. Munich: Piper.

Layard, R. 2005. *Happiness: Lessons from a New Science*. London: Lane.

Mounier, E. 1936. *Manifeste au service du personnalisme*. Paris: Aubier.

L. Bouckaert, H. Opdebeeck, and L. Zsolnai. 2008. *Frugality: Rebalancing Material and Spiritual Values in Economic Life*. Oxford: Peter Lang.

Ricoeur, P. 1990. *Soi-même comme un autre*. Paris: Seuil.

Rousseau, J.-J. 1755. *Discours sur l'origine et les fondements de l'inégalité parmi les hommes*. Amsterdam: Michel.

Toulmin, St. 2001. *Terug naar de rede*. Kapellen: Pelckmans.

Wilkinson, N. 2008. *An Introduction to Behavioral Economics*. Basingstoke: Palgrave Macmillan.

Chapter 11
Out with the Old, In with the New? From Conceptual Reconstruction in Philosophical Anthropology to a Realistic Theory of Change

Wesley J. Wildman

Abstract Philosophers have solid analyses of defective understandings of the human condition and regularly propose inspirational alternatives that would seem to have the promise of changing the fortunes and fate of our species. But philosophers sometimes over-generalize in their criticisms, attributing to a vast cultural complex a specific anthropological understanding when in fact any large culture plays host to a large variety of mutually inconsistent anthropological visions. Moreover, philosophers rarely demonstrate that a culture-level change in anthropological understandings would have the effects they claim and they virtually never spell out a theory of change by which such a culture-level transformation could ever be realized. This paper begins in philosophical anthropology, spelling out two specific problematic aspects of contemporary western human self-understanding: individualism and cognitive error; two corresponding correctives: relationality and self-awareness; and two spiritual translations of these corrective measures: love as *agape* and *karuna* and wisdom as knowledge and humility. The argument then transitions to practical questions about what differences the envisaged transformation in ideas about human nature might be expected to make on socioeconomic conditions and how such changes might be implemented to realize the envisaged changes. The conclusion is that the anthropological insights of philosophers would be best served by a partnership with education and policy experts that would add realism about the conditions for social change to the generative creativity of philosophical analysis.

W. J. Wildman (✉)
Boston University, Boston, MA, USA
e-mail: wwildman@bu.edu

J. van Nes et al. (eds.), *Relational Anthropology for Contemporary Economics*,
Ethical Economy 61, https://doi.org/10.1007/978-3-030-84690-9_11

11.1 Pinning Down a Slippery Problem

Philosophers aren't very important as agents of social change. Maybe they never were. After all, Confucius was reportedly frustrated at not being able to realize his vision for ancient Chinese society and Plato's Republic never made it off the page. Even Karl Marx's socioeconomic vision was realized very differently than he had intended, in every instance. If there were past eras when philosophy had a large voice in social organization, philosophers certainly seem to have little impact on socioeconomic realities these days. The great idea brokers of our time are public intellectuals who blend a dash of philosophical insight with impressive depth and breadth of knowledge and a formidable talent for communication. We call them thought leaders and opinion makers because they influence the way regular people think.

Yet, philosophers have always had great ideas, and that's as true today as it has ever been. The danger of people blessed with splendid ideas is that they can overestimate the social influence of great ideas in the past. They can also harbor unduly optimistic estimations of the social potential of their own ideas today. Just as moral reasoning for most people is a process parallel to and somewhat independent of nearly automatic moral appraisals and actions, so philosophical reflection on what society most needs appears to be a process parallel to and somewhat independent of the reflexive operation of a society. Philosophy happens but with uncertain causal influence, at best.

For example, did John Stuart Mill's understanding of human beings as what his critics would later call *Homo economicus* – "a being who desires to possess wealth, and who is capable of judging the comparative efficacy of means for obtaining that end" (Mill 1836) – have any determinate effect on the way regular people behaved in society? I think few people ever bought into it back in the nineteenth century nor at any time since. An informal survey of my acquaintances reveals that most people think of it as ridiculously reductive and contrary to the way they behave – and that's true even of those among them who are personally oriented to wealth accumulation. Even Mill treated the definition as an abstraction intended to indicate the scope of the emerging science of economics, as the preceding part of the sentence demonstrates: "Political economy ... does not treat the whole of man's nature as modified by the social state, nor of the whole conduct of man in society. It is concerned with him solely as a being… [etc.]." He's giving a definition of political economy, not of human beings; his view of human beings as such was far richer. To my way of thinking, Mill was postulating the abstracted definition of human being as a premise for further analysis and reflection specifically within the science of economics. Not many people are perfectly rational actors, solely concerned with accumulating wealth, yet that assumption can found a science of economics that generates a flurry of new and powerful insights. This hypothetical, almost experimental, limitation on the scope of economics became a pillar of economics textbooks for decades after Adam Smith and Mill but even that didn't cause most regular human beings suddenly to conform to that definition of their economic nature. There are so many more pressing issues impacting economic behavior than what a bunch of nineteenth- and early twentieth-century economists and philosophers said about the best abstractions for leveraging insight-generating analyses of economic systems.

I'm not arguing that all causes for socioeconomic behavior are proximate and none distal. On the contrary, a large body of well replicated experimental work in social psychology has demonstrated that people unconsciously react to awareness of finitude and death with aspirational life projects that bolster self-esteem, with investments in close relationships for comfort and material support, and with vigorous defense of worldviews (for an overview, see Solomon et al. 2015). These are distal effects and they are not detectable until some time passes after experimental subjects are primed with thoughts about death. But they are powerful contributing factors to a host of socioeconomic realities, from building up a business to maintaining safe family neighborhoods, to xenophobic reactions toward refugees taking jobs that locals might have had. Those unconscious behavioral strategies for managing death anxiety no doubt partially underwrite the kind of single-minded wealth acquisition and rational maximization of means to that end that Mill had in mind. I feel confident that such real-life motivations, conscious and unconscious, dwarf in magnitude whatever influence Mill's understanding of the scope of the science of economics may have had on western socioeconomic practices.

Nevertheless, I think there's a broad consensus that contemporary western societies confront daunting threats, some global in scope, that seem to be traceable in part to a deeply flawed operative understanding of human nature implicit within our societies and economies and politics. I doubt that these flaws can be traced back to the conceptual model of human beings as rationally choosing, wealth-maximizing economic actors, because that was never much more than a premise for limiting the scope of the discipline of economics in its early years and has been routinely contested ever since, inside and outside of economics. Moreover, there are countless examples of economic cultures that operate very differently, on principles of reciprocity, or honor, or morally inflected indebtedness that underwrite very different visions of the economic aspects of human being. It follows that the problem of flawed anthropological concepts does not lie in the science of economics, however flawed that may or may not be as a science, and it won't be the same problem in every culture, because cultures vary rather colorfully in their visions of human nature, even though every culture has some operative means of economic exchange. Focusing on North Atlantic cultures and the associated democratic, capitalist socioeconomic systems adds some welcome and needed specificity.

In western settings, the deep flaws in the operative understandings of human nature implicit within our societies and economies and politics relate primarily to individualism and cognitive error, in my view.

By *individualism*, I refer to a structure of rationalization, a pattern of thinking in forms of socioeconomic coordination that easily leaves vulnerable people behind in ways that might seem cruel to an outsider. Within the cultures where this occurs, individualism effortlessly rationalizes such behavior with an emphatic assertion of rights, rewards, and responsibilities articulated primarily at the individual level. That is: I as an individual have the right to as much wealth as I can or want to accumulate; I as an individual deserve whatever wealth and privilege I can amass; I as an individual am responsible primarily for myself and only secondarily, in circles of attenuating intensity, for my family, my neighborhood, my society, my nation, and my planetary habitat. Most western nations have taxation systems and government-funded safety nets designed to mitigate the problem of the marginalization of the vulnerable to some degree. In some nations – the United States in particular – indignant, individualistic moral rationalizations for neglecting and oppressing poor and vulnerable human beings are pervasive. Such individualistic rationalizations express a particular understanding of fairness: not fairness as "From each according to his ability, to each according to his needs," which was a slogan popularized by Marx, but fairness as "people who are the most talented and the most hard-working should be paid the most," which is constantly on guard for freeloaders who would benefit from social goods without contributing. Individualism is a crucial rationalizing adjunct to this understanding of fairness.

By *cognitive error*, I refer to our cognitive limitations in the face of the enormously complex socioeconomic systems we have built. We have terrible difficulty understanding the causal processes driving the emergent features of these complex systems and cling to simple but false explanations to ease cognitive load when analysis and prediction would be better served with a cognitively more demanding approach to complexity. The result is baffling and frustrating. Good-hearted people can end up perpetrating devastating socioeconomic violence on others and really have no idea how to stop, even though they would never willingly harm people in that way if they had greater control over their situation. Even generally selfish people wouldn't normally harm themselves in the manner of human-abetted climate change, but the climate system is formidably complex, the links to socioeconomic systems incredibly tangled, the cognitive challenge seemingly insurmountable, and solutions profoundly disruptive and painful. It is easier to deny the problem or to satisfy ourselves with simple actions such as recycling, telling ourselves that we are doing our part, even though such actions are largely irrelevant to solving the underlying problem.

If the line of my reasoning to this point is sound, then philosophers face an interesting puzzle. We certainly should not stand idly by and fail to engage with threats such as climate change or economic injustice, particularly since philosophers can offer potent alternatives to the unhealthy prevailing concepts of human nature that directly address the problems of individualism and cognitive error. But the threats are urgent enough that there is little point in thinking philosophically about reconstructing concepts of human nature in these two dimensions if we don't also have a practical plan to change the socioeconomic practices that most concern us. If we ignore the need for change, philosophers pondering human nature may end up being the philosophical equivalent of Wallace Hartley's band playing soothing music on the Titanic even as the great boat filled with water and everyone scrambled to escape. Thus, I believe we need both conceptual reconstruction *and* a theory of change.

Typically, philosophers are very good at conceptual reconstruction and very bad at generating feasible theories of change. Fortunately, educators and policy professionals arguably need help with conceptual reconstruction and are often excellent at generating practical methods for social change. A strategic partnership seems called for, as a result. Admittedly, philosophers may need educators and policy professionals more than those two groups need philosophers. After all, without professional help, the best philosophical ideas remain inert outside of specialized communities of philosophical debate, whereas educators and policy professionals may feel that philosophical niceties run a distant second to creating literate human beings and leveraging positive social change. Nevertheless, I find a partnership between philosophers and educators and policy professionals to be an intriguing possibility and well worth pursuing.

The June 2019 *Homo Amans* symposium in The Netherlands represented an opportunity to move from conceptual reconstruction of "human nature" to a feasible theory of socioeconomic change. Perhaps the downstream consequences of that symposium will include philosophers working with educators and policy professionals on shared goals for worldview restructuring, synchronized with socioeconomic transformation. Arguably, in the era of the Anthropocene, which is already manifesting perilous socioeconomic side effects of climate change, nothing could be more important.

11.2 Conceptual Reconstruction

Let us begin in the domain of philosophical anthropology, asking about ways of thinking that we imagine might improve human life if they were incorporated into the living imaginaries of our time. For now, we can set aside the realism-drenched question of how any concrete changes might actually be achieved.

11.2.1 Framing Considerations

There are numerous definitions of the human being, each attempting to capture the essence of our species. In my own work in philosophical and theological anthropology, I have declined the temptation to offer an essentializing definition, instead focusing on species-wide characteristics and patterns of individual and cultural variation (Wildman 2009). The species-wide characteristics are a rich array of evolutionarily stabilized features ranging from cognitive capacities, including cross-cultural tendencies to cognitive error, all the way to recurring cultural features, such as means of exchange and regulation of sexual activity. Individual variations stretch from gender and sex to personality and intelligence. Cultural variations extend from language to religion. Species-wide characteristics might be thought of as essential, in the sense of almost universally present, and could be the basis for an essentializing definition if you wanted one, but the individual and cultural variations are just as important for generating a reliable understanding of the nature of our species, and they tend to be masked when the focus is on assertions of a human essence.

For this reason, I prefer a multi-vocal approach to articulating human distinctiveness, one that keeps the biological and cultural dimensions of human life tied closely to one another, and human beings in their complex bodily reality firmly rooted in the rest of physical nature. Doing this well demands the participation of numerous university disciplines – in fact all disciplines that have anything to say about human beings. It may not be possible always to harmonize everything that academic disciplines say about human beings but, all in all, I find there is an impressive convergence of angles of analysis in what I have called the "modern secular interpretation of humanity." This relative (not perfect!) consensus begins to break down as we move to richer levels of interpretation, where we grapple with human beings as meaning-making animals whose adventures in meaning are borne within cultural trajectories of world exploration. This is where we see profound and probably irresolvable disagreements about the origins and destiny and meaning of human beings, expressed in potent stories that enliven various cultural forms even as those stories slowly mutate over time to accommodate new socioeconomic and cultural realities. And yet, these days, the modern secular interpretation of humanity exercises a profound regulative effect on these stories, causing some to die if they pass too far into the territory of implausibility, and others to adapt so as to maintain plausibility for those who find the stories to be life-giving.

With those framing assumptions in place, I'll take up the two themes of individualism and cognitive error, in light of the modern secular interpretation of humanity. I'm interested in the implications of these two concepts for our self-understanding as socioeconomic beings. I'm equally interested in what would happen if new ways of thinking supplanted these aspects of our self-interpretation as human beings and were incorporated into living imaginaries, from where they could impact socioeconomic behavior. The attendant changes are critical for the human future. I'll defer discussion of that until the next section. In this section, attention is on philosophical anthropology.

11.2.2 Individualism, Relationality, and Love as Agape *and* Karuna

Individualism in the sense I give it above is somewhat novel in the history of our species. Other hyper-social species, such as bees, consist of individual bees, in a sense ultimately underwritten by physically distinct bodies that are born, move, and die – this despite their profound dependence on one another in everything from the microbial to the social dimensions of bee life. Despite similar connections and dependencies among human beings, the complexity of human minds, the hiddenness of our thoughts from others, and the way we hold individual human beings responsible for their actions, jointly invite an intensification of individualism. Most human cultures balance that individualizing tendency with religiously and politically enforced moral norms about obligations toward others that bind individual identity to satisfying those obligations. What's interesting and exceptional about western cultures after the solidification of capitalism and democracy is the partial severing of individual identity from social obligations, permitting individualism to attain degrees of intensity rarely or never seen in the long history of our species. For instance, young people in western cultures are now expected to become independent of their parents, financially, emotionally, and in terms of end-of-life care. Western individualism is not so extreme that we dispense with social obligations; after all, laws are enforced, schooling is a social-hive activity, and the vast majority of parents teach their children to be other-regarding. But individualism is still unusually powerful in the west, not least because of its function in articulating and justifying a particular understanding of fairness, as noted above.

Running counter to western individualism, insights from the modern secular interpretation of humanity assert a profound relationality with the power to contest and correct the socioeconomically inspired hyper-individualism of western cultures. Numerous disciplines attest to the presence of intensive relationality at the root of life in general, and within human life in particular, but they do so in very different ways. Philosophical anthropology is a useful venue in which to attempt to assemble an interpretation of relationality that can benefit from and respond creatively to those varied disciplinary perspectives. These insights have the potential to transform human self-understanding, both in terms of the way we conceive our relationships with one another and in terms of the way we picture our relationship with the wider world of nature. Here are a few of those worldview-transforming insights, from the domain of the very small and very old to the domain of the very human and very recent.

- From physical cosmology and elementary particle physics, we learn that every aspect of material reality comes from the same source. Very early in the history of our universe, even the forces we now think of as separate – the gravitational force by which mass-energy warps space-time, electromagnetism that underwrites atomic structure and chemistry, the weak force associated with radioactive decay, the strong force that binds atomic nuclei – were indistinguishable. *We are all related by virtue of coming from the same matter-energy.*
- Though the early universe could only create light atoms (isotopes of hydrogen, helium, lithium), stars formed from those elements were able to generate a range of heavier but still relatively light elements, explosions of those stars produced enough energy to forge still heavier elements, and a second generation of stars with solar disks containing those heavier elements formed planetary systems and ultimately all of the lifeforms teeming over our planet. *We are all related by virtue of coming from the same star-born atoms.*
- The geological formation of planet earth is intimately related to the emergence of microorganisms, which both adapted to the planetary environment and transformed ecological conditions. Just as geology and microbiology are intimately bound, so that union is the condition for the possibility of more complex organisms to emerge. *We are all related by virtue of the intimacy of organic and inorganic matter.*

- Biochemistry has revealed the mechanisms of intergenerational genetic transmission and protein expression, through which it has become clear that all earth organisms share the same deep biochemistry even when cellular chemistry changes among large classes of organisms. *We are all related through participating in the same biochemical nexus of DNA and amino acids.*
- Evolutionary biology has taught us about the intricate process by which complex organisms emerged from simpler lifeforms, uncovering a range of mechanisms of genetic change, including natural selection, which crafts adaptive bodies from environmental constraints, including social realities that underwrite stunning exhibitions of gene-culture co-evolution. *We are all related by virtue of the evolutionary process.*
- The energy processing factories within cells exist because of a symbiotic relationship with primitive bacteria, which were absorbed into cells and brought their ATP engineering capacities in with them. *We are all related by virtue of sharing evolutionarily stabilized metabolic processes.*
- The study of organism microbiomes shows that the life of any given plant or animal critically depends on a network of living organisms. No organism exists without intricate relationships with other organisms, including for food, and human beings die without the microorganisms that live in and on them. *We are all related by virtue of being dependent on other life forms for our very existence.*
- Attachment theory within psychology has revealed the potency of relationships between parents and their offspring, particularly within mammals and especially in primate species. Those formative attachments are critical for physical wellbeing and mental health. *We are all related by virtue of our strong emotional links with other people.*
- Life in social species is all about adapting to and thriving in novel environments through cooperation and problem solving. Group selection effects within evolution incentivize groups to minimize free-riders and embrace ritual strategies that encode group norms and bind us to one another for the sake of survival and protection. *We are all related by virtue of our commitment to group-defining moral norms.*
- Human beings are intelligent enough to tell and remember stories and to orient one another to life challenges by means of those stories. Such stories convey history and knowledge, hopes and dreams, cultural practices and social norms. *We are all related by virtue of our investment in and reliance on culturally constructed imaginaries.*
- Crossing back into physics, quantum entanglement has demonstrated that the commonsense view of local realism – that particles have definite properties and causes operate locally (no faster than the speed of light) – contradicts experiment. All viable interpretations of the quantum formalism, whether deterministic or indeterministic, are non-local, which entails a subtle and strange form of connectivity beneath the surface appearances of the ordinary world. *We are all related by virtue of entanglement.*
- Cognitive science of human beings has demonstrated cross-cultural similarities in cognitive operations. The stable species-wide character of human cognition is

the basis for a significant degree of intelligibility and translatability despite notable differences in language, culture, religion, morality, personality, and ideology. *We are all related by virtue of our evolutionarily stabilized brains.*

The modern secular interpretation of humanity has generated an impressive consensus. By itself, this suggests that the relationality inherent in human life is multidimensional, consistent, irreducible to a single perspective, and extremely profound. Western hyper-individualism seems a particularly extreme and ultimately unsustainable adventure in the social construction of human nature in light of this rich perspective on relationality. We might regard the conception of socioeconomic fairness that hyper-individualism rationalizes – people who are the most talented and the most hard-working should be paid the most, and freeloaders should be identified and penalized for betraying their individual responsibilities – as similarly extreme. Arguably, that extremity is a sign of western cultural greatness. But maybe it is also the great weakness of western forms of socioeconomic cultural organization. I think the historical record demonstrates that extreme ideas often function as both enablers of novelty and seeds of self-destruction.

Moving beyond the powerful consensus within the modern secular interpretation of humanity to the more controversial territory of metaphysics, this depiction of relationality leans heavily away from the Aristotelian vision of "things" as substances that bear properties and toward the relational vision of "things" co-constituting one another in webs of mutually dependent co-arising. This radically intimate vision of relationality at the ontological root of every part of reality, if correct, would powerfully reinforce the relationality affirmed within the modern secular interpretation of humanity (Scaringe and Wildman 2020). In any event, there seems to be no question that the modern secular interpretation of humanity demands some kind of relational ontology (Wildman 2010). Relational ontologies do not outrightly contradict western hyper-individualism, but they do make hyper-individualism fundamentally implausible as a way of conceiving human nature, and thus offer conceptual resistance to the socioeconomic enshrinement of hyper-individualism whenever and wherever it occurs.

Within the moral and spiritual domains, an apt expression for the kind of relationality portrayed within the modern secular interpretation of humanity and its metaphysical extensions is *love*. Now, love is a famously complex and multi-faceted concept, so a word of clarification is in order. To begin with, human beings have three distinguishable neurological love systems: sexual attraction (mediated especially by testosterone), infatuation (mediated especially by dopamine), and bonding (mediated especially by oxytocin) (see a summary of these systems in Wildman 2019). These are something like the atomic components of the molecular formations of love in the evolutionary realities of reproduction and parental investment in offspring. There are also higher-order, phenomenologically distinguishable types of love, from love of friends to love of animals and from love of music to love of sports. Longstanding traditional typologies of love often begin at this level, understandably silent on what we have discovered about the neurology of love in recent decades.

The morally and spiritually most profound types of love are of two main types. One is resolute benevolence, an alignment of intention and action for the benefit of others. The other is universal compassion. The first kind of spiritual love, often called *agape*, is more a matter of virtuous will than emotion. It first presupposes and then actualizes a profound relationality between persons that befits underlying relationality, conceived differently in the varied spiritual worldviews of our planet – this is the very relationality disclosed in reality through the modern secular interpretation of humanity. The second kind of spiritual love, often called *karuna*, is the fruit of spiritual practices that express a profound awareness of relationality, an awareness that can be cultivated in meditative states. Importantly, while the two types of spiritual love overlap, they are distinguishable. *Agape* does not require *karuna*, though feelings of empathy and compassion can be powerful motivators toward realizing the unconquerable benevolence of *agape*. Similarly, *karuna* does not require *agape*, but ordinarily universal compassion should lead outwards to precisely the kind of benevolent actions that *agape* prizes.

I contend that cultivating these two types of love is the spiritually most relevant and profound response to the disclosure of relationality within the modern secular interpretation of humanity. The vision of the human person expressed in the union of *karuna* and *agape* goes well beyond anything envisaged within that consensus interpretation from the contemporary university disciplines but they are conceptually consistent and mutually resonant.

11.2.3 Cognitive Error, Self-Awareness, and Wisdom as Knowledge and Humility

Let's turn to cognitive error. The human brain is phylogenetically dependent on a long process of brain evolution in other species. Critical tasks for the brains of most species include keeping the body running (e.g. autonomic nervous system), making sense of situations quickly enough to take effective action (e.g. rapidly changing bodily function in response to life-threatening dangers), and managing procreation (e.g. finding mates and protecting offspring). In human cognition, an overlay of higher cortical functions launches cognition into unprecedented realms of complexity. Memory is more powerful, simulation of future situations is more extensive, and information processing to interpret a situation is more intricate. For many purposes – indeed, for most purposes within the small-scale cultures of the era of evolutionary adaptation – human cognitive capacities were well suited to the natural hazards and social demands that human beings had to navigate. In complex cultures, however, where cognitive demands are much higher, our memory, our interpretative abilities, and our decision systems are often stressed. That's when we make mistakes, mistakes that we often don't recognize and typically can't avoid or fix.

These all-too-human tendencies to cognitive error have been studied exhaustively during the last century of research in cognitive psychology and documented voluminously (see Fig. 11.1 for the Codex of Cognitive Bias, which I prefer to call

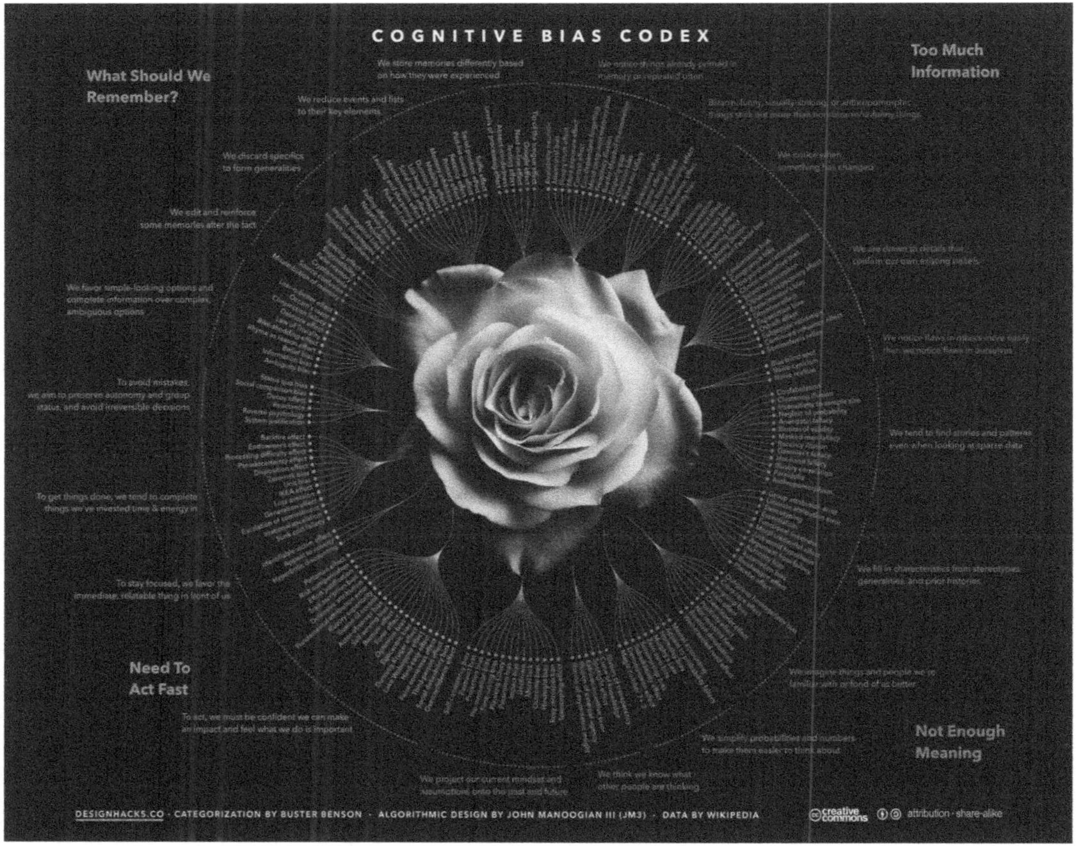

Fig. 11.1 Cognitive Bias Codex, aka the Codex of Tendencies to Cognitive Error, presenting a variety of empirically confirmed biases in the human cognitive system, categorized by similarity of cognitive operation. (Reproduced under a Creative Commons license ("attribution and share-alike"))

the Codex of Tendencies to Cognitive Error, emphasizing *tendencies*). Some of them are amusing: think of a magician taking advantage of the way human beings are known to interpret sensory information and doing something that appears impossible but in reality is merely deceptive. Other tendencies to cognitive error can be deadly: picture one group of people settling for cognitively easy negative generalizations about another group in lieu of detailed person-to-person information and then using those oversimplified generalizations to rationalize violence against the group they malign. Of course, there are lot of cognitive errors whose importance lies somewhere in between amusement and genocide (for application to human inquiry, see Wildman 2009).

In the case of attempting to interpret and transform the socioeconomic practices of western capitalistic democracies, tendencies to cognitive error play a critical role. Formally complex systems – e.g. large economies – display several mind-bending properties that play havoc with human cognition. Under some circumstances, they become highly unpredictable, which makes human beings extremely nervous because methods for satisfying their survival needs become fragile. The nexus of causes involved in a complex economic system is only partially understood, making interventions potentially perilous and always debatable, which also makes people nervous. Moreover, interventions can backfire producing unintended consequences, which can be very dangerous.

At a more personal level, since we lack control over the economic system as such, we cannot act meaningfully to improve the economic practices we don't like. We can complain and protest, of course, but it is extremely difficult constructively to contribute to a solution. That kind of despair is a rational reaction to being unwillingly caught up in perpetuating economic injustice and the resulting dissonant state of mind is difficult to tolerate so we tend to narrate our way out of the impasse with stories about other people's badness or about us doing our part. They might even be convincing stories at some level but they are fundamentally evasive and self-exculpatory, and they are oriented more to alleviating cognitive dissonance and moral anguish than to solving socioeconomic problems.

Naturally, the inevitable failure of experts to possess a sound grasp of a complex socioeconomic system leads to economic disasters and popular mistrust. That's a rational reaction, amounting to coming to terms with the complex nature of a modern economy. But experts are the only people able to gain much of a sense of the levers of a socioeconomic system, so an opportunity for cognitive error lurks nearby: we can all-too-easily generalize from skepticism about complete knowledge to wholesale mistrust in all experts, and thereafter agitate to replace so-called experts, who actually do possess the best knowledge available, with populist demagogues, who typically possess little relevant expert knowledge at all.

How do we mitigate the problems associated with being a species whose cognitive powers are optimized for cultural worlds far simpler than the one in which we actually live? The answer, surely, is a specific kind of self-awareness, one that recognizes the ever-present tendencies to cognitive error, inspiring us to regulate emotion and behave accordingly; one that recognizes the presence of a complex system and proceeds cautiously; one that is ready for the possibility of unintended, unwanted side effects of even the cleverest interventions.

Consider a side effect of the advent of the internet, which revolutionized the global economy. Nobody boosting the internet imagined a massively amped-up market in every country and locality for the commercial sexual exploitation of children, linking buyers with sellers with an efficiency that was formerly impossible. Now that we do know about that unintended consequence, we are struggling to find effective ways of battling the problem. People self-aware in the way I'm now describing would have detected the opportunity for cognitive error lurking. They'd have been on the lookout for unintended side effects and they'd have been warning people in advance to expect them, even if they didn't know precisely what they would be.

Within the moral and spiritual domains, this kind of self-awareness might be called wisdom, and it has two important aspects: knowledge and humility. The knowledge aspect of this kind of wisdom involves knowing a lot, including and especially about tendencies to cognitive error. Acquiring knowledge requires training – a great deal of training – in cognitive science, logic, probability, ethics, and also in specific subject matters, such as political economy or climate science or whatever the specific problem in view may be. It also involves building character, which takes us to the humility aspect of this kind of wisdom. The humility aspect of wisdom is powerfully akin to what Christians might call consciousness of sin, what Buddhists might call right mindedness, and what secular humanists might call the ethics of systems thinking.

Wisdom recognizes the complexity of vast human social systems, and is resolutely skeptical about every kind of hubris, particularly those on a civilizational scale with the potential to impact billions of people and other animals besides us. Both the knowledge and humility dimensions of wisdom are virtues that can be cultivated – and absolutely must be cultivated if human beings are to successfully navigate the challenges we now confront.

11.3 Theory of Change

Love as *agape* and *karuna,* and wisdom as knowledge and humility are capable of confronting rampant individualism and unchecked tendencies to cognitive error within contemporary western socioeconomic systems. I think philosophers feel sure of this; after all, someone who has truly learned the lessons of love and wisdom is very unlikely to fail to notice side effects of socioeconomic hubris such as marginalization of the economically vulnerable and the crazy careening of civilization into a climate catastrophe. But there are not many such virtuous souls. So where else does this confrontation actually happen? I think that this confrontation happens mostly in our heads, which is to say, in the heads of philosophers who think deeply about the way human beings understand themselves. But that's not enough, particularly given how urgent the problems are. Once again, it really doesn't matter how clever and potentially revolutionary our anthropological ideas are if they remain socially and politically inert. So now we need to discuss the move from conceptual reconstruction in philosophical anthropology to a theory of change.

I want to suggest five directions of change, as follows:

- education about complex social systems, relationality, and species-wide cognitive error,
- activating religious and humanist communities as sites of virtue cultivation,
- strategic policy deployments to counter socioeconomic hubris and its effects,
- advertising campaigns to explain the importance of love and wisdom, and
- explicit political rhetoric about the problems of individualism and cognitive error.

To pull any of this off, partnerships are critical. Philosophers need to team up with educators and policy professionals because philosophers will not achieve practical results of this kind by themselves. I think the main impediment to such partnerships lies in the ability of philosophers to convince practically oriented change agents and on-the-ground stakeholders that philosophical anthropology has anything of importance to offer. So let's start there.

How do philosophers make the case to practically minded change agents such as educators and policy experts that visions of the human person powered by the virtues of love and wisdom can effectively confront the problems associated with invidious individualism and chronic cognitive error? It sounds like a pipe dream, or perhaps some kind of religious vision. Wouldn't it be better to focus on economic prosperity, calming people's anxieties, and projecting strength on the world stage? Isn't expecting people to become enlightened enough to qualify as loving and wise asking way too much? Anyway, why would anyone trust a philosopher who claims that the virtues of love and wisdom can make all the difference in a life-and-death confrontation with the problems that beset us?

There are ways for philosophers to navigate around their well-earned reputation for being irrelevant to socioeconomic challenges. But they will make most philosophers nervous. The trick is to *engage* policy experts and educators by *showing* them the difference that love as *agape* and *karuna* and wisdom as knowledge and humility can make. Because nobody will trust a philosopher to experiment in the real world, that difference will have to be demonstrated in some other way, and I want to suggest four such methods.

First, philosophers can demonstrate the difference their ideas can make using inspiring word pictures capable of captivating the imagination of journalists and educated readers. This is one method by which powerful ideas spread. Of course, the directions and extend of spread critically depends on the nature of communication and the stakeholders involved. So consider a few examples.

The Berggruen Prize for Philosophy and Culture is an annual "award for major achievements in advancing ideas that shape the world" (https://www.berggruen.org/prize/). Three philosophers have won that prize, each invested in partnerships that spread powerful ideas and create conditions conducive to socioeconomic change, but the way those partnerships work has been quite different. Canadian philosopher Charles Taylor has primarily influenced other university intellectuals but he is also a public intellectual with a strong media presence striving to support conditions he thinks will unify societies in the face of increasing cultural diversity. British philosopher and public servant Baroness Onora Sylvia O'Neill has brought her philosophical-ethics perspective to policy and politics in the UK House of Lords, raising consciousness and creating positive change on everything from bioethics to civic life. American philosopher Martha Craven Nussbaum has combined the highest scholarly standards with a role as a public intellectual, partnering with economist Amartya Kumar Sen to create an intellectual framework for welfare economics (the capability approach) that has had a profound effect in numerous policy directions, including the design of the United Nations' Human Development Index. In all three cases, these philosophers maintain a complex web of partnerships that give practical leverage to their profound ideas about the human condition.

Similarly, the Templeton Prize recognizes people from a wide variety of disciplines who have "made an exceptional contribution to affirming life's spiritual dimension, whether through insight, discovery, or practical works" (http://www.templetonprize.org/purpose.html). Sometimes a philosopher is a recipient of the Templeton Prize (e.g. Alvin Plantinga, Jean Vanier, Tomáš Halík, Michael Heller, Charles Taylor, Michael Novak) and in each of those cases there is a key dimension of public influence that involves partnerships beyond philosophy to leverage creative philosophical ideas for meaningful social change. Sometimes the partnership takes the form of a media presence, spreading potent ideas in persuasive ways; sometimes the partnerships are with change agents and other kinds of intellectuals to spread ideas and social change strategically.

Many media venues focus on the power of ideas to change self-understanding and behavior, and ultimately to transform socioeconomic values and practices. Articulate philosophers sometimes participate in such processes of public education and transformative enlightenment. Consider just one example: the National Public Radio (NPR) program "On Being," hosted by Krista Tippett (https://onbeing.org/). This Peabody Award-winning radio show and podcast asks: "What does it mean to be human? How do we want to live? And who will we be to each other?" and has an inspiring mission: "Pursuing deep thinking, social courage, moral imagination, and joy, to renew inner life, outer life, and life together." Airing on more than 400 public radio stations across the United States, On Being's podcasts have been downloaded or played online more than 200 million times. And who is listening? NPR as a whole classifies its audience into six groups – the business leader, the cultural connoisseur, the educated lifelong learner, the civic leader, the sustainability champion, and the curious explorer – and makes the following claims about its audience:

> Across platforms, NPR reaches the nation's best and brightest. On air and online, the NPR audience is influential and curious. They are learning more and leading more. Connected to their local communities and tuned in to the latest public affairs and cultural conversations, the NPR audience embodies the thought and opinion leader. (https://www.nationalpublicmedia.com/npr/audience/)

Presumably it would be a subset of that group who engages with On Being. The kind of flow of ideas represented here is therefore top down, penetrating not far beyond the realm of opinion leaders and educated elites. These are the people most influential on policy, to be sure, but it is very different from the kind of bottom-up idea-flow seen in recent American political campaigns, such as those of Barak Obama, Donald Trump, and Bernie Sanders. There is nothing wrong with top-down communication focused on cultural elites and this is probably the best philosophers can hope for but it is also important to recognize the limitations of that kind of idea flow, if only to avoid over-idealization and self-deception about influence of bright and shiny philosophical conceptions of the human being.

Second, philosophers can demonstrate the difference their ideas make by partnering with educators to design new kinds of curricula for schools and informal education settings for both children and adults. I am not thinking here of philosophy of education, which is an important part of the academic fields of both philosophy and education, and a notable focus of philosophical literatures in many cultures from Confucius and Plato down to the present. Rather, I have in mind the *content* of educational practice, regardless of the prevailing normative educational philosophy. Philosophers could partner with educators on many fronts, helping to raise consciousness and to make the case for reforming educational practices.

Consider the sobering fact that there is not a single educational program in existence that systematically teaches students (either children or adults) about their tendencies to cognitive error and equips them with the skills needed to contest those tendencies. We have known about most of the tendencies on the Codex of Tendencies to Cognitive Error for the better part of a century at this point and we have had solid empirical evidence on all of them for several decades yet cognitive psychology and philosophy (especially epistemology) have not been able to create the kinds of partnerships with educators that would put in place the educational processes that are so clearly needed. Doing so would be the single most important contribution we could make to improving the civility of public discourse and resisting the biases that are both the enemy of sound policy debate and the ally of populist xenophobic nationalism. Of course, individual lines of training achieve something in this direction, as when historians are trained out of tendencies to anachronism, scientists are taught not to mistake correlation for causation, mathematicians become expert in interpreting statistics, and humanities training helps people acquire skills for critical reasoning and hermeneutical sophistication. But this merely describes a piecemeal approach to an educational challenge that should be confronted comprehensively, with philosophers helping to drive the process of educational reform.

Third, philosophers can demonstrate the difference their ideas make by partnering with change agents such as non-profits and politicians to change public rhetoric about socioeconomic systems. Martha Nussbaum's collaboration with Amartya Sen is a fine example, producing a better way of thinking about social welfare and a more accurate way of measuring human development. The work of the Center for Mind and Culture includes partnerships between philosophers and scientists aimed at increasing public understanding of complex dynamical systems and thereby spreading awareness of the challenges associated with so-called "wicked problems" that resist neat solutions and frequently involve unintended side effects.

Much more of this could be done. The critical factor in how much actually occurs, I suspect, is the intention of philosophers. Change agents operate at some distance from the intricate qualifications and careful conceptual analyses of university philosophers. They look for the neat turn of phrase that captures attention, whereas the typical philosopher finds such simplifications irksome at best and tendentious at worst. Philosophers could wash their hands of such practices but, in so doing, they impoverish the work of such change agents. Some philosophers – those who want their work to influence public discourse, public policy, and the thinking of regular people – need to get engaged and make their philosophical skills count for formulating less misleading slogans and better material to back up those slogans, increasing depth and breadth of intellectual vision without sacrificing focus and reach of the message of change.

Fourth, and here we come to something quite radical, philosophers can use *virtual societies* to demonstrate the difference philosophical ideas can make. Seriously?! Yes: computer simulation is a valuable path to rehabilitating the public image of contemporary philosophical anthropology as socially useless. When a policy expert challenges philosophers who are swept away by their own rhetoric to make good on their seemingly outrageous claims about how to improve socioeconomic systems, computational modeling and simulation may be the only feasible option.

I'm referring to something like computer games, but where the aim is accuracy rather than entertainment. If philosophical recommendations are actually sound and worth the attention philosophers think they deserve, then it ought to be possible to rise to the policy expert's challenge by building a multi-agent artificial intelligence computational model of artificial societies with and without the envisaged change in human self-understandings. Calibrate the model against the world the way it is now and then see what happens when you increase the frequency of people who understand relationality and cultivate the virtue of love, and people who are self-aware about cognitive error and cultivate the virtue of wisdom. Does the world get better in the expected way or not? And what are the precise pathways of change? Then turn the challenge around and demand that the policy experts implement their own proposals for the way the world is supposed to improve and see which vision of the human future fares better.

Computational simulations are ideal for studying complex adaptive social systems, which is why the field of social simulation has been growing for several decades. After all, it's a matter of using a virtual complex system to model a real-world complex system. The subfield of human simulation is particularly relevant because that's where computer engineers engage the arts and humanities disciplines such as philosophy (see Diallo et al. 2019). Human simulation is the ideal venue for helping philosophers make good on their claims about the importance of their conceptual reconstructions in philosophical anthropology and earn their way into public policy and education debates. If Plato and Confucius had computer simulations to work with, they could have implemented their vision of human life in an artificial society and decided that they were being too idealistic, or that they should tweak their ideas a bit, or that they should drive on toward implementation as quickly as possible.

But is this really feasible? Here's what John Teehan, a philosopher at Hofstra University in New York, said after working with one of our computational modeling and simulation teams at the Center for Mind and Culture (CMAC):

> After two (intense) days with the people at CMAC, going through the process of translating my hypothesis about religion and empathy into the language of computer modeling, it all began to make sense … Because of this method, we will actually be able to bring some data into a debate that would otherwise remain largely in speculation … It forced me to formulate my ideas in such precise and concrete terms (so they could be coded for) that I came away with a better understanding of my own theory. (mindandculture.org)

Making use of human simulation is one way for philosophers to win the attention of educators and policy professionals. Once a partnership is forged, anything can happen. All five directions of change I listed earlier are well and truly on the table for discussion and action, along with other possibilities that policy experts and educators will be a lot better at dreaming up than an idealistic philosopher. After that, the game really is afoot!

11.4 Conclusion

The five directions of change and the four types of partnerships I have discussed are fertile soil for growing collaborative ventures with genuinely transformative potential, all directed by realistic theories of change. I wish there were many recent and relevant and renowned examples of innovations in philosophical anthropology impacting social policy in western capitalist democracies. I'm aware of only a few but I have pointed to partnerships in which philosophers engage educators and policy professionals on questions rooted in philosophical anthropology, trying to create the right kinds of impacts. Along with the organization I lead, the Center for Mind and Culture, I'm involved in several such partnerships studying a variety of pressing social issues where philosophical visions of the human condition play critical roles: commercial sexual exploitation of children, the integration of non-western immigrants and refugees in western cities, the crisis of rural suicide, the social and economic consequences of climate change, and others. For us, human simulation is a key tool used to translate from the conceptual domain to the practical domain, creating the possibility of winning the attention of educators and policy professionals in those projects. That method got us into the debate by demonstrating that our ideas aren't just speculative talk; we gave the change agents a reason to look twice and engage us directly. Not every philosopher can build computational simulations or create partnerships with educators and policy professionals, but not every philosopher needs to; it's a task for a team. Experts in philosophical anthropology can design models with computer engineers who build them, and that's just the beginning of fruitful partnerships. Philosophers can consult on educational curricula with educators, and on advertising campaigns with politicians and non-profits, while policy professionals add realism and relevance and thinking about strategic change.

Reconfigured philosophical ideas about human nature can't make any difference unless philosophers partner with change agents. Change agents can't change anything in a good way unless it is thought through soundly first, and nobody is better than philosophers at thinking carefully about things. The era of the solo intellectual is over for scholars who want to influence a troubled world. We have entered the era of collaborative research. And we as philosophers need to engage, and stay engaged, if we want to be relevant. Working with others, under the aegis of realistic theories of change, philosophers have a lot to say about the problems of individualism and cognitive error plaguing western socioeconomic practices and about the virtuous ideals of love and wisdom that are capable of transforming those practices.

References

Diallo, S.Y., W.J. Wildman, F. LeRon Shults, and A. Tolk. 2019. *Human Simulation: Perspectives, Insights, and Applications*. Leiden: Brill.

Mill, J.S. 1836. On the Definition of Political Economy, and on the Method of Investigation Proper to It. *London and Westminster Review* 4.

Scaringe, S.A., and W.J. Wildman. 2020. Biological Mutualism: A Notable Advance and a Hint of Things to Come. *Theology and Science* 18 (2): 211–225.

Solomon, S., J. Greenberg, and T. Pyszczynski. 2015. *The Worm at the Core: On the Role of Death in Life*. New York: Random House.

Wildman, W.J. 2009. *Science and Religious Anthropology: A Spiritually Evocative Naturalist Interpretation of Human Life*. Aldershot: Ashgate.

———. 2010. An Introduction to Relational Ontology. In *The Trinity and an Entangled World: Relationality in Physical Science and Theology*, ed. J. Polkinghorne and J. Zizioulas, 55–73. Grand Rapids: Eerdmans.

———. 2019. Love and Desire, Human and Divine: A Trans-religious Naturalist Account. In *Theology Without Walls*, ed. J. Martin, 138–150. New York: Routledge.

Chapter 12
Personal Leadership: How to Change What Cannot Be Changed: A Response to Wesley Wildman's Out with the Old, In with the New?

Joke van Saane

Abstract In agreement with Wildman's statement about the structural failures in human functioning caused by individualism and cognitive errors, a new concept is introduced. This is needed because of the risk of generalizing with easy solutions, in so doing neglecting the basic human drives of self-enhancement, connectedness, and mastery. It is better that we acknowledge our individualism and failing cognitions, because this acknowledgment creates room for change. Here, the concept of personal leadership is introduced. Change can start with ourselves as the real game changers. The opportunities for personal leadership are based upon spirituality and spiritual concepts: self-knowledge, self-confidence, norms and values, openness, learning, and imagination.

It is an honor for me to respond to Professor Wildman's argument elsewhere in this book. Under an intriguing chapter title, he offers an even more intriguing idea.

Very roughly summarized, Wildman notes that there are two general biases in the human condition. According to Wildman, you could say that people make at least two structural errors: he shows that people are constantly driven by individualism and that people constantly make cognitive errors. And not just a bit, the illustration of the Cognitive Bias Codex is really discouraging. How do we ever think we can produce reasonable thought?

According to Wildman, these two structural errors are to blame for the fact that it is extremely difficult to change humanity. Change, however, is really needed. Wildman quite rightly refers to the enormous socio-economic problems in Western societies, the global climate threat and the unjustified inequality between people around the globe. Our tendency to individualism and the persistent cognitive errors prevent us from finding fundamental solutions for these huge problems. We cannot jump over our own shadow; we cannot manage to let the public interest prevail over our own; not even if that public interest is under such pressure that there are risks to

J. van Saane (✉)
University of Humanistic Studies, Utrecht, The Netherlands
e-mail: J.vanSaane@UvH.nl

J. van Nes et al. (eds.), *Relational Anthropology for Contemporary Economics*, Ethical Economy 61, https://doi.org/10.1007/978-3-030-84690-9_12

personal survival. Individualism falls short when it comes to solving complex global problems, individuals simply do not overlook them.

Wildman proposes two possible solutions to overcome this impasse, fundamentally caused by the human condition wherein we are cognitive and individual organisms. He looks at philosophy for the first type of solution. In his view, philosophers can help with the development of new concepts. Conceptual reconstruction, for example, reveals that the biological and cultural dimensions of human life are strongly interrelated and cannot be dismantled. *Homo economicus* and *Homo amans* are not available separately; as humans we cannot choose to be one or the other. We can, however, choose what we give priority to in our self-understanding as persons. Reflection on the frames and the concepts can reinforce this self-understanding and lead to more conscious forms of desired behavior.

And Wildman shows, very convincingly in my opinion, that no completely new fields of research are needed in order to arrive at that conceptual reconstruction. To be able to give relationality a place in the concept of humanity in addition to individualism, we only have to take seriously what is happening in research areas outside of philosophy. Chemistry, physics, geology, evolutionary biology, biochemistry, neurological psychology, etc. prove that people are not only individualistic organisms, but (also) fundamentally relational: to each other, to the world, to ourselves. Wildman shows that we are related at a fundamental level, because we are all human beings, sharing the same evolutionary processes and physical laws. So, it is rich and multi-dimensional relationality that proves to be fundamental for humanity, not individualism.

In other words, there seems to be a great deal of consensus on the modern secular interpretation of humanity in which relationality is central. Western hyper-individualism must therefore be seen as an extreme and ultimately unsustainable social construction of human nature. Although dominant, hyper-individualism is, according to Wildman, fundamentally implausible in the light of the research results in other domains, as a result of which individualism is corrected by relationality. The spiritual translation of relationality can be found in the domain of metaphysics, in which there is such a thing as selfless love, love as *agape* and *karuna*. Deploying this love can lead to a reduction in (the effects of) individualism. I like the translation of the corrective into a spiritual virtue, because spiritual virtues imply the opportunity to learn, to practice, and to share. If the corrective was only philosophical or cognitive, one dimension would be replaced by another one. But by adding the notion of spirituality Wildman really opens up something new, something healing.

Wildman proposes something similar for the bias of cognitive errors. He shows that increasing self-awareness contributes to reducing the impact of cognitive errors. People can learn, and people can consciously avoid certain pitfalls. The corrective of self-awareness is translated spiritually by Wildman as wisdom, wisdom in the form of knowledge and humility. This wisdom, just like love, is a spiritual virtue and can also be learned, practiced, and emphatically developed. Putting it this way, by bringing in metaphysical concepts Wildman opens up – without reflecting on it – the possibility of growth and change.

Although this is already an impressive reconstruction of concepts, Wildman acknowledges that this will not be enough to bring about real change in society, given the complexity of the problems humanity is facing worldwide, and in particular in the West. For change to happen you need a philosophical basis, but especially to have that in partnership with other actors. In Wildman's words, some reality must be added to philosophy. Education, religion, politics, and marketing are important areas for making the change happen. Within these areas, philosophers must join forces with other professionals, and arrive at concrete actions together, and this is what will really make a difference. I am not quite sure if advertising campaigns or explicit political rhetoric – examples sketched out in Wildman's chapter – will actually help, but I really appreciate the idea and especially the optimism contained in this idea.

Up to this point, we can say "amen" to Wildman's argument. His reflection about the shortage of solutions to real complex global problems is based upon a solid package of both empirical and theoretical research. But I am not fully convinced that this combination of philosophical reconstruction and the development of broad partnerships will actually lead to the real change we so desperately need in our contemporary societies.

As a matter of fact, the separate elements that need to be in place for this reconstruction of reasoning are so massive and unchangeable that reconstruction and partnerships will not be sufficient to bring about change.

To start with, I would like to emphasize how deeply rooted the failures in human structures are. After all, individualism and cognitive errors are fundamental parts of the human condition. Within psychology, many research studies (e.g. Smith and Mackie 2007[1]; Mullen and Riordan 1988; Kaplan and Wilke 2001) show that human beings are characterized by a few basic drives that are very important for our functioning, both on the levels of cognition and emotion as well as on the level of behavior. I summarize these basic human drives here as self-enhancement (or the self-serving bias), connectedness, and mastery, explicitly in this order (see van Saane 2010). Self-enhancement is safeguarding self-interest, working on a positive self-image, and avoiding negative experiences about the self. The individualism that Wildman observes can be seen as a result of this self-enhancement. Besides, individualism – contrary to Wildman's suggestion – is not equivalent to pure self-concern and selfishness. It is the fundamental urge to live and survive. This basic drive of self-enhancement can be mirrored in the fear of death, the fear of one's own mortality. This fundamental human drive can be understood as the ultimate reason behind human inclination to cognitive errors.

At the same time however, just as fundamentally, people are driven by the need for connectedness, or, in other words and expressed by, the fear of isolation. People are relational beings who care firstly about themselves, but also constantly seek to connect with others. Fear of isolation and fear of loneliness are strong incentives for

[1] The textbook of Smith and Mackie (2007) offers a thorough overview of the state of art in cognitive social psychology. The three motivational principles form one of the basic lines of argument in this overview (cf. Smith and Mackie 2007, p. 17).

behavior. This very fundamental basic human drive opens up relationality as characteristic of humanity, not as a corrective for individualism or self-enhancement, but as a fundamental keystone of our psychological system.

And the strive for mastery can be added to these two basic drives of self-enhancement and connectedness. Human beings are self-concerned and they are connected. These drives are influenced by the continuous search for certainty and predictability. People have a hard time dealing with uncertainty, with not knowing what to expect. If this third drive for mastery is put under pressure, the first drive of self-enhancement becomes more dominant as a strategy for coping with unpredictability and fear. From this perspective of the basic need for mastery, it is therefore very understandable that people are overwhelmed by the complexity of contemporary global problems such as socio-economic relations and climate issues. Delving into these problems leads, by definition, to uncertainty and unpredictability for people. This tempts us to ignore or simplify these problems. And in turn, it tempts us to prioritize the drive for self-enhancement (individualism) and the drive for connectedness (withdrawing into our own social group).

I am not so optimistic about our ability to change or correct these fundamental tendencies. There is plenty of research (e.g. Alicke and Sedikides 2010; Smith and Mackie 2007) showing that these basic drives are rooted in biological, evolutionary, and neurological mechanisms that we should regard as given, rather than as accidental characteristics.

This persistence of human characteristics and basic psychological drives will also play a role in those strategic and practical partnerships proposed by Wildman. We remain human beings, even if we come from other areas such as education or politics, and even if we are willing to cooperate. We always, and inevitably, will continue to put our own individual interests first. And if there is a lot of uncertainty to be reduced, these mechanisms of self-enhancement or individualism and withdrawing into our own community to feed the drive for connectedness will only become more dominant in our cognitive system, both on a conscious as on an unconscious level.

So, the old cannot simply be replaced by something new, no matter how philosophically brilliant the new concepts may be. People are, so to speak, trapped in their own human condition. The same could be said for the problems that confront humanity. After all, these problems are in part the result of unashamed and unimpeded submission to basic individual needs. All these individual tendencies towards self-interest naturally exclude each other and are the building blocks on which the self-destructive capacity of humanity develops. Indulging in individual interest ultimately harms humanity as a whole. The human shortage is a reflection of human capacity, and this means that human shortage is just as firm and unavoidable. The complexity of the global problems does not help. They are monsters that have grown completely over our heads and now threaten to crush us.

I would not look for the potential for change so much through philosophical reconstructions, followed by strategic and practical partnerships, but rather in the real acceptance of this fundamental human condition. Only if we dare to face human reality, does room appear to develop strategies that might possibly mitigate the consequences of humanity's failures. No unfounded optimism or naivety, but realism and a mature attitude of self-reflection.

In my opinion, we can introduce the concept of personal leadership here. To do so, let us dig a bit deeper into the discipline of spirituality. Wildman translates the correctives of individualism and cognitive errors (respectively relationality and self-awareness) into the spiritual concepts of love as *agape* and *karuna* and the virtue of wisdom. In my opinion however, this is only a start: more discussion and more thorough thinking about spirituality is needed if we are to arrive at sustainable change and transformation.

For the definition of spirituality, I follow the philosopher Roothaan, (cf. van Saane 2019) who defines spirituality as an attitude of openness, attention, and consciousness (Roothaan 2007, p. 65). This attitude may be based on a philosophical or religious worldview, but that need not be the case. Spirituality can also be rooted in a more secular worldview.

Defined in this way, spirituality can be seen as an ongoing process of seeking meaning, with an open attitude, a focus on sustainability and credibility, rooted in self-knowledge and in the desire for growth and development. At its core, spirituality is about this fundamental search for meaning. And it is important to realize, spirituality is also always connected with morality, with norms and values that set the public interest against the satisfaction of one's own need.

To see how spirituality can help in bridging the gap between structural human failures such as individualism and cognitive errors and the need to find sustainable solutions for complex global problems, I like to underscore the fact that within spiritual traditions, truth can only be personal truth (van Saane 2019). Abstract general truth can be nice to hear, or to study, but will be powerless when we are seeking real change. Then, we need personal truth. This truth should not only be found, but also constructed by the seeker who is flexible and open in nature. Personal truth offers a renewed perspective on someone's life and world. Truth must be involved constantly in one's own life and in one's own context. This is what we learn in studying spirituality: abstract truth, even if it is spiritual or religious i.e. absolute truth, as such, is meaningless. Developing personal truth is a process of construction and connection that is, in principle, infinite: one never reaches the point that the search can be stopped. Finding personal truth is an ongoing journey.

It is not so easy to develop personal truth – we know this from different spiritual traditions. It takes a whole process of reflection, meditation, discussion, and practice. In the first place, we need a rather high level of **self-knowledge**. We need to know our own strengths and weaknesses, where the pitfalls lie and how our personal experiences influence behavior. Lack of self-knowledge will result in lack of knowledge of the other; knowing yourself leads to knowing the other. However, self-knowledge is not the only contribution from spirituality. Secondly, spirituality makes clear that we benefit from **self-confidence**. Self-confidence is self-knowledge in combination with acceptance of yourself. Within spiritual traditions this is an important element, because self-confidence is part of the perception of yourself through the eyes of the other, and through the eyes of God. The perspective of God as an absolute reality also leads to a third element of spirituality worthy of taking into consideration here: **norms and values**. The preference for individual interest rather than the general interest of humanity as a whole can easily result in immoral behavior. In almost all spiritual traditions it is a recurrent refrain: do good, take care of the other person, put the other person before yourself. We certainly need **openness** to new experiences and the capability of **learning** if we are to meet these spiritual standards. Learning is the connecting and fundamental concept here. The core of learning is in itself a process of change and transformation. Learning is not easy, it requires participation, hospitality, willingness to question assumptions. Transformation costs time and effort, change provokes resistance. Developing personal truth, learning about yourself and the world around you, is not at all easy.

The last important element of spirituality that I want to examine as a building block for inspiration and change is **imagination**. In Wildman's approach, imagination appears at the end, in the form of computer simulation games as virtual learning labs, a space for trying things out. I think imagination is more than that, and deserves a more fundamental role here. Imagination enables one to rise above the everyday perspective, to imagine the apparently impossible, and to be capable of acting from an ideal and visionary perspective. Within spirituality, we know that imagination flourishes from irrational forms of knowledge; imagination can involve creative and intuitive thinking (Van Saane 2012, 2014; Verstraeten 2003).

Reflection on these spiritual dimensions is required – obviously far more thoroughly carried out than in this chapter – on self-knowledge, self-confidence, norms and values, openness, learning, and imagination, for example, when we are thinking about a transformation from *Homo economicus* to *Homo amans*, something which is very much needed in our times. For me, this reflection and these forms of learning are part of a form of leadership, known as personal leadership (van Saane 2015, 2017). Personal leadership can be defined as knowing yourself, controlling yourself, your personal environment, and your life as a whole.

In my opinion, personal leadership is the gateway to real transformation. It is inextricably linked to a mature attitude to life, leaving room for responsibility and sensitivity, for resilience. By learning to accept oneself, by establishing good relationships with others, by getting the best out of yourself, by giving meaning to your life, and by maintaining a certain autonomy, regardless of the context, you can use your full potential, on an individual and social level (Ruijters et al. 2015; Ryff and Singer 2013; Ryff 2014).

So, in conclusion, I agree with Wildman about the inevitability of the structural errors of man as subject. I do not agree about the possibility of correctives for that. We are better to acknowledge our individualism and failing cognitions, because this acknowledgment creates room for change. Hoping for correction erects a barrier to change. If that happens, we will be disappointed, time and again.

I am not saying that there is no hope for change. I am not stepping back from responsibility. I do not think that we can never tell others to change their behavior. Yes, we can. But we have to start with ourselves. We need personal leadership. Be realistic, embrace the human shortage and look for ways to connect people with themselves and with others. Look for ways to make people at peace with loss and sorrow. Look for ways not to lose courage but to tackle the problems. Don't look at the other, or the system, or the science. Look, and start, with yourself, by pursuing personal leadership. Don't complain, don't be fatalistic, don't be naïve or too optimistic. Just start with yourself, do something good, and be an inspiration for others.

Where I do want to join with Wildman is in his plea for imagination to have a role. He outlines the possibilities of computer simulation in a game context. This seems to me to be similar to other forms of artistic expression. Within the psychology of religion it is widely understood: creativity is a means for thinking of the impossible as possible, or even to experience it, to give space to personal needs and desires, to overcome paradoxes. Computer simulation, artistic expressions, rituals, narrativity, spiritual exercises in love and wisdom: we should cherish them all and let them grow, because these provide the opportunities for humanity's future.

In its psychological function, imagination is similar to therapy and to religion. Imagination, artistic expression, therapy, and religion enable people to accept reality, and the brokenness of human beings. Imagination can bridge the gap between the shortcomings of human psychology and the enormous threats from outside. Imagination does not lead to easy solutions, or quick fixes, but by imagination we can literally see potential solutions. Imagination provides for a try-out, virtually. We need imagination to come up with real and new solutions, to get beyond human limitation. If we focus on the development of personal leadership and mature attitudes towards mankind, change can happen. It can start within imagination, and be continued in reality.

In summary, I fully agree with Wildman about the structural failures in human functioning. And yes, individualism and cognitive errors are important examples of these failures. I also agree about the necessity of a multi-disciplinary approach, combining philosophy with actors in different domains. The risk of this approach, the generalization of easy solutions, can be overcome by focusing on personal leadership. Change does not start with the other, nor with the world around us, but with ourselves. We, as individuals, are the real game changers. And we can do it, because with personal leadership we can base our approach on spirituality and spiritual concepts, well-proven for hundreds of years. Nothing new, nothing unreachable, but practical and hopeful.

References

Alicke, M.D., and C. Sedikides. 2010. *Handbook of Self-Enhancement and Self-Protection*. New York: Guilford Press.

Kaplan, M.F., and H. Wilke. 2001. Cognitive and Social Motivation in Group Decision Making. In *The Social Mind: Cognitive and Motivational Aspects of Interpersonal Behavior*, ed. J.P. Forgas and K.D. Williams, 406–428. New York: Cambridge University Press.

Mullen, B., and C.A. Riordan. 1988. Self-serving Attributions for Performance in Naturalistic Settings: A Meta-analytic Review. *Journal of Applied Social Psychology* 18: 3–22.

Roothaan, A. 2007. *Spiritualiteit begrijpen: Een filosofische inleiding*. Amsterdam: Boom.

Ruijters, M.C.P., et al. 2015. *Je Binnenste Buiten: Over professionele identiteit in organisaties*. Deventer: Vakmedianet.

Ryff, C.D. 2014. Psychological Well-being Revisited: Advances in the Science and Practice of Eudaimonia. *Psychotherapy and Psychosomatics* 83 (1): 10–28.

Ryff, C.D., and B.H. Singer. 2013. Know Thyself and Become what you Are: A Eudaimonic Approach to Psychological Well-being. In *The Exploration of Happiness*, ed. A. Della Fave, 97–116. Dordrecht: Springer.

Smith, E.R., and D.M. Mackie. [3]2007. *Social Psychology*. New York: Psychology Press.

van Saane, J. 2010. *Religie is zo gek nog niet: Een introductie in de godsdienstpsychologie*. Utrecht: Ten Have.

———. 2012. *Geloofwaardig leiderschap*. Zoetermeer: Boekencentrum.

———. 2014. Spirituality and the Psychology of Leadership Credibility: An Analysis from the Psychology of Religion. In *Leadership, Spirituality and Innovation*, ed. J. Barentsen and P. Nullens, 41–56. Leuven: Peeters.

———. 2015. *Geloofwaardig onderwijs: Van kennis naar persoonlijk leiderschap*. Inaugural address. Vrije Universiteit Amsterdam.

———. 2017. From Cognitive Science to Personal Leadership: The Role of Religion and Personal Life Orientation in Curriculum Development Processes within the Domain of Religious Studies. In *Religion and Higher Education in Europe and North America*, ed. K. Aune and J. Stevenson, 181–190. London: Routledge.

———. 2019. Personal Leadership as Form of Spirituality. In *Leading in a VUCA World: Integrating Leadership, Discernment and Spirituality*, ed. J. Kok and S.C. van den Heuvel, 43–58. Dordrecht: Springer.

Verstraeten, J. 2003. *Leiderschap met hart en ziel: Spiritualiteit als weg naar oorspronkelijkheid*. Tielt: Lannoo.

Chapter 13
A Relational Anthropology for Contemporary Economics? Concluding Reflections

Patrick Nullens, Steven C. van den Heuvel, and Jermo van Nes

> *"How selfish soever man may be supposed, there are evidently some principles in his nature, which interest him in the fortune of others, and render their happiness necessary to him, though he derives nothing from it except the pleasure of seeing it."*
>
> *Adam Smith (Opening sentence of The Theory of Moral Sentiments (1759).)*

13.1 Introduction

In one way or another, all of the contributions in this volume respond to the opening paper in which we addressed the need for refining the Homo *economicus* model and explored the potential of a modified version preliminarily entitled *Homo amans*. We sincerely thank all respondents for their worthy contributions and their thinking along with us, whether in supportive or critical ways. Some engage directly with our discussion paper in a way that implicitly or explicitly support our thoughts on the *Homo amans* model; others also express concerns and raise critical questions. In this final paper, we take the opportunity to discuss some of these, using them to refine and reshape our thoughts on the *Homo amans* model. These final thoughts will be shared in the conclusion.

P. Nullens (✉)
Evangelische Theologische Faculteit, Leuven, Belgium

University for Humanistic Studies, Utrecht, The Netherlands
e-mail: Patrick.nullens@etf.edu

S. C. van den Heuvel · J. van Nes
Evangelische Theologische Faculteit, Leuven, Belgium
e-mail: Steven.vandenheuvel@etf.edu; Jermo.vannes@etf.edu

J. van Nes et al. (eds.), *Relational Anthropology for Contemporary Economics*, Ethical Economy 61, https://doi.org/10.1007/978-3-030-84690-9_13

13.2 Discussion

1. *Should anthropological models be imposed on free human beings?*

The contributions by Dennis Krebs and Deirdre McCloskey evoke the question of how biological determinism, free will, and moral responsibility are interrelated. While giving an answer to this question is beyond the scope of this essay,[1] it is important to say a bit more about the notion of freedom. McCloskey in her contribution praises the benefits of capitalism, being a strong advocate of free market economy without government interference. This position implies that the idea of *Homo amans* could be an obstacle as it imposes an idealistic anthropology on persons operating in free and neutral markets. For the rational *Homo economicus*, there are no restrictions on what sort of preferences are admissible. Adam Smith's emphasis on self-interest endorses the freedom of the individual. The contractual relationship between different parties guarantees basic equality and freedom of choice. So why interfere ideologically if it limits our freedom?

The problem, however, with a neo-liberal view on the human person is that it tends to reduce the meaning of freedom. Already in 1969, Isaiah Berlin (2002) helpfully distinguished between negative and positive liberty. Negative liberty is the absence of external constraints, obstacles or blockades. Positive liberty is the possibility of acting as an agent, to control one's life and realize one's primary purposes. Capitalism tends to focus exclusively on negative freedom, a "freedom *from*…" being rid of obstacles; positive freedom is a freedom of becoming, a "freedom *to*…". Theorists of negative freedom start from the postulation of the heterogeneity of human ends and preferences. Non-interference and absence of coercion is fundamental to freedom. Theorists of positive freedom believe that it is possible to distinguish a moral end, or at least some set of potentialities for people to pursue. McCloskey's focus on negative freedom and liberal allergy to coercion fuels her negative attitude towards government interferences. This bias makes it difficult to see the importance of positive freedom.

The *Homo amans* concept as outlined in the discussion paper understands freedom as both negative and positive within a context of community and relationality. The socio-psychological analysis of freedom by Erich Fromm (1941) may be of help here. His research was driven by the shocking impact of fascism in the 1920s through 40s in Italy and Germany. Fascism took everyone by surprise because man's rational side, based on calculated self-interest, was taken for granted. However, fascism relied on an appeal to irrationality, fear, and romantic nationalism. So, what is freedom in light of ideology? Fromm (1970) built on Freud's basic understanding of unconsciousness, which he criticizes, and turned psychoanalysis into a social heuristic tool. Individuals have "dark passions" and these need to be suppressed by society. This need for suppression creates culture. Capitalism is a form of culture dealing with our needs. This creates a paradox – the more we

[1] For a recent study, see Willmott (2016).

suppress our desires, the more culture we create, but the higher the risk of neurosis, because the individual only has a certain propensity to cope with the suppression of his/her desires; the more freedom we are allowed to get, the less culture we create.

In his book *Escape from Freedom*, Fromm (1941) gives a profound social and historical analysis of freedom in modern society. For most of human history, man saw himself as part of nature, being one with it and driven by survival instincts. Yet culture developed and people were freed from the bonds of nature, which created a pre-individualistic society. In a pre-individualistic society a person is conscious of themself as a member of the community. In this case, the person's actions are not based on self-realization. In other words, the person is still related to the world by primary ties as they do not yet conceive of themself as an individual agent apart from their social roles. Freedom is defined by a sense of belonging, providing security, and identity. This notion of pre-freedom is seen, for instance, in tribal and medieval cultures. In extreme forms, the person was not an individual, but understood their duty in the community hierarchy and submitted to external forces, often confirmed by religious structures.

During the Renaissance and Reformation(s), the focus was on negative liberty as people tried to free themselves from social and religious coercion. The emergence of capitalism demolished the old securities of the medieval social system. The individual was left to themself. Everything depended on their own effort and no longer on the security of their traditional system. However, everyone experienced increasing insecurity and anxiety. Capital and entrepreneurship had now become the suprapersonal force determining society and personal fate. Again, this is a paradox as capitalism shaped a world that was both limitless and threatening at the same time. Individual freedom, even though it brought independence and reason, isolated people as they became anxious and powerless. This isolation was hard to bear, and the alternatives were either to escape from the burden of freedom into new dependencies and submission, such as fascism, or to advance to the full realization of positive freedom which is based on the uniqueness and individuality of man. Since there is the danger of some kind of relapse into pre-individualism, Fromm argues, the only healthy way forward is that man forges new productive relations in love.

Against Fromm's reading of history and cultural evolution, the *Homo amans* concept should not be understood as a relapse into a pre-individual society. In that case, it becomes an escape from freedom and a coercive ideology. In a marketing driven society the person tries to adapt themselves to a sick society. Their role is defined by what they do, what is desired from them, they are as a commodity on the market. According to Fromm, the psychodynamics of marketing bear a certain relationship to the authoritarian character of political ideologies. Both orient themselves towards an object outside the person. In the marketing orientation, this object is not a leader or an institution, but rather the anonymous and constantly shifting authority of the markets. A narcissistic character can function well in such an environment. It is only from a deeper understanding of love that a new sense of identity and individual freedom can develop (Fromm 1956). A mentally healthy person is a person who lives by love and respects life, not only that of his own but also that of his fellow man. These type of characteristics are required for a sane society (Fromm

1955). Hence the idea of *Homo amans* is not meant as a means to limit freedom, but to help people become free persons.

2. *What about the nature of love? Is love a stable virtue inherent to human nature, or a structural dynamic to emerge in and through social interaction?*

In response to our argument in the discussion paper that love denotes a fundamental characteristic of human beings, Rebekka Klein remarks that ". . . the view that love is a general trait of human persons or actions is not helpful but only obfuscates the study of its phenomenality." She then draws on Kierkegaard in emphasizing that love is complex and requires a special form of phenomenology. Making reference to various behavioral and neuroscientific investigations, she argues that love should not be seen as an innate virtue. "Love," she argues, "is not a stable core of human nature or a character trait which can be educated or trained. Rather, it should be seen as a dynamic structure at work in human attitudes and behaviours, which arises out of a change of perspective concerning the world, oneself and others. This change of perspective cannot be determined but happens out of contingent reasons."

Let us first clarify that, to us, faith, hope, and love are not descriptions of the essential nature of human beings; we are, of course, more than questing, longing, and loving beings. Wesley Wildman also warns against such an essentializing definition of the human person. We do believe, however, that the traits of faith, hope, and love are foundational to our relational constitution as human beings. Yet Klein's Kierkegaardian view of love touches upon a weakness in our position, which is that we have not adequately taken into account the bipolarity of virtues, including that of love. We do not believe that love is an innate virtue that is stable throughout one's life, but that all human beings from birth onwards have an innate potential to love. Whether or not external factors determine an act as an act of love, the very fact that people can act as such proves their ability to do so. We believe this is a capacity common to all human beings.

Perhaps some further thoughts on the nature of love are helpful here. Very often a contrast is drawn between an ethics of love as an unreal ideal and egoistic tendencies in terms of hedonism. This focus on contrast is a common pitfall in theological ethics. McCloskey in her contribution refers to the theologian Paul Tillich as an advocate of the contrast between "Christian love" and "economic and political egoism," when she quotes from his co-authored essay: "The spirit of Christian love accuses a social order which consciously and in principle is built upon economic and political egoism, and it demands a new order in which the feeling of community is the foundation of the social structure." Behind this contrast are some theological misunderstandings that are widely spread. Nicholas Wolterstorff (2011) refers to this approach as "agapism." This approach was mainly influenced by Søren Kierkegaard and even more by Anders Nygren. Klein draws on Kierkegaard and distinguishes the uniqueness of Christian love from universal human need-loves. Kierkegaard (1874, pp. 86–89) distinguishes agapic love from natural loves. Christian love is unnatural, and foremost a radical change of perspective rather than a character trait. It is seeing the other as an equal child of God, which helps the human being to acknowledge the nearness of love and also its practicability. Christian love is a dynamic structure at work in human attitudes and behaviors, arising out of a change of perspective concerning the world, oneself, and others. This type of love, according to Kierkegaard, is not spontaneous; it is a matter of duty. As Klein rightly observes, Kierkegaard's understanding of love is deep and complex. Nygren goes a few steps further than Kierkegaard. His influence on modern agapism can hardly be overestimated. He believes that all forms of natural love are manifestations of *eros*, which are types of need-love in search for satisfaction and completion. Agapic love is a mystery and essentially different in nature. It is demonstrated in love for the enemy and it does not recognize any valuable quality in the object; it is pure benevolence (Nygren 1969, p. 78, 215). Agapic love is motivated by God's unconditional forgiveness. It is fundamentally different and cannot co-exist with natural self-love and our love preferences. It even goes beyond justice and principles. Agapic love is gratuitous generosity and not based on the requirements of justice. It is not based on the justice requirements of the other, it is not based on law at all. God chooses love over justice. According to Nygren (1969, p. 75), agapic love needs to be spontaneous, since God's love is spontaneous.

We believe that Wolterstorff rightly points out that this popular disconnection between love and justice is theologically and philosophically problematic. Agapic love incorporates justice and human dignity. It seeks to promote the good in the life of the other. Even more so, it incorporates *eros*-love and self-love (Wolterstorff 2011, pp. 93–100). Wolterstorff (2011, p. 101) describes this broad understanding of agapic love as "care": "Care combines seeking to enhance someone's flourishing with seeking to secure their just treatment." This tendency to care is quite natural. Yet there is malformed care, such as paternalism, or preferential and well-formed care which "incorporates reverence, respect for the recipient of one's care" and does not wrong others (Wolterstorff 2011, p. 102). Well-formed care, incorporating justice, natural love, and the overall well-being of others are very important for understanding love. In that sense love is always doing what justice requires.

The interesting point of an ethics of care is that it gives prominence to our capacity of concern and empathy. Interdisciplinary research indicates that our innate ability to empathize with other people is what makes us relational beings (Slote 2007). As primatologist Frans de Waal (2012) points out, we – like other primates – are strongly inclined to bond, to reach out, and to have empathy. This testifies (although it does not "prove") to the deep-seated potential to love, which we posit as important to appropriate in a new economic anthropology.

3. *Does the* Homo amans *model aim to replace that of* Homo economicus*?*

Klein discerns a "strict opposition" in the way we have presented the *Homo amans* concept in relation to that of *Homo economicus*. It also strikes her that we seem to devalue the contents of the *Homo economicus* model on the basis that it appeared somewhere in the history of ideas. Consequently, Klein wonders whether some truth in the *Homo economicus* model can be found. These are all important observations, which need some clarification from our side.

First of all, we acknowledge that a phrase like "viable alternative" implies opposition. At the same time, however, we have stated that the *Homo economicus* model is in need of "modification" and that we aim to develop "a more refined anthropological model". So, we answer in the negative the question of whether we see a strict opposition between *Homo economicus* and *Homo amans*. What we argue is that *Homo amans* is a necessary adjustment of *Homo economicus*, supposing that we are both rational and relational beings. The latter, we believe, is not sufficiently taken into account in the *Homo economicus* model. As such, the *Homo amans* model is complementary to that of *Homo economicus*.

This implies, second, that we do acknowledge that there is certainly some truth to the *Homo economicus* model. Admittedly, this is not sufficiently stressed in the discussion paper. In his recent book, Michael Pirson (2017) – on the basis of studies by Paul Lawrence and Nitin Nohria – argues that there are four core human drives that account for the complexity of human thinking and behavior: (1) the drive to acquire (Lawrence 2010), (2) the drive to defend (Lawrence and Nohria 2002), (3) the drive to bond, and (4) the drive to comprehend (Lawrence and Nohria 2002). The former two refer to things that people need, and need to protect, in order to survive. As such, they fit the *Homo economicus* model. The drives to bond and comprehend fit the *Homo amans* model as they refer to people's sociality and desire to understand themselves and their environment. From this perspective, *Homo economicus* and *Homo amans* are complementary models.

Finally, we consider any normative anthropology to be the product of its time, and so we do not consider the *Homo economicus* model to be inaccurate simply because it is a late eighteenth century idea. We do think it is inaccurate, because scholarly research across various academic disciplines has revealed that there is a social component to human nature that is not sufficiently taken into account in the *Homo economicus* model.

4. *Is the* Homo amans *model descriptive or prescriptive in nature, or both? Should it be studied from more distinctive perspectives?*

The response paper by Gerrit Glas provokes the question of whether the *Homo amans* model is descriptive or prescriptive in nature. Like the *Homo economicus* model, it is both. In this respect, as Glas rightly points out, our research moves within the broad philosophical tradition of eudemonic ethics. A statement about "the good life" is both descriptive and prescriptive. But recognizing this brings us into conflict with two important propositions that are currently seen as important. First, there is the well-known criticism of the "is-ought fallacy" as introduced by David Hume. Second, there is the argument about the role and moral scope of different scientific disciplines, in particular the scope of social sciences. It is not possible, in the confines of this essay, to address both issues in depth, but given the weight of both objections some clarification is needed.

Concerning the epistomological is-ought fallacy, or what G.E. Moore (1903) later called the "naturalistic fallacy,'" Glas is absolutely correct to say that we should not uncritically draw values from facts, certainly not from religious motives. But while this is an important warning, the potential of the naturalistic fallacy does not ask for a complete overhaul of our project; it is possible to argue for a connection between ontology and ethics; but this is not an automatic or self-evident connection. Hume's original argument was not about the epistemological impossibility of moving from an "is" to an "ought" (Smith 2010, pp. 386–96). He simply noted – and he was right to do so – that this is not a self-evident deduction. However, this epistemic criticism does not necessarily mean that we have to completely disconnect "is" from "ought," nor that one is scientific and the other quasi-religious. Recognizing the naturalistic fallacy simply means asserting that there is a step to be taken between "is" and "ought"; this calls for a normative premise. The teleological approach that we are introducing, by means of our conception of *Homo amans*, is meant precisely to form such a bridge from "is" to "ought." The "ought" has its *raison d'être* in a goal category: In order for agent A to achieve goal B, A reasonably ought to do C. Or, in other words, a knife *is* a sharp object that *ought* to cut through the apple. This goal approach to the problem was elaborated by, among others, Alasdair MacIntyre (1981) who mainly relies on Aristotle. It is precisely our criticism of the one-sidedness of *Homo economicus* and so-called "value-free scientific naturalism" that relates to this epistemological axioma. Especially in our times, with the earth being in danger of collapsing, we need to look more closely at how life is structured and what this means for our moral actions. We consider such a qualified relationship between "is" and "ought," therefore, to be not only possible, but also an urgent task for ethics.

Acknowledging the warning about the naturalistic fallacy, there is also the criticism that the task of social sciences is purely descriptive and not prescriptive. We tend to disagree. A human ontology (or anthropology) is always implicitly present and must now be made explicit and questioned on a coherent and factual basis. Charles Taylor (1989, pp. 2–8) points to the exaggerated fear of the connection between ontology and ethics in the current world of human sciences. He speaks of a suppression, an avoidance of the "inescapable frameworks," as if articulating the fundamental question of the essence of man is a legacy of an outdated pre-scientific past. Such a deliberate avoidance of normative frameworks is also criticized by Christian Smith (2010, pp. 78–88). He notes that while social scientists avoid ontological-ethical questions, they do not shy away from making powerful moral statements about what is conducive to human flourishing and what is not. They invoke equality, freedom, and human rights, but fail when it comes to providing an ontological basis for these (Smith 2010, pp. 3–5). According to Smith, this is a form of schizophrenia caused by a dominant reductionist methodology of the natural sciences. According to him, the gap between "is" and "ought" can be closed through the development of a teleological moral framework, which he then contributes to, describing individuals as "centers with purpose".

In terms of method, Glas proposes a multi-perspective vision taking into account the perspective of one's life- and worldview, the perspective of philosophy (core concepts; conceptual frameworks; paradigms; argumentative structures), the perspective of theoretical knowledge, and the perspective of practical (professional) knowledge and know-how. These four perspectives give the impression of a separation of estates and assume that each area uses a generally accepted methodology.

But is this really the case? Does Glas not have his own views on these four perspectives? To give an example, existential and phenomenological philosophers will have reservations when it comes to the distinction between experienced worldview and theoretical conceptual knowledge. The separation between science and practice also seems to us to be rather artificial and too much influenced by a scientific paradigm. Charles Taylor (2004), for example, refers to modern social imaginaries. These are not "worldviews," but rather frames of reference or assumptions of social practices. Here, too, we see how perspectives merge together.

Glas sees value in the clear distinction between perspectives and is critical when it comes to "logical transitions." He claims: "For the understanding of the current project, the above implies that there are no such (logical, deductive) relationships between economic theory and economic practice, between philosophical views on man and labor and economic theory; nor between the images of man based on life- and worldview and economic theory." His separation of "is" and "ought" leads, among other things, to statements such as: "Understanding how empathy develops does not lead to recognition of empathy as moral virtue." While this is true, it does say something about how empathy can develop as a virtue, and this development or character growth is the very essence of virtue ethics. There is an intuitive linkage between understanding the phenomenon and normative valuation. But even more so, we see effectively that people living without empathy show destructive behavior. Integrating these themes is not a "dreaming away" but an existential necessity. Reducing the logical step towards ethics to a question of "moral and religious reasons" ignores the great impact that scientific insights have on our contemporary moral positions.

According to Glas, if we understand him correctly, the place where different perspectives would come together is in professional practice. This is a very interesting idea that fits in with the global crises as we are currently experiencing them. When we talk about an economy that takes into account the limits of growth (Raworth 2017) or an economy at the service of the common good (Felber 2019), we are indeed talking about the need to change our current practices. But these innovative practices are supported by an implicit vision of human happiness and man's place in nature. Reality thus forms a whole, and the problem is that economic science has lost this breadth and is now trapped in its own reductionist perspective, the dead alley of a science that does not want to contribute to the articulation of what is, or is not, humane.

5. *How will the philosophical concept of* Homo amans *bring about social transformation in terms of economic action?*

This question is asked in various ways, especially by Hendrik Opdebeeck, Gerrit Glas, and Wesley Wildman. The latter, for example, warns us against philosophical overreach, i.e. in reality, policymakers and educators do not get their ideas from philosophers. Instead, he notes, philosophers need policymakers and educators more than the other way around. We tend to disagree, but Wildman is certainly right to wonder about the real-world implications of the *Homo amans* model (but see the contribution of James Van Slyke, who gives a good practical example). It reminds us of Marx's famous words that "[t]he philosophers have only interpreted the world, in various ways. The point, however, is to change it" (Marx 1845, p. 535). In recognizing this, we admit that the discussion paper does not contain much concrete advice on how *Homo amans* is to bring about social transformation.

However, we certainly had social transformation in mind when we wrote the discussion paper, and we will endeavor to operationalize the ideas contained in it towards realizing social transformation. However, before indicating further how we envision this, we would like to first challenge Wildman's thesis that in reality, philosophers primarily play a second-order role. While it is true that ideas often seem to be second-order, theoretical reflections of already established practices, this does not make philosophy the handmaiden to practice. The history of philosophy has shown that a philosophical view can also strongly shape human attitudes towards practice, both for good and for bad. This can be illustrated by means of a reference to the inception of the capabilities approach by the Indian economist and philosopher Amartya Sen (1980) who developed this new approach to human development based on extensive field research which he did in India. It was in pondering the realities of deep poverty and inequality that he realized the need for a new approach, which he then began to develop theoretically. His extensive research earned him the Nobel Prize for Economics in 1998. In this new approach, the focus on growth of GDP is complimented with a focus on the empowerment of human capabilities. The primacy of either theory or practice is hard to establish in the development of the capability approach, but the overall model was, in the end, a result of the interaction between theory and practice.

This is a positive example of how new thinking in the face of old realities can lead to changed practices. However, history teaches us that this mechanism can also have detrimental results. When it comes to economics, for example, there is evidence that students of economics experience a marked drop in their level of altruism during their studies. In effect, they become more selfish, in various ways, as has been illustrated by different studies (see Frank and Schulze 2000; Wang et al. 2012; Frank et al. 1993).

These examples show that theory matters to socio-economic life, either for good or bad. The second example, in particular, illustrates the importance of education. It is a long-established truth that education plays a major role in either bringing about or in stifling social change (Burns 2002). We therefore recognize it as a challenge, not only to nuance and further develop our concept of the human person as a *Homo amans* but also to develop a concrete training program for faculties of economics and for business schools. As such, we hope to stimulate and empower students of economics and business to develop a richly sourced anthropology, drawing on various academic disciplines, in order to challenge them to resist reductionism and dogmatism of any kind.

13.3 Conclusion

Given the contemporary challenges in society, we hope to foster an increasing awareness of the importance of anthropological assumptions in economic thinking. Because the dominant paradigm of *Homo economicus* is too narrow a basis for a just and well-functioning society, it must be seriously called into question. This quest leads inevitably to an interdisciplinary dialogue and a prominent role for the humanities. We are human beings or persons in an evolving cultural community. However, the overall conclusion of this multidisciplinary dialogue is that reforming anthropology in contemporary economics is anything but easy. Questioning the accuracy of the rational *Homo economicus* model, we have started the conversation by introducing the *Homo amans* model, suggesting that people are socially conditioned in their natural ability to search for meaning ("to believe"), to project their longings unto the future ("to hope"), and to relate meaningfully to others ("to love"). The following lessons have been learned from our conversation with the respondents in this volume:

- *Homo amans* as an isolated concept cannot serve as an independent model for a more humane economy. It is a crucial element of a much-needed change in social imaginary. However important the traits of faith, hope, and love for the social condition of man, there is more to human beings that needs to be taken into account. As such, *Homo amans* cannot but serve as a complementary model to that of *Homo economicus*. What needs more study is the exact relationship between the rational and relational qualities of people in relation to trust. As Harry Hummels remarked in his foreword to this volume, "[a] dialectic relationship, leading to a constructive discourse between the self-interested *Homo economicus* and the other-oriented *Homo amans*, is more likely to clear the path towards the change that is needed in our current society."
- In light of this, perhaps the term *Homo amans* should be dropped altogether. It focuses too much on the quality of love, which in the discussion has turned out to be a complex and ambiguous virtue for economics. We have also learned that it should not be equated with altruism as there is more to love, including justice and human dignity. We suggest that perhaps the term *Homo florens,* as once used by Cicero (Romeo 1979, p. 50), more accurately focuses on the goal of the project, allowing more room for the rational qualities of man and also giving more prominence to the virtues of faith and hope. However, what is crucial is that the idea of *Homo florens* is not perceived as an isolated individual looking for calculated self-interest, but a person who lives in a complex network of trust relationships. The broad ethical concept of care, integrating justice and love, might be an interesting avenue for further investigation. The ethics of care does not start with our individuality but with relationality. It recognizes that human beings are highly dependent for many years of their lives and only partly dependent for the rest. Progress is only possible if we take into account the needs of those who are dependent on us (Held 2007). Our broad understanding of care can be integrated with the capabilities approach in economics. Are we naturally caring beings

seeking to enhance not only our own well-being but, driven by empathy, also the flourishing of others? In short, "do we care?"

- In our discussion paper, too little attention was given to the dark side of *Homo amans*, namely that the wrong loves can obstruct or even destroy human flourishing. Virtues, including that of faith, hope, and love, are bipolar. The life sciences, in particular, have shown that we are biologically preprogramed to search for meaning, project our desires, and relate to others. Yet we should be careful about thinking that everyone cannot but develop into a *Homo amans*. Future research may want to focus on how people can be encouraged to search for meaning, to hope, and to love in the context of work, and how developing into the opposites of these can be prevented.
- The *Homo amans* model potentially has transformative power. What we need, as Emilio di Somma demonstrated in his paper, is a change in our epistemic structure or social imaginary. This transformative process can start as a set of claims belonging to a restricted group niche and then expand to embrace the whole community. Therefore, a theory of change needs to be developed in order to harvest the fruits of the *Homo amans* model. Yet along with theory there is a need for praxis. Our focus should be on what the philosopher Hanna Arendt (1960) calls not the contemplative live but the "active life," our lives as citizens, workers, consumers, caregivers, teachers, policy makers, etc. Praxis is not simply applying some theory. Praxis is the cyclical process by which concepts such as human flourishing and *Homo amans* are embodied and realized. And through this process of embodiment our theories adapt continually. Accordingly, more attention will have to be given to how the model can be implemented in the curricula of management and business education, and how future leaders and policy makers can embody the model. Ultimately, it is about creating influencers who are able and willing to situate their own professional mission within a broader framework of human dignity, trust, sustainability, and relationships.

These thoughts will certainly not settle the debate, but hopefully will be taken into account when we continue to explore relational anthropology for a more humane and sustainable economy.

References

Arendt, H. 1960. *Vita activa oder Vom tätigen Leben*. Munich: Piper.

Berlin, I. ^{2}2002. *Liberty: Incorporating Four Essays on Liberty*, ed. H. Hardy. Oxford: Oxford University Press.

Burns, R.J. 2002. Education and Social Change: A Proactive or Reactive Role? *International Review of Education* 48: 21–45.

de Waal, F.B.M. 2012. The Antiquity of Empathy. *Science* 336: 874–876.

Felber, C. ^{2}2019. *Change Everything: Creating an Economy for the Common Good*. London: ZED Books.

Frank, B., and G.G. Schulze. 2000. Does Economics Make Citizens Corrupt? *Journal of Economic Behavior & Organization* 43 (1): 101–113.

Frank, R.H., T. Gilovich, and D.T. Regan. 1993. Does Studying Economics Inhibit Cooperation? *The Journal of Economic Perspectives* 7 (2): 159–171.
Fromm, E. 1941. *Escape from Freedom*. New York: Farrar & Rinehart.
———. 1955. *The Sane Society*. New York: Holt, Rinehart & Winston.
———. 1956. *The Art of Loving: An Enquiry into the Nature of Love*. New York: Harper.
———. 1970. *The Crisis of Psychoanalysis: Essays on Freud, Marx and Social Psychology*. New York: Holt, Rinehart & Winston.
Held, V. 2007. *The Ethics of Care: Personal, Political, and Global*. New York: Oxford University Press.
Kierkegaard, S. 1995 [1874]. *Works of Love*, ed. and transl., H.V. Hong and E.H. Hong. Princeton: Princeton University Press.
Lawrence, P. 2010. *Driven to Lead: Good, Bad, and Misguided Leadership*. San Francisco: Jossey-Bass.
Lawrence, P., and N. Nohria. 2002. *Driven: How Human Nature Shapes Our Choices*. San Francisco: Jossey-Bass.
MacIntyre, A. 1981. *After Virtue: A Study in Moral Philosophy*. Notre Dame: University of Notre Dame Press.
Marx, K. 1845. Theses on Feuerbach. *Thesis* 11. https://www.marxists.org/archive/marx/works/1845/theses/theses.htm. Accessed 18 Aug 2020.
Moore, G.E. 1903. *Principia Ethica*. Cambridge: Cambridge University Press.
Nygren, A. 1969 [1938]. *Agape and Eros*. Transl. P.S. Watson. New York: Harper & Row.
Pirson, M. 2017. *Humanistic Management: Protecting Dignity and Promoting Well-Being*. New York: Cambridge University Press.
Raworth, K. 2017. *Doughnut Economics: Seven Ways to Think Like a 21st Century Economist*. White River Junction: Green.
Romeo, L. 1979. *Ecce Homo! A Lexicon of Man*. Amsterdam: Benjamins.
Sen, A. 1980. Equality of What? In *Tanner Lectures on Human Values*, ed. S. McMurrin. Cambridge: Cambridge University Press.
Slote, M. 2007. *The Ethics of Care and Empathy*. London/New York: Routledge.
Smith, C. 2010. *What is a Person? Rethinking Humanity, Social Life, and the Moral Good from the Person Up*. Chicago/London: The University of Chicago Press.
Taylor, C. 1989. *Sources of the Self: The Making of the Modern Identity*. Cambridge, MA: Harvard University Press.
———. 2004. *Modern Social Imaginaries*. Durham/London: Duke University Press.
Wang, L., D. Malhotra, and J.K. Murnighan. 2012. Economics Education and Greed. *Academy of Management Learning & Education* 10 (4): 643–660.
Willmott, C. 2016. *Biological Determinism, Free Will, and Moral Responsibility: Insights from Genetics and Neuroscience*. Cham: Springer.
Wolterstorff, N. 2011. *Justice in Love*. Grand Rapids/Cambridge: Eerdmans.

www.ingramcontent.com/pod-product-compliance
Ingram Content Group UK Ltd.
Pitfield, Milton Keynes, MK11 3LW, UK
UKHW021035050925
462611UK00011B/885
* 9 7 8 3 0 3 0 8 4 6 9 2 3 *

Redistribution

A Silent Counter-Revolution

Michael Barratt Brown

Socialist Renewal

third series, number 8
£2.00